Gates County North Carolina Deeds

- 1833-1839 -

(Volume #6)

Compiled by:
Mona Armstrong Taylor

Southern Historical Press, Inc.
Greenville, South Carolina

This volume was reproduced
from a personal copy located in
the Publishers private library

Please direct all correspondence and book orders to:
SOUTHERN HISTORICAL PRESS, Inc.
PO Box 1267
Greenville, SC   29602-1267

Originally printed: Harker Height, TX 1985
Copyrighted 1985 by: Mona A. Taylor
Copyright Transferred 2005 to:
    Southern Historical Press, Inc.
ISBN #978-1-63914-155-5
Printed in the United States of America

TABLE OF CONTENTS

Notes..................iii
Book 15................ 1
Book 16................ 56
Index..................130

Notes

This is my seventh volume of the deeds of Gates County, North Carolina and it is my hope that it may be of some help to those researching ancestors in that part of the state. As in previous deeds many inhabitants of nearby Nansemond County, Virginia are mentioned, as well, as those in Hertford and Chowan counties in North Carolina.

I have tried to include all names and places written in the deeds and as much land description as possible without the repetition that is always present in the records. No doubt some initials and names have been mis-read and typing errors have been made but I have been as accurate as possible. In all cases the deeds end with "and back to the first station," which I have left off in interest of space and time.

One deed was omitted from Book 14, page 80 (deeds page 412) of which I am sorry, and will be found at the end of this volume. It is from Sarah Parker to John Matthews.

MJT

BOOK 15

Page

7 19 Nov 1833--John R. Norfleet and his wife, Harriett W., to
Elisha Umphlett...$250...200 acres adjoining Etheldred Cross, heirs
of John Beeman, Abraham Crafford and others, known by name Two Tracts,
given by Abraham Cross in his will to his daughter, Harriett; more
fully described in two deeds from Abram Curl to Abram Cross, dec...
                                                John R. Norfleet
Jno. O. Hunter
Martha Parker   Harriett W. Norfleet

8 12 Nov 1833--William Bush of Chowan to Abram Davis...$300...80
acres beginning at white oak on road running SE and then SW to cor-
ner of Jesse Hobbs, NE to James Bakers and down run to Catherine
Swamp, corner of said Baker and John Hurdle...
                                                  William Bush
Isaac Williams
Henry R. Pugh

8 12 Nov 1833--Treasy Walton to William Bush of Chowan...$130...120
acres beginning at white oak on road running SE to corner of Jesse
Hobbs to run of Catherine Swamp to a corner of Amos Hobbs...
                                                  Treacy(x)Walton
Joseph(x)Lilley
Jno. Bush

9 31 May 1833--John R. Norfleet to John R. Felton...$38.88...71 acres
whereon Jesse S. Hare now lives, which was sold by sheriff to pay
taxes due in 1822, and bought by said Norfleet...beginning at road
in Parker Jones line to Jordon Parker's line by meeting house to
Humphrey Parker's line and down run of Orapeak Swamp to James Morgans.
Wm.W. Stedman   John R. Norfleet
Jos. Gordon

10 18 Dec 1832--Jasper Trotman to Jethro H. Riddick...$400...95
acres, all the balance of land given to him by his father, Elisha
Trotman, beginning on S side of Cross Swamp, a corner of Joseph
Hurdle and Bushrod Riddick, nearly S to a red oak, a corner of
Riddicks and Gilliams line to main road and across swamp to James
Brinkley's line to a corner tree of Brinkleys and Drew Trotmans...
                                                  Jasper Trotman
Jesse R. Kee
Jason Riddick

11 10 Sep 1833--James Baker Sr. to James Baker Jr....$160...400 acres,
all that tract of land in Juniper Swamp, lying on Bennetts Creek, be-
ginning at Old Canal Road at high land running to Old Ferry Road, up
Juniper Swamp to W end of Pugh Bridge...   James Baker Sr.
Abel Rogerson
Shadrack(x)Stallings

12 14 Nov 1833--John Ellen to James Boothe...$141...110 acres for-
merly belonging to estate of Susan Odom, dec., lying in and near head
of Middle Swamp, and commencing at hickory in Nisum Cuff's line along
Mallica Cuff's to Henry Willey's except 6 acres near center of tree

sold by said Ellen to Blake Baker, where Thomas Peal now lives...
John (x)Ellin
Allen Smith
William Boothe

12 23 Sep 1833--Isaac P. Freeman of Elizabeth City to Miles Parker..
$124.67...62 1/3 acres, one-third of a tract beginning at black gum
in run of Cypress Swamp NE to Dunn's corner to Joshua Lang's corner
to Elizabeth Lee's...
C.R. Kinney   Isaac P. Freeman

13 8 Oct 1833--John Benton Jr. to Jesse Benton...$150...93½ acres
on W side of main road that leads from Benton's Creek to Gatesville
beginning at pine in corner of Lemuel Bentons and then SW and a
second lot of 99 3/4 acres beginning at corner of Margaret Bentons
then SW ...   John Benton
William Hudgins
Jas. E. Matthews

14 8 Nov 1833--Abraham Riddick of Nansemond to Kedar Ellis...$100...
100 acres joining lands of Riddick Jones, Jesse Matthews, Abraham
Riddick, Polly Matthews and Lewis Jones heirs and running SW...
Riddick Jones   Abraham Riddick
James D. Perry

15 17 Nov 1832--Amos Hobbs Sr. to his son, Guy Hobbs...gift of 31¼
acres beginning at red oak in Mordecia Perry's line running N to
Jacob Hobbs and then NE to Jesse Hobbs to William Boyce's to Kedar
Hurdle and James Boyce corner and then Nw...
Joseph Hurdle   Amos Hobbs
Jordon Hobbs

15 24 Apr 1832--Riddick Gatling to John Lee...$28...9 acres on S sid
of John Gatling's plantation beginning at run of Rogers Branch near
black gum and down run and N...
John Sparkman   Riddick Gatling

16 12 Sep 1833--William Goodman to Jason Roundtree...$24.75...24 3/4
acres beginning in Little Causeway, a corner of Jethro Teabout and
Jason Roundtrees and down run of branch to outside swamp to red oak
in Mills Eure's line, a corner of Jethro Harrells and said Roundtree
SW to Thickneck Branch to John Roundtrees then NW...
J.B. Baker   William Goodman
Dempsey Goodman

17 12 Sep 1833--William Goodman to John Roundtree...$41.75...41 3/4
acres beginning at small black gum in Thickneck Branch, corner of
Jethro Harrells NE to pocosin...   William Goodman
Dempsey S. Goodman
Edward S. Neal

18 12 Sep 1833--William Goodman to Jethro Harrell...$130.50...130½
acres beginning at red oak in outside pocosin, Jason Roundtree's
corner tree to Barnes Creek...   William Goodman
Dempsey Goodman
J.B. Baker

19 24 Nov 1832--William Goodman to Lewis Green...$30...30 acres be-

ginning at outside pocosin in Mills Eure's line running to Jethro Teabout's line to Jason Roundtrees to Little Causeway...
John Harrell   William Goodman
Jethro D. Goodman

20 19 Mar 1834--Mary Taylor to Thomas W. Stallings...$350...Four Negroes Prissilar, Sally, Jane and Mary, and 1 white mare...
Frederick Rooks   Mary(x)Taylor
Whitmill Stallings

21 1 Apr 1834--Law. S. Daughtry to Jeptha Fowlkes as trustee...$10 2 Negroes and household furniture listed in next deed...
                                                        Law.S.Daughtry
Jas.C.Riddick   Jeptha Fowlkes
Wright Hays   H. Gilliam
                                                            W.G.Daughtry

22 8 Mar 1834--Isaac F. Stafford to Jeptha Fowlkes...$5.00 and whereas: said Stafford is a member of firm of Stafford and Daughtry and to insure payment of following debts: Isaac Fryer $1350, Willie McPherson $600, Capt. Charles Fowler $75, Myers & Hodges $25, John Roberts $200, Wm.G. Daughtry $300, Wm.E. Pugh $60, L.S. Daughtry for board of hands, Pryor Savage for shop rent, Fowler & Speed for medical services, Wm. H. Moore for notes to Henry Gilliam, Jesse Brown, Jno. Savage, Henry Bond, Jno. Lovet, Asa Hill, David Parker, James Harrell, Isaac Fryer, Treadwell & Kissam, Boush & Fourney, Emersons, M.A. Santos, Bernards, John Forbes, Benjamin Sutton and H. Bond....
grey horse, 2 beds and furniture, 12 chairs, 1 table, 1 doz. plates, ½ doz dishes, 12 knives and forks and all household and kitchen furniture and all interest in firm of Stafford, Daughtry & Co....
                                                            Isaac F. Stafford
E. Slocum   J. Fowlkes

24 31 Mar 1834--Abraham Morgan to Jesse Wiggens...$1.00 and to make safe note of $874.68 to Noah Harrell...200-acre tract, formerly owned by John Duke, adjoining lands of Wills Cowper, Rizop Rawls and others and Negro woman Pheraby and her daughter, Mary...
                                                            Abraham Morgan
Willis F. Riddick   Noah Harrell
Sam'l R. Harrell   Jesse Wiggens

26 28 Apr 1834--Abraham Morgan to Jethro Willey...$1.00 and to make safe to Seth R. Morgan as security for notes to David Benton for $578.95 and James Morgan for $235...9 Negroes Hannah, Julia, Moses, Priscilla, Rose, Reuben, Stephen, Lewis and Adeline...
                                                            Abraham Morgan
John Willey   Jethro Willey
                                                            Seth R. Morgan

27 30 Apr 1834--Abraham Morgan to Wills Cowper...$1.00 and to make safe notes to Josiah Holley of Bertie Co. $512, James Goodman of Nansemond $561, and Riddick Arnold $105...Four tracts of land... The Old Place whereon Thomas P. Morgan now lives bounded by lands of Wilie Riddick on N, creek on E, tract formerly own by Seth Morgan on S and James Benton on W...contains 190 acres. Second tract called The Harbour of 41 acres is bounded on N by said Benton land, E by land formerly owned by said Seth, S by swamp and W by David Riddick.

Third tract, called Arnold's, has 38 acres and is bounded on N by Arnold heirs, E by Davis pocosin, S by Bentons and W by land of Pruden's heirs. The fourth tract, called Davis Pecosin, bounded by lands of James Benton and Wilie Riddick, contains 20 acres. Also, 4 brandy stills, 3 mules, 5 horses, 3 yokes of oxen, all cattle and hogs, 45 head of sheep, carriage and harness, carts and wheels, carry log, blacksmith tools, ploughs and farm utensils and Negro man, Spencer...

John J. Granbury
Seth R. Morgan

Abraham Morgan
Wills Cowper Jr.
Thomas P. Cowper

28 4 Jan 1834--Rizop Rawls to Henry Costen...$1.00 and to make safe to James Costen as his security for note of $2481.10...500 acres whereon said Rawls lives and formerly belonging to James Barnes, dec. and adjoining lands of Thomas Twine, heirs of John Granbury, dec., Richard H. Parker and others...

Docton(x)Alpin

R. Rawls
Henry Costen
James Costen

29 1 May 1834--Abraham Morgan to Rizop Rawls...$1.00 and to secure to said Rawls for note made to Jethro Willey for $1000... two tracts of land...first one of 305 acres that said Morgan purchared of Jane A. Gregory and called Gregory Land and the second tract, called The Barnes Land, on which William S. Barnes, dec. lived, and containing 190 acres. Also Negroes Granville, Haywood, Sam, Robin, Jim (Jim Arnold), Washington, Austin, Harry, Harrison, Chaney, Warren, Big Ned, Almond, Rachael, Abigail, Agga, James Madison, Mary, Sophia, Malviney, Mourning, Armsted, Ailey and Lucy...

Wills Cowper Sr.
John J. Granbury

Abraham Morgan

31 27 Mar 1834--Abraham Morgan to Wiley Riddick as trustee...$1.00 and to make safe to Ann Wiggens debt of $1330...land formerly owned by Noah B. Hinton adjoining land of Seth Benton's heirs, containing 170 acres. Also Negroes, Madison Sr., Isaac and Flucher...

Samuel R. Harrell
Jesse Wiggens

Abraham Morgan
Ann Wiggens
W. Riddick

32 3 Dec 1833--Henry S. Spivey to Nathan Riddick...$1.00 and to make safe to Jethro H. Riddick as security for note to Isaac Harrell for $225...40 acres beginning at Sandy Cross running road towards Chappel E to lane S to Joel B. Hurdle's line to Jacob Nixons line and W to road...

Quinton H. Trotman
J. Riddick

Henry S. Spivey
Jet.H.Riddick
Nathan Riddick

33 21 Feb 1833--George Ferebee, clerk and master of Court of Equity for Camden County and Augustus Coriell of Norfolk Co., Virginia to wit: Mary V. Proctor by Willie McPherson, guardian, petition to sell land at Canal Bridge, adjoining land of Mills and Josiah Riddick, called The Granbury Track...½ of tract or 1500 acres for $1672.50

beginning in E and W line of Jno. Fontaine's patent along Riddick's
line and running S...
                Geo. Ferebee,
J.N. McPherson   Clerk

34 4 Mar 1834--Willie M. McPherson and George Ferebee of Camden
and Thomas Pool of Pasquotant, executors of will of Samuel Proctor,
dec., late of Camden, to Augustus Coriell of Norfolk petition to sell
swamp lands as authorized in said Proctor's will and divide equally between his 5 children: Frederick S, Ann E., Albert G., Samuel and
Lovely L. Proctor and his wife...land called The Granbury Tract, adjoining lands of Mills and Josiah Riddick and beginning in Carey Weston
and James S. Seguin's lines on E and W line of John Fontaine's patent and to Riddicks on S and E...$1672.50...
                Thomas Pool
                W. McPherson
J.N. McPherson   Geo. Ferebee

36 20 May 1834--Abraham Morgan to John Walton...$1.00...two tracts
and to insure a debt of $4092.60 to John Walton..one where he now
lives purchased from Jane A. Gregory, widow of Richard B. Gregory,
and another formerly belonging to William S. Barnes, 190 acres bought
at a sheriff's sale...
                Abraham Morgan
W.S. Riddick   J. Walton

38 23 May 1834--Abraham Morgan to Wilie Riddick...$1.00...deed in
trust for Nancy Wiggens...land and slaves described in within deed...
Samuel R. Harrell   Abraham Morgan
David F. Felton   W. Riddick

39 23 May 1834--Abraham Morgan to Jesse Wiggens...deed in trust
for Noah Harrell...land and slaves described in within deed...
                Abraham Morgan
Samuel R. Harrell
David F. Felton

39 1 Aug 1834--James T. Freeman and Clement Hill to John Roberts
$12.00...6 acres on S side of Roberts large ditch beginning at a
gum then running S and West...
                James T. Freeman
John Walton   Clement Hill
G. Hofler

40 10 Nov 1833--Mary Brisco to Mary Hudgins...$23...6 acres adjoining said Hudgins, Job Blanchard, Henry Bond and others...
John Blanchard   Mary (x)Brisco
Tim. Walton

40 28 Jun 1834--Abraham Morgan to Jesse Wiggens: Whereas: said Morgan
is indebted to John Savage, guardian, with David Benton as security
for $445.62, 12 Dec 1826; balance due on note to Ann Wiggens for $716.12
12 Jun 1834; note to William Hinton for $400; note to John W. Parker
and endorsed to Hardy D. Parker for $500 due 12 Mar 1834 and credit
of $162.50 6 May 1834; balance due on note to Charles Fowler and Josiah Coffield for $500; $68.43 in judgment in Chowan at instance of
J.H. Fareboult and James Coffield and paid by John Popleston as security; also said Morgan is desirous to pay John Savage, Ann Wiggens,
Henry Bond, administrator of William Hinton, Hardy D. Parker, Charles
Fowler, Josiah Coffield and said Popleston...to said Wiggens...$5.00

and settlement of debts...three tracts of land: 1st, Barnes Tract of 190 acres, adjoining John Granbury, dec; 2nd tract of 350 acres is called Gregory Tract, whereon said Morgan resides and 3rd tract called Old Plantation is where he formerly lived, containing 500 acres and adjoining James Benton and Wilie Riddick. Also, Negroes Hardy, Chaney, Sophia, Robin, Mourning and Rachael...
Thomas E. Riddick
H. Gilliam
Abraham Morgan
Jesse Wiggens

42 16 Jun 1834--John B. Baker to Prior Savage...$1.00...his rights in 800 tract adjoining Kicheon Norfleet, Ann Harvey and John D. Pipkin to secure said Savage for said Baker's note of $633 to John Roberts...
Jno.B.Baker
H. Gilliam
Tho. Riddick

43 16 Jun 1834--William Cowper to Joshua M. Harrell of Nansemond $1.00 and to insure to Wills Cowper $350 note made to the Bank of Virginia at its branch in Norfolk and due this month...two tracts, one purchased by his father, John Cowper, and his grandfather, John Cowper, purchased second tract.
Wm. S. Cowper
Bn.B. Ballard
A.R. Harrell

44 9 Jul 1834--Simmonds Roundtree to Abraham W. Parker...$5...Joseph J. Barnes right to Negro Edey...
T. Saunders
Simmonds Roundtre

45 10 May 1834--Joseph Gordon to Andrew R. Harrell...$500...230 acres formerly belonging to Abraham Harrell beginning at red oak on S side of public road in John Alpin's line S to land formerly belonging to Henry Harrell, dec. (now William Harrells) to Creecy's line, along this line N to road...
Jos. Gordon
John Liles
Willis W. Harrell

47 3 Mar 1832--Exum Lewis to William W. Cowper...$250...87 acres beginning at persimmon tree in Mrs. Martha R. Sumners line and down ditch NE to Mills Swamp to a gum in Isaac Pipkin's line SW to a pine, corner of Mrs. Nancy Riddicks...
Exum Lewis
Peter Piland
Blake Brady

48 17 Feb 1834--Thomas Saunders and wife, Sarah B. to Exum Jenkins of Nansemond...$500...tract set apart to Sarah in division of estate of her father, Francis Speight, Survey No. 5 beginning at a pine corner on W side of Old Road running SE to an oak and SW to a White oak at Holly Island, Henry Goodman's corner, now William Goodman, on his and Jesse Saunders line, now Willis Cross line NW to Old Road...250 acres...
T. Saunders
Sarah B. Saunders
Edward Howell
John W. Darden
John A. March
Wm.W. Stedman, clerk,
Henry Gilliam, d.c.
attested to Susan's free consent

49 26 Oct 1833--Abraham W. Parker to William L. Boothe...$5.00
33 1/3 acres in branch at road near the white oak , up branch to
a pine in Mrs. Mary Cullens dower up branch to sweet gum in John
Riddicks line to red oak in edge of road and down road. Land was
conveyed in deed to said Parker by Henry Gilliam 6 Feb 1833...
Jno. Riddick   A.W. Parker
Elisha Parker

50 10 Mar 1834--John Cuff to Nancy Eads...$10...4 acres beginning
at pine a corner in Cuffs line E to post oak and N to a red oak SW
to a persimmon tree in cornfield and to mulberry near house...
John Figg   John(x)Cuff
Lem. Riddick

50 2 Nov 1833--Hardy Williams to Moses D. Hare...$250...100 acres
binding on lands of Levi Creecy, Hillory Willey, Jonathan Williams
Sr. and Robert Rogers...
Nathaniel Doughtie   Hardy(x) Williams
B. Goodman

51 30 Mar 1831--Absolom Blanchard to Miles M. Davis...$300...50
acres beginning at a pine, corner of William Blanchard's heirs
opposite Meeting House to edge of Beaverdam Swamp to fork of
branch at Pearce's line...being plantation whereon Benjamin Blanchard Sr. formerly lived...   Absolom Blanchard
Miles Brown
William Blanchard

52 20 Jan 1834--Miles M. Davis to William Pearce...$225...50 acres
adjoining lands of Samuel or Benjamin Brown, heirs of William Blanchard, dec. and others, being land where Davis now lives and formerly owned by Benjamin Blanchard Sr....
J. Walton   Miles M. Davis
Willis I. Riddick

52 20 Jan 1834--Willis I. Riddick to William Pearce...all rights in
above mentioned tract conveyed to him as trustee to secure debt of
said Davis to said Blanchard...   Willis I. Riddick
J. Walton
Miles M. Davis

53 30 May 1832--John Sparkman to Riddick Gatling...$40...20 acres
that Lewis Sparkman purchased of Rodon Odom on E beginning at
white oak in Abraham W. Parker's line running line to John King's
to small red oak, a corner of said Gatlings to a pine, a corner
of the Isaac Carter tract and SE...   John Sparkman
John (x)Lee
H. Gilliam

54 5 Feb 1834--Levin Cuff to Miles Parker...$175...two tracts of
41 acres each; the first beginning at red oak in Henry Willey's
line E along line of marked trees to Daniel Cuffs to Kicheon Norfleet's line to William Parker's line. Second tract begins at a
pine joining land of Henry Willey along his line E to Cuff's own
line to said Norfleet's line W to Demsey Parker's purchase of
Simpson and wife (former Penny Parker) to pine in said Willeys...
                                                        Levin Cuff
Jethro Willey
H.G. Williams

55 31 Jan 1834--Edwin Smith of Nansemond to James Sumner...$156.50 160 acres as trustee for Hardy Cross by deed of trust executed by William Davidson to secure payment of debt to said Cross; being land formerly owned by David Boyt, dec. adjoining land of Henry Jones, dec., Miles Parker and others...
                   Edwin Smith
George W. Smith
Demsey Parker

55 8 Feb 1833--Abraham Spivey to Thomas Twine...$300...50 acres on Watery Swamp joining lands of Timothy Spivey, Timothy Walton, George Brooks and said Twine...
                   Abram(x)Spivey
Daniel S. Ward
I.S. Harrell

56 6 Jan 1834--Abraham Baker to James Baker...500 pds...18 barrels of brandy, 2 horses, 1 colt, 1 gigg and harness,1 horsecart and wheels, 1 cow, 2 sows and pigs, 2000 juniper shingles, all household and kitchen furniture, farm utensils and 1000 ___pork, 15 barrels of corn...to secure debts to said James...
                   Andrew Baker
Daniel Hobbs
Hardy Baker

57 16 Feb 1833--Mary Taylor to Nathaniel Taylor...$1500...4 Negroes Priss 18, Sally 14, Jane 11 and Mary 3...
                   Mary(x)Taylor
Seth Spivey
Wesley Spivey

58 1 Jan 1834--Andrew Baker to James Baker...$1.40...1 yoke of oxen, cart and wheels, tumbler cart, plank and scanthing...
Daniel Hobbs   Andrew Baker

58 13 Feb 1830--Humphrey Parker to Miles Parker...$35.37½...1 sow and pig, bed, bedstead and furniture, pine chest, looking glass, 3 common chairs, 1 iron pot, 1 skillet and 1 spider...
                   Humphrey(x)Parker
James Perry
William Parker

58 20 Feb 1830--Abram Parker to Miles Parker...$53...1 bed, 6 chairs 1 pine table, 2 iron pots, 1 spider, 1 skillet and 13 hogs...
                   Abram(x)Parker
James Perry
Humphrey(x)Parker

59 21 Oct 1833--Jacob P. Jones to Humphrey Parker...$120...100 acres called White Oak Ridge beginning at corner pine in James and Charles Jones line W to Britton Barrs line N to John R. Barrs to David Bentons and E; it being a piece of land bought by Elisha Hare, dec., formerly Demsey Odoms...
                   Jacob P(x)Jones
John Barnes
Joshua Jones

60 30 Oct 1833--Andrew Baker to James Costen Jr. ...$750...150 acres adjoining land of Walton Freeman, Timothy Walton, Henry Walton's heirs and Thomas Harrell...
                   Andrew Baker
Gilbert Harrell
David(x)Hobbs

61 17 Sep 1833--John O. Hunter to E.R. Hunter...$800...300 acres formerly belonging to Christopher and Henry Riddick beginning at black gum, corner tree in Figgs line on SE side of Honey Pot Swamp at place called Old Flax Hole, running by line of marked trees NE to sweet gum in Miles Parkers line W to a pine, Norfleets corner, on Parkers Path to head of branch and S to 3 oak saplins, a corner and E to Figgs line up SE side of swamp...
                                                   Jno. O. Hunter
Bn.B. Ballard
Tho.E. Powell

61 29 Nov 1833--William Moore to Jonathan Williams...$30.50...15 acres beginning at a pine on edge of new road NW to red oak to a sweet gum in run of Long Branch along Williams line and NE...
                                                 W.K. Moore
Henry Willey
Levi Rogers

62 1 Nov 1832--Lassiter Riddick to Job R. Hall...rent or let farm formerly belonging to Taylor Cross and lately in occupancy of Etheldred Cross, adjoining lands of said Cross, Thomas Saunders and others...for five years...
                                               Lassiter Riddick
Wm.L. Boothe
Simmonds Roundtree

63 14 Feb 1834--Elisha Hunter to Nathan Riddick...$125...47 acres on N side of Catherine Creek beginning at black gum, Milton Eason's corner and along his line N to James Brinkleys to red oak, W to Henry Kings line S to Ezekiel Trotman's to Catherine Creek Swamp and to middle of swamp...
                                             Elisha R. Hunter
Milton Eason
Jasper Trotman

64 19 Feb 1829--Alexander Freeman of County of Monroe in Georgia to James T. Freeman...$330...125 acres in Indian Neck on S side of Mill Swamp beginning at a pine and up swamp to Juniper Branch along James line to head of Poley Bridge Branch and down branch binding on John Whites line to a gum a corner tree between heirs of Riddick Trotman, dec., White and Thomas Spivey; being whereon James Freeman, dec. formerly lived and was purchased by Henry Hurdle of Chowan and then given to said Alexander Freeman...
                                           Alexander Freeman
John Roberts
Timothy Hays

65 1 Apr 1833--Ann Bond to Elizabeth G. Bond...gift of land on N side of Bennetts Creek in fork of Honey Pot and Indian Road bordering on land of Bryant Brothers, John Matthews, John Gatling and John Brown and up said Brothers land...
                                       Ann Bond
Henry E. Blanchard
Easton Blanchard
Sarah(x)Blanchard

68 Feb Ct. 34--James R. Riddick, sheriff, to Acrhibald Jones...$73 57 acres belonging to Henry Speight, adjoining land of Joshua Allen, Richard Smith and others...
                                       J.R.Riddick
Jos. Gordon
Henry S. Briggs

69 22 Dec 1831--James Boyce and wife, Deborah, and Thomas Ward to John White...$200...50 acres beginning at maple in Spivey's

line down branch to Mary and William White's line, along White's line to Elmira Ward's line...

P.B. Minton
Reuben Blanchard

James Boyce
Deborah(x)Boyce
Thomas N. Ward

69 18 Jan 1834--Riddick Trotman to William Harrell...$120...30 acres beginning at sassafras and along ditch then N to white oak and down line of marked trees S, joining Pheraba Trotman on E and land of William and Benbury Griffin...

Riddick Trotman

Thos. R. Costen
M. Hudgins

70 8 Dec 1832--James Eure and wife, Mary, to Martha Taylor...$15... 5 acres beginning at corner pine in line of heirs of John Beeman, dec. to corner post oak in Mills Eure's line along his line to Sarum Creek Road...

Jas.(x)Eure
Mary(x)Eure

Wm.L. Boothe
Peter Piland

71 22 Jan 1834--Miles Parker to Henry Carter...$374...187 acres beginning at black gum in run of Cypress Swamp NE to popular called Jason Saunders corner, NE to spanish oak to lightwood stake, Gilbert G. Saunders corner, SW to an ash in Cypress Swamp, corner on Nathaniel Eures and down swamp...

Myles Parker

R. Gatling
Peter Eure

72 8 Feb 1834--Jesse Mathias and wife, Julie, to Benjamin Brinkley...$85...16 acres beginning at white oak, corner of Col. Josiah Riddicks and Polly Newsoms S adjoining lands of Miles Brinkley, dec. heirs and James Brinkley, dec. heirs W to corner of said Polly and said James and NE...

Jesse Mathias

Jet. A. Ballard
Demsey Vann
Edwin Mathias

72 8 Feb 1834--Benjamin Brinkley and wife, Penny, to Jesse Mathias...$175...30 acres beginning at sweet gum corner of lands of Jesse Mathias, purchased of Kedar Ellis, running E and then N to land formerly belonging to Miley Tooley and W to post oak and S...

Jas.A.Ballard
Demsey Vann
Edwin Mathias

Benj. Brinkley

73 4 Sep 1833--Kedar Ellis to Jesse Mathias...$9...tract beginning at water oak in ditch adjoining lands of Benjamin Brinkley to lands of Elisha Brinkley's heirs to lands of Mills Riddick and W; being S end of ridge land...

Kedar(x)Ellis

Jas.A.Ballard
Demsey Vann
Riddick Jones

75 21 Jan 1834--Clement Hill to Clement Lassiter (son of Henry B. Lassiter)...gift of 15 acres to his relation...land in Indian Neck

where said Henry B. lives, beginning at pine at corner of Mrs. Parker's land on road leading from Parkers Landing along Hills avenue to a pine, across and S...
Clement Hill
J. Walton
Henry B. Lassiter

75 28 Dec 1832--Somerton: Jas. C. Smith to Jos. J. Barnes, agent for Jeptha Fowlkes...$125...Negro woman, Edith...
Jas. C. Smith
Ed. Shaw

76 1 Aug 1834--John Jones to James and David Parker, as trustees... $10... to secure notes of $53.77 and $115...land bounded by James Boothe, Nath'l Jones, Riddick Smith and William Jones, and is land he purchased from Riddick Smith and Mills Riddick, and also land devised to him by his father, and his interest in Negro women, Rose and Rachall and her four children, Washington, Nelson, Mills and Hester; Negro man Toney, all his crop or corn, peas and potatoes, all stock of horses, cattle and hogs, cart and farm utensils and household and kitchen furniture...
John Jones
James Parker
David Parker
Chas. R. Kinney

77 1 Aug 1834--Thomas Bagley to Timothy Walton...$1.00 and to insure a note of $108.13 and another for Sarah Blanchard (who afterward intermarried with him) made to Benbury Walton for $16.10... his equity in Negro woman, Esther and her four children, Daniel, Harriett, Dave and Jane or any interest his wife may have in estate of her former husband, William Blanchard, dec...
Thomas(x)Bagley
W. Walton
Willis I. Riddick

78 19 Aug 1834--John B. Baker to John Walton to secure notes of $1000 to John Roberts...Negroes: Rosella, Washington, Thomson, Carlos, Carolina, Bolivar, Jackson and Samson...
J.B. Baker
J. Walton
Burwell Brothers
John Roberts

79 27 Sep 1834--David Cross, agent for David Lewis, to Jethro Willey...$450...2 Negroes Milia 14 and Aggy 12...
Nancy Smith
David Cross

79 8 May 1833--Henry Gilliam to Law. S. Daughtry...$3858.00 in notes one of which is payable 1 Jan 1834 and rest severally for $400...lease for 9 yrs 7mos and 23 days all his tavern houses with stables, lot and garden attached and land adjoining...
Law.S. Daughtry
Jno. Bond
H. Gilliam

81 3 Oct 1834--George Freeman to Henry Gilliam to secure notes for $204.50 to John Roberts, $50.40 to John Walton and to Jeptha Fowlkes $42.90...67½ acres adjoining Frederick Pearce, Reuben Hinton and also horse and gigg, crop of corn, fodder and potatoes..
George Freeman
B. Walton
Henry B. Lassiter

82 18 Sep 1834--James R. Riddick, sheriff, to Walton Freeman...
$42.65...400 acres belonging to Robert Parker, dec., adjoining
lands of John Walton, David Parker and James Smith. Land was sold
by court order recovered by judgment against said Parker brought
by Timothy, John and Benbury Walton, executors of John B. Walton,
for $30 and interest...
H. Gilliam   J.R. Riddick
Jet. H. Riddick

83 2 Oct 1834--Timothy, John and Benbury Walton, executors of
John B. Walton, dec. to Elizabeth Hofler...$51...400 acres, form-
erly belonging to Robert Parker and described in above deed...
                                                        Tim. Walton
H. Gilliam   J. Walton
Jet.H.Riddick
                                                        Benbury Walton

84 18 Sep 1834--Hance Hofler and wife, Elizabeth, to John Walton...
$54...18 acres on SW side of main road leading from Gatesville to
Sunbury beginning at a gum and pine, a corner in said Waltons and
NW and then NE along old dividing line to corner of Elizabeth's
fence...
                                                        Hance Hofler
H. Gilliam   Elizabeth Hofler

85 18 Sep 1834--John Walton to Elizabeth Hofler...$3.00...1 acre
beginning at post oak on main road leading from Gates to Sunbury,
corner between said John and lands formerly owned by William
Gordon, dec. and now in possession of heirs of Frederick Hinton,
dec., S to said Elizabeth's fence and E...
                                                        J. Walton
Jet.H. Riddick
H. Gilliam

86 10 Feb 1830--Jesse Piland and wife, Pleasant; Peter Eure and
wife, Nancy and James and Henry Carter to Richard Curl...$20...
14½ acres beginning at a gum in run of Cypress Swamp and being
piece of undivided land that Annis Carter, dec. heired from her
father, James Carter, dec...   Jesse Piland
                                                        Pleasant(x)Pilar
                                                        Henry Carter
Abrm.W.Parker   James Carter
Demsey Parker   Peter Eure
                                                        Nancy(x)Eure

88 1 May 1834--John Mathews to Henry Gilliam, Joseph Riddick and
John D. Pipkin, commissioners to purchase land for parish...$573.50
96 acres, known as the Robert Parker Tract, adjoining Bryan Brothers
Thomas Saunders, Elizabeth Bullock and others; boundries of which
may be known by referring to deeds of Thursey Parker, John Evans
and wife, Ezekiel Lassiter and wife, Nancy Bond, Elizabeth and
Louisa Parker, Penina and Sophie Parker, Briant Brothers and wife,
Willis Brown, Abraham and Sarah Parker, Theophelus and Sydney
Parker and James Brown, all executed to said Matthews...
Jet.H. Riddick   John Matthews
George Costen

88 20 May 1834--William Overman to Joseph Riddick...$50...½ of
100 acre tract, known as the Griffen Place and formerly belonging

to Thamer Briggs, dec. and given to said Overman and John B. Griffen to be divided in Thamer's will, beginning at corner of William Harrell's along his line to Pherba Trotman, dec. line to Ezekiel Trotman, dec. line to Jacob Walton's heirs line...
Charles Overman   William Overman
Jethro H. Riddick

88 6 May 1834--Edward Hobbs to Henry Stallings and wife, Peggy...
gift of all his land and property to maintain him out of said property...10 acres whereon her father, Shadrack Stallings, now lives and for which he has a life lease, and all household furniture and to said Henry...balance of his land, his half as it has been divided by marked trees and the plantation where he lives beginning at mouth of branch at Warwick Swamp to Mitchells line SE to William Perry's line S to swamp; all hogs, hand mill and tools...
Jno. Mitchell   Edward(x)Hobbs
Jno. Kelly   Henry Stallings
Thomas(x)Hurdle   Peggy(x)Stallings
William(x)Spivey

90 29 Mar 1834--John Sparkman to Dempsey Parker...$339.75...56 acres beginning at red stump in Parkers line NE to a pine, SE to a sweet gum and SW and then NE to an oak stump, a corner of said Parkers and David Lewis, dec. NW to black gum to a white oak, a corner of A. Beeman's, dec. SW and along road to Britton Smiths and NW to a red oak in James Eure's line SE and then SW to run of swamp and back to road...   John Sparkman
Thos. Hoggard
A.W. Parker
Wm. L. Boothe

91 29 Nov 1833--John Roberts to Benbury Walton and John Bond...$900 1 acre lot in Gatesville, that Mills Riddick purchased of Isaac R. Hunter, executor of Isaac Hunter, Sr., dec. and conveyed by John Gatling and said Mills to said Roberts; one of lots being that on which store and warehouse now stands beginning 21 ft S of store piazza on main road N 144 ft, W 108 ft. S 136 ft. and E 108 ft. Also another acre lot known as Wharf on Bennetts Creek bounded on E by lands of Thomas Saunders, N and W by Henry Gilliam and S by oak...
Henry Bond   John Roberts
Law.S. Daughtry

92 15 May 1832--Walton Freeman to Jethro H. Riddick...$600...Negro woman, Agga 34, Boy Isaac 4 and Henry 1 yr.10 mos.
George Costen   Walton Freeman
Burwell Brothers

92 15 May 1832--Mourning Williams to Henry G. Williams...$100... all her interest in land adjoining Levi Creecy, Hillory Willey, Levi Rogers and said Henry G.; being tract that was given to heirs of Demsey Williams, dec. by Jonathan Williams in his will, and said Mourning, one of heirs of said Demsey...
Miles(x)Parker   Mourning(x)Williams
Levi Rogers

93 18 May 1834--Margaret Parker to John Matthews...$18...4 acres
bounded on E, W and N by lands of said Mathews and S by land of
Nancy Bond...
James Smith　　　　　　　　　　　　　　　　　　　　　Margaret(x)Park
Henry Riddick of Ro.

94 13 Feb 1834--Jason and Gilbert G. Saunders to Willis Cross...$55
125 acres known as part of tract bought by Jesse Saunders Sr. from
John Copeland and given to his son, Robert Saunders, in his will...
on E side of Chowan River and beginning at river and running SE
to small cypress near Speights Mill Pond SE to a hickory NW to
river and binding on lands of Thomas Saunders, Hare and others
and on lands of Benjamin and James Saunders(formerly)now said
Cross, and being part of same tract...　　　　　James Saunders
Miles Howell　　　　　　　　　　　　　　　　　　G.G. Saunders
H.H.C.Jones

95 13 Feb 1834--Jason and Benjamin Saunders of Nansemond to Willis
Cross...$120...185 acres on Sand Banks; it being their interest in
will of Jesse Saunders Sr. and given to Briant Saunders, his son,
and which was purchased by said Jesse from John Copeland, beginning at Chowan River running SE to spruce pine, corner of Goodmans
and Speights to river and along river and binding on lands of William Goodman, Thomas Saunders, Willis Cross and others...
H.H.C.Jones　　　　　　　　　　　　　　　　　　Benja. Saunders
Miles Howell　　　　　　　　　　　　　　　　　　Saunders

95 21 Apr 1834--William E. Pugh, clerk and master of court of equity
to Ezekiel Trotman...30 acres sold by petition of Riddick Trotman,
etal...adjoining lands of Elisha Hunter, Henry King and others...
　　　　　　　　　　　　　　　　　　　　　　　　Wm.E.Pugh
Lassiter Riddick

96 15 Nov 1834--William Petty to Wm.G. Daughtry and Jeptha Fowlkes
and to pay debts of $350 to said Daughtry; $260 to said Fowlkes;
$200 to Mills Roberts; $153.70, with $100 credit, William Pugh;
$11.30 accepted order of Wm.E. Pugh; $192.17 to Wm.P. Vincent; $85
to John H. Wheeler with David Cross as security; $60 to Thomas
Shepherd of Norfolk...100 acres bought of Kedar Green; all stocks
of goods on hand consisting of dry goods, crockery, hardware, salt,
groceries, lumber; corn fodder, peas, 3 giggs, 1 horse, 1 piano
forte, secretary, table, cart and bull, books and accounts, notes
and constable receipts...
　　　　　　　　　　　　　　　　　　　　　　　　Wm. Petty
Wm.E. Pugh　　　　　　　　　　　　　　　　　　J. Fowlkes
　　　　　　　　　　　　　　　　　　　　　　　　W.G. Daughtry

97 12 May 1834--Jesse Hobbs to son, William...gift of 26 acres
on S side of Catherine Creek Swamp joining lands of Simon Stallings, dec. Seth Roundtree, dec. on side of swamp and line of
Christian Hobbs and Thomas Hobbs...　　　　　　Jesse(x)Hobbs
James Boyce

98 14 May 1834--Nathan Ward to William Hobbs...$55...24 acres on
S side of Catherine Creek Swamp beginning at Jesse Hobbs line to
Thomas Hobbs and to Elizabeth Hobbs...
　　　　　　　　　　　　　　　　　　　　　　　　Nathan Ward

99 5 May 1832--Cyprian Cross to John Vann of Hertford...$9.00...
½ of land purchased by said Vann and Abraham Cross, late of Gates,
at or near foot of Winton Causeway...for particular reference to
deed made by Mills Riddick, clerk, 23 Dec 1826; it being sold by
court decree by petition of heirs of William Crawford, late of
Gates...
Albert G. Vann   Cyprian R. Cross

100 5 Mar 1834--Job R. Hall to John Roberts...$370...Negro woman,
Rachael and child, Leah...
Jno.B.Baker   Job R. Hall

100 2 Jan 1834--John Matthews to Robert Parker...$100...20 acres,
being part of tract formerly belonging to Robert Parker, Sr.,dec.
it being shares of Henry, Cherry, Sarah, Thomas Collins and wife,
Nancy, and Robert Parker, heirs of said Robert Sr...
H. Gilliam   John Matthews
Soloman Roundtree

101 10 Sep 1834--Jesse Harrell to James Harrell...$50...75 acres
beginning at a pine at head of Middle Pocosin down line of marked
trees to head of Sarum Creek and down creek to gut and across plantation...
A.W. Parker   Jesse(x)Harrell
Stephen(x)Piland

101 29 Nov 1834--William Petty to Robert Booth of Edenton and David
Cross of Hertford: Whereas said William is indebted to Jonathan H.
Haughton and Robert H. Booth, merchant traders under firm Haughton
& Booth, on merchantile transactions...an unsettled account of $600
and they are security for $750 debt to Thomas White of Cambridge,
Md....for $1.00...land in Northampton County which was given by
Nicholas Tines to said Petty's wife, Sarah, reserving for himself
a life estate and all rights in personal estate that descended to
Sarah by death of her sister, Lucy Sowerly. Also Negro woman, Amy,
and four children; three orders given said Petty by said trustees;
debt of $450 to Dr. Thomas V. Roberts, $80 to Abraham C. Morgan
and John Popelson and $80 to Charles C. Taber...
                                                       Wm. Petty
R.B. Parker   Robt.H.Booth
Wm.E. Pugh   D.C. Cross

104 16 Dec 1832--Demsey Parker to Daniel Cuff...$55...41 acres beginning at white oak on Henry Willeys line S on his line to Mary
Parkers line to Kicheon Norfleets line, a corner maple, and along
Norfleets line to Levin Cuffs and said Willeys...
                                                    Demsey(x)Parker
Mills R. Fields
Harrison Vann

104 17 May 1834--Jesse Savage to James Savage...$250...120 acres
bought of Thomas G. Benton beginning at Col. Jethro Sumners Mill
Pond binding on lands of Abram Riddick and others W to small sweet
gum NW and along newly marked trees to a sweet gum in Bay Branch...
Caleb Savage   Jesse Savage
Jesse M. Savage

105 17 May 1834--Jesse Savage to Jesse M. Savage...$250...196

tract formerly belonging to Nathaniel Doughtie beginning at a
sweet gum near run of Big Mare Branch, along a line of marked
trees, along fence to N bar post near barn to N gate post at
road, down small lane a straight course to a line of land belonging to heirs of David Parker, dec. to red oak in heirs land
to road and up road to John Savage line and along his line W to
a pine in Miles Bentons and John H. Haslett's line and along line
N to Great Mare Branch and down run...
                 Jesse Savage
Caleb Savage
Jas. Savage

106 14 Dec 1833--John Coffield and wife, Elizabeth, to James
Boyce...$35...9 acres...
                John(x)Coffield
Amos Hobbs   Elizabeth(x)Coffie
Barnes Goodman and W.F. Riddick certified
said Elizabeth signed freely.

107 19 May 1834--Dempsey Flood and wife, Mary, to Abraham Pruden..
$20...land, yet undivided, that descended to said Mary by death of
her father...
                Dempsey(x)Flood
Thomas Hoggard   Mary(x)Flood
Marmaduke Baker

108 28 Nov 1833--Zachariah Hayes and wife, Lovina, to Robert Hayes
$250...40 acres beginning in Hawtree Branch at main road down run
to popular, a corner tree, W along John Hofler's line to main road
and up road to said branch...
                Zacara Hayes
Noah Harrell   Lovina Hayes
Willis R. Hayes

109 28 Nov 1833-Andrew Eason and wife, Agatha, to Riddick Trotman
$130...45 acres beginning at mouth of Poley Branch running up branch
W to a gum, N binding on land of Hance Hofler to a post oak and E
bordering on land of Ezekiel Trotman to a cypress on Catherine Creek.
J. Riddick   Andrew Eason
W.F. Riddick   Agatha Eason

110 28 Nov 1833--Willis F. Riddick and Hardy D. Parker, j.p. attested said Agatha signed freely...

110 18 Aug 1834--Nathaniel Taylor to William Bush...$800...4 Neg-
roes Priscilla, Sally, Jane and Mary, and 1 gray mare...
Abraham Twine   Nathaniel(x)Taylor
Wm.(x)Bogue

111 15 May 1834--John G. Liles to Riddick Hunter...$1.00 and to
make safe to Joseph Gordon and Willis W. Harrell as his security
for a note given to John C. Gordon, guardian to heirs of Henry
Lassiter, dec. for $356.18...118 acres whereon said Liles now
lives; it being lots 1,2, and 4 in division of estate of William
Brothers, dec. Also Negro Matilda and child, Willis...
                John G.Liles
Jas. P. Small   Riddick Hunter
Geo.G. Harvey   Jos. Gordon

112 1 Oct 1834--William Marshall to David Parker...$1.00...and to
insure note of $40 made 18 Aug 1834...2 acres whereon said Marshall

lives and 2 beds and furniture, 6 chairs, 1 pot, 1 dutch oven,
1 chest, 3 barrels of corn and 450 ft. flooring plank...
                  Wm.(x)Marshall
James Parker

113 24 Nov 1834--William Cowper to Wills Cowper...$1.00 and to
secure to Robert W. Bowden of the borough of Norfolk a note of
$638.84 dated 19 Mar 1834...lien on tracts of 260 and 50 acres;
the first purchased by John Cowper, father of said William, from
James Gordon 3 Jan 1805 and the latter in Dismal Swamp purchased
by John Cowper, grandfather of said William, from John Small...
Wills Cowper   William Cowper
Jno. Davis Day

114 1 Sep 1834--Frederick Morris to Willis I. Riddick...$1.00 as
trustee for note of $62 to James T. Freeman...37½ acres in Indian
Neck beginning at a gum a corner of John Morris line to the pocos-
in and to John Roberts line...
              Frederick(x)Morris
Jno. Wiggens   James T. Freeman
Joshua Jones   Willis I.Riddick

117 28 Dec 1832--Joseph T. Hurdle to Jethro H. Riddick...$1.00 and
to make safe to Abraham Hurdle two notes, one to Isaac S. Harrell
for $72.96 and one to Joseph Riddick for $53.75, both witnessed by
Joel B. Hurdle...53 acres beginning in Nathan Riddicks line to James
Brinkleys line, 3 beds and furniture, 1 table, 1 desk, 6 windsor
chairs, 1 mare, cart and wheels, 11 head hogs, 1 cow, 2 blade stacks,
40 barrels corn, 1 pot and 1 dutch oven.... Jo.T.Hurdle
Joel B. Hurdle
Moses Griffith
J. Riddick

118 10 Jun 1834--William King to Jethro H. Riddick...$1.00 and
to insure to Jesse Hobbs bond of $51...45 acres known as Simon
King Tract joining lands of Samuel Hobbs, Dec. and Norman King; it
being lot of land said William drew in division of his father's
estate and whereon said Simon formerly resided...
               Wm(x)King
Whit. Stallings   Jesse(x)Hobbs
Sarah(x)Perry

119 5 Mar 1834--John B. Baker to Job R. Hall...$370...Negro,
Jenny, and child, Fanny...
               Jno. B. Baker
John Roberts

119 4 Jan 1834--James Bond to Job R. Hall...$1040..Negroes,
Rachael, Annis, Agga, Winney, Matilda and Old Man Ben...
H. Gilliam   James Bond

120 12 Apr 1832--William Hofler to John Roberts...$300...Negro
man, Bob...
               Wm. Hofler
James Bond

120 27 May 1834--Abraham Morgan and H. Gilliam to Fisher Felton...
$437.50...Negro man, Ben...
            Abraham Morgan
Seth R. Morgan   H. Gilliam

120 31 Aug 1833--John Felton to John Hunter for Timothy Hunter...
$1.00 Negro girl, Lecrecy...
Elisha R. Hunter   John Felton
Whitmill Hill

121 12 Jun 1834--J.R. Riddick, sheriff, to Jethro Willey...$319...
Negro girls Julia and Rose, by virtue of a court execution against
Abraham Morgan...
                     J.R. Riddick
H. Gilliam

121 12 Jun 1834--J. Walton, trustee of Abraham Morgan, to Jethro
Willey...$435...Negro boy, Almond, 15 years old...
                     J. Walton
H. Gilliam

121 16 Jun 1834--Law. S. Daughtry to Seth R. Morgan...$125...
Negro boy, Stephen...
                   Law.S.Daughtry
H. Gilliam

122 16 Jan 1835--Jeremiah Rogerson to Isaac S. Harrell and Thomas
R. Costen, merchant traders under the name Harrell and Costen...
$1.00 and to secure note of $210.76...500 acres in Perquimans County beginning in Reuben Nixons lane running to Daniel Stallings
line along his line to Willis Riddicks line and along his line
back to said Nixons. Also Negroes Cela, Rose, Amas, Jack, Sam,
Charles, Ritty and Jimmy...
H. Gilliam   Jeremiah Rogerson
Rufus K. Speed   Harrell & Costen

123 2 Oct 1833--John Gatling to William G. Daughtry...$1000...2
tracts; the first 140 acres begins at white oak on main road leading from Somerton to Gatesville, a corner in William Browns line,
binding on his line to Honey Pot Road and binding on road to a branch in line of Willis Parker's heirs to the road, corner of Willis
Brown's fence. Second tract of 10 acres begins at a black gum, a corner, between Abram Parker and first tract and running a line of
trees to an oak, a corner tree between above tract and William
Brown and running E...
                     Jno. Gatling
Ro. Riddick

124 27 Aug 1833--Kedar Ballard to loving granddaughter, Mary Jane
Ballard (daughter of Alfred and Margaret Ballard)...67 acres adjoining lands of David Benton on S, Jordon Parker on E, Kedar Taylor on
N and heirs of Alfred Parker on W and is same tract whereon Alfred
Ballard now resides...
                     Kedar Ballard
T.W. Carr
Margaret Ann Ballard

125 19 Aug 1834--J.R. Riddick, sheriff, to Jesse Wilson, agent...
$5.00...two tracts of land; the first 80 acres ½ of tract adjoining land of Miles Parker, Gilbert Sanders and Nancy Glover and the
second tract of 100 acres adjoins said Parker near road leading to
Manneys Ferry. Sale results as result of a levy made by Wm. H. Savage, constable, for May Court 1833 against John Jones by writ of
John A. Anderson...   J.R. Riddick
Jesse Wilson

125 22 Jan 1835--Clement Hill to James T. Freeman...$1.00 and to
satisfy debt of $950 to Mills Roberts...200 acres called Davis Tract adjoining lands of John Roberts, William Hinton and others; all
stock of horses, sheep, hogs and cattle, household and kitchen furniture and farm utensils...
                     C. Hill
Benbury Walton   Mills Roberts
J.W. Bond   Jas.T.Freeman

127 16 Jun 1833--Kedar Briggs to Miles Briggs...$18...50 acres devised to him in will of his father, Solloman Briggs, dec. and after Kedar's death to be given to his son, Wesley, dec....
R.H. Ballard   Kedar(x)Briggs

127 Aug Ct 1834--James R. Riddick, sheriff, to Jonathan Williams... 91¢ for 1831 taxes...15 acres belonging to Monica Cross, dec. on S side of Long Branch joining land of Edwin Cross and Hillory Willey and beginning at a pine corner of said Edwin's line and running NW.
Jno. H. Haslett   J.R. Riddick
Daniel Williams

128 24 May 1833--James Duke and wife, Sophia, of Nansemond to John Small...$75...two tracts of land that she heired from her father, Moses H. Small...130 acres of high land and 50 acres of desert adjoining, it, whereon said James formerly lived; adjoins lands of John Small on S, Thomas Swann on N and John C. Gordon on W...
John Hofler   James Duke
Jacob Brothers   Sophia Duke
(This deed is also registered in Bk. 14 pgs. 569 and 570)

129 18 Aug 1834--Robert Hays and wife, Ann, to Nancy Bond...$87.50 35 acres adjoining land of Demsey Bond, dec., land of heirs of Hance Hayes and estate of Reuben Hinton and others...
Timothy Hays   Robert Hays
Richard Cross   Ann(x)Hays

130 Aug Ct 1834--J.R. Riddick, sheriff, to John W. Odom...$1.02½ tract of land of Martha Horton, sold for 1831 taxes; on N side of James C. Smith's mill pond beginning at a pine standing in state line, corner of Samuel Cross, running E to a black gum in a small branch and then SE...
Jonathan Williams   J.R. Riddick
Elbert H. Riddick

131 19 Aug 1834--Isaiah Riddick to son, William, gift of 200 acres beginning at corner of Nathan Wards, along his line to Abner Easons to Andrew Easons to a row of beech trees to lane that leads to main road W and then N to Joseph Riddicks line and on his line to Jet. H. Riddicks; also 20 acres, being ½ of tract given to said Josiah by his father, lying on main desert...
J. Riddick   Isiah Riddick
John Riddick

132 6 Sep 1833--Samuel Brown to Wesley W. Speight...$81...40½ acres including part of Great Marsh beginning at a water oak, corner of Benjamin Brown, John Lassiter and Timothy Spivey, running SE along a ditch to another ditch, said Samuel's corner thence SE and then NW to a dead pine to corner of Jethro Blanchards to corner of said Spivey and Blanchards...
Benbury Walton   Samuel(B)Brown
Henry Hofler

133 8 Jan 1834--Ro. R. Smith and Benjamin Saunders to Hiram Loomis...$100...10 acres known by Name Lumberton and on record in deed from Myles Parker and wife and Thomas Saunders to said Smith and Saunders...   Ro.R. Smith
H. Gilliam   Benja. Saunders
Robert Rogers

133 12 Mar 1834--Wills Cowper to Seth R. Morgan...$20...3 acres beginning at post on road near Cowpers house W and along road and then along old road...
John Willey
Edwin Copeland
                             Wills Cowper

134 11 Aug 1834--Henry Hare to Miles Parker...$50...22 acres, being land which he heired from his father, John Hare, dec. and adjoining land of John P. Benton, Demsey Knight, Bryan Hare and others...
Humphrey(x)Parker Jun.
Alfred Ballard
                             Henry(x)Hare

135 1 Jan 1833--Jet. H. Riddick to Jasper Trotman...$15 yearly for 10 years, ending 1 Jan 1843...land adjoining lands of H. Gilliam, Nathan Riddick and others; being part of tract whereon said Trotman lives and lying on side of road where buildings stand...
                             Jet.H. Riddick
H. Gilliam   Jasper Trotman

136 25 Feb 1834--Elisha Umphlet to William Savage...$140...18½ acres beginning at persimmon tree, John Eure's corner and standing on Brittian Smith's across road to a field to a post oak, along line of marked trees to a cypress in run of Big Cypress Swamp to John Sparkman's line to said Smiths to the mulberry tree at the graveyard and back to Smiths...
John R. Norfleet   Elisha Umphlet
Thomas Hoggard

136 15 Nov 1827--John Powell to James Powell...$20...10 acres beginning at black gum on W side of main road, James Gwinn's corner, along his line NW to white oak, said John's corner, and S to said James...
Daniel Powell   John Powell

137 15 Aug 1834--Mary Eure, Cyprian Eure, John Hinton Sr. and Susannah Lassiter to John Morris...$100...30 acres in Indian Neck beginning at mouth of Fort Branch running up branch to James T. Freeman's line to John Roberts and along Roberts line to Frederick Morris to pocosin and along pocosin to mouth of aforesaid branch...
                             Mary(x)Eure
Jas.T.Freeman   Cyprian(x)Eure
                             John Hinton
                             Susanna(x)Lass

138 17 Jul 1834--Kedar Ellis to Riddick Jones...$150...18 acres beginning on W by land of Lewis Jones, dec. heirs N and E by land of Jesse Mathias and land where he now lives...
Miles Briggs   Kedar(x)Ellis
Demsey Vann

17 Jul 1834--Kedar Ellis to Riddick Jones...$150...100 acres known by name The Ridges and beginning on S by lands of Jesse Mathias, W by land of Edwin Mathias, N by Simeon Brinkley, dec. heirs and Mills Riddick...   Kedar(x)Briggs
Miles Briggs
Demsey Vann
(note: This deed was made by Kedar Ellis but the signature is Kedar (x)Briggs) M.J.T.

139 1 Mar 1834--Benjamin Williams to Allen Williams...$170...two lots drawn by said Benjamin and Jordon Williams in division of real estate of their father, Mills Williams, dec.: No. 5, 28 acres drawn by said Jordon and sold to Benjamin, and No. 6, 34 acres, drawn by Benjamin; adjoining lands of Sophia Williams and Lovinia Williams.
James Williams   Benjamin Williams

139 20 Jul 1834--Law. S. Daughtry to Henry Gilliam and William G. Daughtry...$200...lease of lot and tavern...
                                                      Law.S. Daughtry
Open court

140 12 Dec 1834--Zaccra Hays to Robert P. Hays...$1.00 and to secure to Timothy and Willis R. Hays notes given to William Ballard and Elijah Harrell for which they are security...tract of 38 acres, where said Zaccra lives, 1 horse, 1 work oxen, 3 beds and furniture, chairs, tables and kitchen furniture...
                                                      Zaccra Hays
                                                      Timothy Hays
J.R. Riddick   Willis R. Hays
Mary E. Parker   Robert P. Hays

142 1 Nov 1834--Abel Rogerson to Henry Gilliam and Jethro H. Riddick...$2.00...two tracts of land and his interest in 9 Negroes and to secure an $800 bond payable to John C. Gordon, guardian to orphans of Henry Lassiter, dec.; 128 acres adjoining lands of Timothy Walton, Nathan Nixon, Absolom Blanchard and others and being same tract set apart in division of late Timothy Walton, dec. to Thomas and William Walton and conveyed to said Rogerson; 60 acres set apart to Lucy Walton, widow of late Timothy, as her right of dower; and interest in Negroes Jack, Amos, Jerry, Sam, Harvey, Celia, Rose, Milly and Ritty...
                                                      Abel Rogerson
W. Walton   H. Gilliam
Henry King   Jet.H.Riddick

143 13 Feb 1835--Hertford Co.: Benjamin Wynns of Gates to James D. Wynns of Hertford; whereas said Benjamin is indebted to William B. Wynns of Hertford by notes of $683 19 Dec. 1827 and $106.30 15 Dec 1831...50¢ and to secure payment...3 mules, 1 mare, 1 yoke of steers, 8 meat cattle, 12 sheep, 30 hogs, 3 carts and wheels, 7 ploughs, 1 mahogny table, 1 mahogny sideboard, 1 desk, 2 bedsteads and furniture, 6 chairs, all household and kitchen furniture and his life estate in land in Gates known by name of Pilands and bounded by heirs of ____Lewis, William W. Cowper, Jones heirs, Parkers and others...   J.D. Wynns
John Deans

145 25 Aug 1832--Elisha H. Bond to Riddick Gatling...$450...220 acres on W side of Suffolk Road beginning in William Goodman's line and along road to Isaac Piplins line to Peggy Hoskins line to Beaver Dam Swamp on line of Richard B. Gatling...   Elisha H. Bond
Henry Gilliam
Jet.H.Riddick

146 18 Nov 1834--James P. Small and wife, Christian, to Joseph

Gordon...$25...9 acres, it being her proportional part of estate of her father, Daniel Duke, dec. and whereon her mother now lives, adjoining lands of James Lassiter and Risop Rawls...
Riddick Hunter   Jas.P.Small
George G. Harvey   Christian Small

147 3 Nov 1834--Jason Roundtree and wife, Elizabeth, to Thomas Hoggard...$60...33 acres beginning at a pine a strait line of marked trees to swamp to run of Cypress Swamp up run to Mary Harrell's corner, out of swamp to a corner of Bray Eure's on Mills Eure's line...
Wiley Carter   Jason(x)Roundtree
Abram Pruden   Elizabeth(x)Round

148 28 Nov 1834--Abraham Pruden and wife, Martha, to Thomas Hoggard...$60...33 acres beginning at a spruce pine in Mills Eure's line, a corner of Jason Roundtrees, a strait line of marked trees to post oak, a corner of said Roundtrees to corner of Bray Eure's SW to juniper, a corner of Margret Green's on side of pocosin to gum in corner of Long Branch...
Wiley Carter   Abraham Pruden
Wm.H. Savage   Martha(x)Pruden

149 18 Nov 1834--Bryant B. Best and wife, Mary, to David Parker $100... said Mary's dower in estate of Reuben Hinton Sr., bounded by lands of David and James Parker, Ann Bond, Frederick Jones and Noah Hinton...
C.R. Kinney   Bryant B. Best
                                                      Mary Best

151 11 Aug 1834--James R. Riddick, sheriff, to Jesse Wiggens...$1445...190 acres; for writs against Abram Morgan for $2746.18 issued by John A. Roberts, Thomas P. Morgan, Seth R. Morgan, John C. Goodman and Jesse Wiggens. Land is known as William Barnes Plantation and begins at several saplins at Wills Cowper and John Granburys corner NE and through Maple Pocosin NW to Abram Morgans line, plantaion former belonged to Richard Gregory...
Jethro Willey   James R. Riddick
I. Riddick

152 18 Nov 1834--David Outlaw, by Timothy Walton, to James Baker $250...Negro man Sam...
Daniel Hobbs   David Outlaw

152 1 Oct 1834--Joel B. Hurdle to James Baker Jr...$425...Negro woman, Mary, and boy, Jery...
Jet.H. Riddick   Joel B. Hurdle

152 3 Nov 1834--Jason Roundtree and wife, Elizabeth, to daughter, Nancy Harrell, gift of 15 acres of land beginning at an oak, a corner in Mills Eures line a strait line to Mary Harrells line to a stob, a corner and along Elisha Parkers line to Bray Eure's..
Thomas Hoggard   Jason(x)Roundtree
Wiley Carter   Elizabeth(x)Round

153 17 Nov 1834--John Eure to William H. Savage $150...18½ acres beginning at a small persimmon tree in Little Field whereon Silvester Lucas formerly lives adjoining lands of Britton Smith, to run of Little Cypress Swamp to Nathan Smiths line of marked trees to Large Cypress Swamp down run to said Savages line, across plantation...
Wm.L. Boothe, Abraham Parker   John Eure

154 10 Oct 1834--Calvin Brinkley to Edwin Mathias...$122...33 acres beginning at sweet gum, corner of Riddick Jones and John Brinkley's heirs, running S adjoining lands of Benjamin Franklin at public road S to a pine adjoining land of Riddick Jones at a sweet gum and along his line; all the land said Calvin heired from his father, Elisha Brinkley, dec. and a part whereon he resided at time of his death...
                                              Calvin R. Brinkley
Benja. Franklin
Jet.H.Ballard

155 9 Aug 1832--Humphrey Parker to son-in-law, James A. Ballard gift of Negro, Milley and her 3 children, Stephen, Mahala and Sarah...
                                               Humphrey Parker
John C. Gordon
T.W. Carr

155 8 Nov 1825--Dempsey Bond to Susannah Lassiter...$50...15 acres on N side of Bennetts Creek beginning at corner pine of John Saunders and John Lassiters running to middle of branch E to forked pine in Jethro Lassiters...
                                               Dempsey(x)Bond
John(x)Morris
Henry Jocelin

156 Nov Ct 1834--James R. Riddick, sheriff, to Edwin Cross...$2.25 for 1831 taxes on 22 3/4 acres belonging to Elizabeth Saunders, dec. on S side of Long Branch adjoining James Rogers, Jonathan Williams and others and beginning at black gum in Rogers' line and up Long Branch to Elisha Cross' heirs land...
                                             J.R. Riddick
J. Riddick
Henry Willey

157 Nov Ct 1834--James R. Riddick, sheriff, to Edwin Cross...91¢ in taxes for 1831 on 24 acres belonging to Sarah Watson, joining land of Jonathan Williams and said Cross and beginning at pine at corner of John Cross heirs NE and then SE to said Williams fence to a white oak to a bay on Hillory Willeys and NW...
Henry Willey   J.R. Riddick
J. Riddick

158 12 Jun 1834--Jesse Wiggens, trustee of Abraham Morgan, to Wills Cowper...$301...60 acres beginning at apple tree near road W to small mulberry tree running a straight line across swamp to main run of creek or Gregory's line along line up to Wiggens corner to main road S...
                                             Jesse Wiggens
John Granbury
George W. Granbury

159 22 Oct 1834--Wills Cowper Jr. to Rachael Yates...$1150...105 acres beginning at a post near Cowper's house running S to Cypress Swamp along run to line of heirs of John Granbury, dec. to road and down road to white oak on N side to Mrs. Elizabeth Granbury's line and down lane to old white oak with large hump on side N to corner of Jesse Wiggens W to large pine former corner of Duke's land to red oak near road and across road to run of creek to a large beach on Gregory's line E to field and to road...
Henry Gilliam   Wills Cowper
Noah Harrell

160 22 Oct 1834--Rachael Yates to Noah Harrell...$1.00 and to secure $200 note to said Harrell 105 acres described in preceding deed...
H. Gilliam   Rachael(x)Yates
Wills Cowper

161 1 Nov 1834--William Walton to Abel Rogerson...$700...128 acres beginning at fork of road at Timothy Walton's line running down avenue to dwelling house binding on Absolom Blanchard's line to Mill Dam then NW down run of swamp S to Henry Bond and Abraham Morgan's line E binding on Nathan Nixons line to branch to plum orchard along marked apple trees and through plantation to road; it being part of land late Timothy Walton, dec. set aside to William and Thomas Walton...
Henry King   William Walton
John(x)Boyce

162 1 Nov 1834--William Walton to Abel Rogerson...$100...60 acres, being part of plantation set aside by late Timothy Walton to his widow, Lucy, as her dower...
Henry King   William Walton
John(x)Boyce

163 12 Apr 1834--Simon Walters, guardian of orphans of Wiley Jenkins, dec. to John C. Jenkins by court order to sell estate of said Wiley...$45...35 acres adjoining land of John H. Haslett, William Babb, James Savage and others...
William Walton   Simon Walters
Henry Willey

163 4 Nov 1834--Daniel Fields to Allen Smith...$25...30 acres on new road leading from Norfleet's Mill to Somerton beginning at a red oak E side, Honey Pot Swamp, corner of said Fields and Smiths and running E along line of marked trees to new road to Cuffs...
                                                        Daniel(x)Fields
Seth Norfleet
Harrison Vann

164 25 Jan 1834--Robert Riddick to James Woodward...$204...102 acres, being part of tract bought by said Riddick of Noah B. Hinton beginning at oak stump in Andrew R. Harrell's line NW to a pine SE to public road...
                                                        Robert Riddick
Jacob J. Harvey
John Alpin

165 18 Nov 1834--Jephtha Fowlkes, guardian to heirs of Reuben Hinton, Jr., to Benbury Hinton...$55...35 acres adjoining Nancy Bond and James Parker...
Jas. T. Freeman   Jeptha Fowlkes
W. Walton

166 19 Nov 1834--Benbury Walton to David Parker...$75...35 acres drawn in division of estate of James Hinton, dec. by Reuben Hinton, dec. beginning at a large white oak, a corner of Noah Hinton Jr. in Fred. Jones line SE to James Parkers line...
Willis I. Riddick   Benbury Walton

167 16 Jun 1834--Hiram Loomis of Norfolk to John L. Griffith... $200...10 acres attached to a fishery and formerly known by name

Copeland's Fishery and sometimes called Gut Landing and now known as Lumberton...on Chowan River and bounded on S by land belonging to Myles Parker, E and N by land of heirs of late Henry Hare, dec.
Jason Saunders   H. Loomis
D.M. Saunders

167 5 Jul 1835--John L. Griffith to Abram Riddick of Hertford...
$200...Lumberton Fishery described in preceding deed...
Jason Saunders   John L. Griffith
D.M. Saunders

167 7 Nov 1834--John Gatling to Nathan Pearce...$200...120 acres, which was purchased by Amos Lassiter of Lassiter Riddick, and then purchased by said Gatling from Thomas and Robert Riddick, heirs of said Lassiter Riddick, beginning at run of Bennetts Creek at cypress in James Costens line then running to mouth of Deep Gut to Moses Lassiters line N to Abram Green's line and down road to John Lassiters line binding on his line to head of Popular Stump Branch and down branch to creek...   Jno. Gatling
Thomas(x)Lassiter
Lassiter(x)Pearce

169 8 Aug 1828--Abner Lassiter to Molly Johnston...$25...16½ acres laid off to him in division of his fathers land bounded by land of Kicheon Howell, Abner Pearce and others...   Abner(x)Lassiter
Rich'd Boyt
Jno.B. Baker

169 20 Oct 1834--Jacob Matthews to Elbert H. Riddick...$14.52...
7 3/4 acres beginning at sweet gum in flat corner of said Matthews and running SW...   Jacob Matthews
David F. Felton

170 1 Oct 1834--Samuel Felton to Elbert H. Riddick...$10...small piece of land in N corner adjoining Thomas old field...
Open court   Samuel Felton

171 5 Nov 1834--Jesse Mathias to Kedar Ellis...$75...25 acres beginning at fork of marsh road, corner of Daniel Ward, Riddick Jones and others, running S and binding on said Jones, to Deep Branch and adjoining lands of John Jones, son of Lewis Jones, dec., down branch to Col. J. Riddicks NW to road and E...   Jesse Mathias
Lem Benton
Jam. Ballard

171 31 Jul 1834--George Harrell of Perquimans to Mary Harrell...$15
17½ acres beginning at said Mary and Elisha Parker's corner, down Parkers line to swamp, S to Jason Roundtree and said Mary's line..
A.W. Parker   George Harrell

172 20 Oct 1834--Abram Pruden to Mary Harrell...$50...15½ acres beginning at a pine, a corner in Isaac Greens thence along Bray Eures line to stob in Elisha Parkers line in corner of said Mary's line to Mills Eures line to Pleasant Taylors...
Thomas Hoggard   Abram Pruden
Wm.H. Savage

172 13 Oct 1834--John Lassiter to Willis Hoffler...lease for 10

years, assigned from 1 Oct 1834, 15 acres for 1/3 of all products after first five years. First five years to be free from rent and said Lassiter to have privilege of firewood and rail timber from land, which is known as the George Brooks Tract and begins at a water oak, a corner tree in dividing line between Timothy Spivey and said Lassiter running N to a corner white oak then E to a corner pine and S by a line of marked trees to a corner pine binding on Margaret Brooks line then W...
Jethro Blanchard
Hance Hofler
John(x)Lassiter
Ann(x)Lassiter
Willis(x)Hofler

173 10 Aug 1830--Division of land of James Piland: Survey No. 1--Seth Piland...56 acres on Coles Creek beginning at a pine near new road SE to a ditch in front of Mills Piland's house to a pine of Prior Savage to John Worrells. No. 2--Elisha Piland...50 acres beginning at a pine near new road N to Seth's lot to Coles Creek and SW along run. No. 3--Isaac Piland...35 acres, the house lot whereon said James lived, beginning at hickory in Thomas Hoggard's line SW to lightwood stob, a corner of said Hoggards NW to a black gum to a road leading to Sarum Creek, along road SW to road leading to house. No. 4--Reuben Piland...45 acres beginning at post on side of road leading to creek to a pine stump, a corner of Bray Eure's and along dividing line. No. 5--James Piland...100 acres beginning at a white bay tree, a new corner made between said Reuben and James along out boundry E to water oak on W side of Coles Creek, a corner in Reuben Harrell's line up run of creek to cornfield to dividing line. No. 6...Jesse Piland...88 acres beginning at post in cornfield along dividing line to gum on Coles Creek and NW. No. 7--Mills Piland...79 acres beginning at post in cornfield along dividing line to Coles Creek to gum in out boundry W to said Hoggards. No. 8--Asa Piland...56½ acres beginning at line of Mills Piland, Joseph Stallings and Miles White on Bee Pond Swamp, prong of Voss Creek
H. Gilliam
Mills Eure
Pryer Savage

177 Nov Ct 1832--Division of estate of Abner Pearce, including plantation of 560 acres and a small tract of 80 acres, conveyed to him by John and Isaac Lassiter, among said Pearce's heirs: Survey No. 1--Abram Pearce...50 acres beginning at a pine blown up in Coldmans Branch, NW to a stake, then NE to a small branch and down branch to run of Watery Swamp to mouth of branch. No. 2--Lassiter Pearce...50 acres beginning at blown up pine in Coldmans Branch, NW to small branch to white oak and SE to large pine in branch. No. 3--heirs of Abner Pearce, dec...66 acres beginning at a white oak corner running to a pine in Waltons line to run of Watery Swamp to a large cypress corner of George Costens SW to red oak. No. 4--Thomas Lassiter in right of wife, Mary...64 acres beginning at a water oak NW to red oak corner of No. 3 and SE along line of marked trees. No. 5--Edward Jones in right of wife, Leah...85 acres beginning at small red oak corner of said Thomas Lassiter running NE to water oak and S to Coldmans Branch and up branch. No. 6--Kedar Lassiter in right of wife, Arey...95 acres beginning at a maple corner of No. 7 to stake in old field to a

pine corner of James Lassiters in old road SE to black gum to a
small maple. No. 7--Enoch Pearce...65 acres beginning at maple
corner of No. 6 running to Jethro Blanchards to head of Coldman Branch to stake in old field. No. 8--Benbury Walton, which
he purchased of Kedar Green and wife, Judith...95 acres beginning at dead pine in Deep Gut, corner of Abram Lassiters SW to
Bond's line and NE to maple corner. No. 9--Nathan Pearce...80
acres beginning at sweet gum in Abram Green's corner on N side
of main road along road to Lassiter Riddicks, dec. to branch in
Bennett Creek swamp, down swamp to Bond Menchews, dec. line S.
No. 1 receives of No. 3 $10, No. 2 receives of No. 8 $10.

John Walton
Henry Bond
Willis I. Riddick
David Parker

Jethro Barnes,
county surveyor

179 19 Feb 1833--Division of estate of Abram Benton, dec. consisting of 219 acres: Survey No. 1--Sidney Benton...30 acres beginning at a gum in Seth Benton's line NE to pine stump of David
Bentons and SW along line of marked trees. No. 2--Joseph Benton...
30 acres beginning at white oak, corner of said Sidney's SW to
small holly on edge of Bennetts Creek along run to road leading
from Wiggens cross roads to Abram Morgans to said Seth Benton's
heirs line. No. 3--Bryant Hare in right of wife...35½ acres beginning at Wiggens road running NW along line of newly marked
trees to a cypress in Bennetts Creek at mouth of Benton's Great
Ditch, includes 6½ acres of pecosin land. No. 4--Elisha Benton...
25½ acres beginning at stake in edge of road along line of marked
trees to Bennetts Creek and SE. No. 5--Benjamin Benton...25½ acres
beginning at stake in road running to corner of David Bentons to
Bennett Creek and also includes 6¾ acres of pecosin land. No. 6--
Susannah Benton...25½ acres beginning at stake in David Benton's
line to run of Bennetts Creek and also includes 6¾ acres of pecosin land. No. 7--James Jones in right of his wife...32 acres
known as Licking Root Tract and conveyed to said Abram Benton by
Gates County sheriff. Sidney to pay Bryant Hare $20 and Joseph to
pay Susanna $10.

J. Barnes
John C. Gordon
Humphrey Parker
Holloday Walton

Richard H. Ballard,
alternate

181 18 Feb 1833--Division of estate of Peter Harrell, dec. includes 222 acres and is made in two divisions: Survey No.1 in 1st
division--Mary Harrell...14½ acres beginning at black oak NE to
pine stump to corner of Pleasant Taylors and Riddick Greens, SE
to persimmon tree to a stake near a cedar corner and along a line
of marked trees; and Lot No. 3 in 2nd division...17¼ acres beginning at stake in corner SW to Brick Hole to run of Cypress Swamp. No. 2 in 1st division--Elizabeth Benton...14½ acres beginning
at black oak corner, NE to stake and NW, also Lot No. 5 in 2nd
division 17¼ acres beginning at run of Long Branch NE to stake and
SE to run of Cypress Swamp and up swamp. No. 3--Bray Eure in right
of wife, Sarah...14½ acres from 1st division, beginning at black

oak corner SE to stake to run of Long Branch and NW to Mills Eure's line and NE; also Lot No. 1 in 2nd division 17¼ acres beginning at stake corner NE to run of Cypress Swamp, along small branch to corner of Riddick Greens SW to pine corner of Pleasant Taylors. No. 4--Nathan Harrell...14½ acres in 1st division beginning at stake corner SE to gum in Long Branch SW to pine corner then NW to stake; also Lot. No. 2 in 2nd division 17¼ acres beginning at stake near cedar corner NE to run of Cypress Swamp and down swamp NW. No. 5--George Harrell...14½ acres in 1st division beginning at pine corner SW to an oak and then NW; also, Lot No. 4 in 2nd division 17¼ acres beginning at stake in corner to run of Cypress Swamp and down swamp SW to Long Branch. No. 6--Margaret Johnson...14½ acres in 1st division beginning at pine corner SE to oak corner then to juniper at edge of pocosin and NE; also, No. 6 in 2nd division 17¼ acres beginning at stake corner at edge of pocosin and NW. No. 7--Abram Pruden in right of wife, Martha...14½ acres in 1st division beginning at pine corner SE to juniper at edge of pocosin to pine corner of Mills Eures and NE; also, Lot No. 7 from 2nd division 17¼ acres beginning at gum in Long Branch corner SE to edge of pocosin. Nathan to pay Elizabeth $6, George to pay Elizabeth $14, Margaret Johnson to pay Bray Eure $10 and Abram Pruden $5.
J. Barnes surveyor
Reuben Piland and Richard Odom,
alternate commissioners

Dempsey Sparkman
Prior Savage
John Riddick

184 Feb Ct 1834--Division of estate of James Jones, dec. and included 247 acres valued at $2.00 per acre. Survey No. 1--Nancy Jones...42 acres valued at $55, beginning at pine stump on Jesse Parkers line SW to corner of said Jesse's and B. Wynns to red oak a new corner between Lots 1 and 2 and NE to swamp. Lot. 2--Whitmill Jones...26 acres valued at $61.75 beginning at red oak corner SW to oak in swamp and along swamp to dividing line. Lot 3--William Jones...22 acres valued at $80 beginning at red oak NW to maple, a new corner and along dividing line NE to swamp. Lot No. 4--Eli Jones...39 acres valued at $61.75 beginning at corner maple NW to dividing line and SW. Lot No. 5--Elizabeth Jones...39 acres valued at $80 beginning at red oak N to dividing line to red oak near head of small branch to swamp and up swamp. Lot No. 6--Nathaniel Jones...39 acres valued at $61.75 beginning at red oak NW to post oak corner to Isaac Pipkins and along dividing line. Lot No. 7--Simmons Jones...19 acres valued at $46.87½ beginning at oak in swamp NE to red oak to maple corner to water oak in swamp and down swamp. Lot No. 8--James Jones...22 acres beginning at water oak in swamp NE to maple corner SE to post oak then to forked white oak, a corner of Robert Rogers and binding on said Rogers line SW to gum in swamp and along swamp...William to pay Nancy $6.75 and Simmons $11.50 and Elizabeth to pay Simmons $3.37½ and James $14.87½.
Isaac William, surveyor
Alternate commissioners
were: John Saunders and John D. Pipkin

R. Gatling
John Willey
Kindred Parker

185 28 Feb 1834--Division of estate of Simon King, dec. and includes 200 acres valued at $3.00 per acres. Lot No. 1--William King

50 acres called the House Lot, where said Simon formerly lived beginning at a black gum in Cabbin Branch, corner of Reuben Nixon's NE to pine corner of Abel Rogerson and along his line SE and back to branch and down branch. Lot No. 2--Norman King...77½ acres beginning at gum in branch running NE to red oak then SE and back to branch. Lot No. 3--Simon King...72½ acres beginning at pine in branch running NE to Joseph Hill's corner and SE to red oak, corner of Guy Hobbs and NW along James Eason's line...

Alternates were:
Joseph Riddick
Nathan Riddick

Whit. Stallings
Jesse(x)Hobbs
Reuben Nixon

188 28 Feb 1834--Division of estate of Nathan Cullens, dec. between his widow, Christian Cullens, and Nathan Cullens, son of Jacob Cullens, made according to his will: Survey No. 1--Christian...160 acres beginning at stake in Nathan Nixon's line on N side of plantation running SW to edge of swamp and N on Nixon's line to fork of creek, down run of Catherine Creek to mouth of Deep Branch, Powell's corner, up Deep Branch to oak stump near where old schoolhouse stood, to a pine Taylor's corner NW by line of marked trees and through plantation including all buildings and orchard, and including swamp land. No. 2--Nathan Cullens...tract beginning at aforesaid stake on N side of plantation in Nixon's line SE through plantation by line of marked trees to Powell and Taylors line to a pine and to a post oak at head of small branch and down branch, Taylor's line, to gum on edge of Catherine Creek to Nixons line...

Benbury Walton, surveyor

Nathan Nixon
Thomas Costen
J. Riddick
I.S. Harrell

189 16 May 1834--Nathaniel Taylor and Seth Spivey of Gates and William Bush of Chowan to Thomas Whitmill Stallings...$75.25...14 1/8 acres beginning at post oak saplin by side of Old Town Road, adjoining land of Joseph Taylor's heirs with their line NE to Taylors and George Outlaws corner tree SE to branch by Old Town Road...

William(x)Spivey
Jonas(x)Spivey

Nathaniel(x)Taylor
William Bush
Seth Spivey

190 6 Apr 1835--Lawrence S. Daughtry assigns enough of his interest in property conveyed to him by Jeptha Fowlkes to secure debt to Jeremiah F. Randolph of firm of Randolph and Disosway for $500 for which William G. Daughtry is his security.

Robert B. Parker

Law.S.Daughtry

190 8 Apr 1835--Lawrence S. Daughtry to Henry R. Pugh...enough interest in property conveyed to him by Jeptha Fowlkes to cover following debts: William Speight for hire of boy Jacob $55, Titus Darden security for $125 and $300 debts to John Roberts, Mrs. Ann N. Harvey $95, John Lovett $70, John S. Roberts $30, Jeptha Fowlkes $30 and W.L. Byrum for $65. John Waddle is executor of Titus Darden, dec.

Robert B. Parker

Law.S. Daughtry

191 3 Apr 1835--Thomas Darden to John Lovett...50¢ and to secure debt of $66.26...household and kitchen furniture consisting of 2 mahogny tables, 1 bed and furniture, doz. windsor chairs, 1½ doz. plates, ½ doz. tumblers, 1 doz. cups and plates, 1 looking glass, 1 dressing glass, 1 bucket, 1 wash basin, 1 pine table, 1 griddle, large bowl, bread tray, coffee mill, pair andirons, set teaware and ½ doz. knives and forks...
R.B. Parker
Thomas R. Darden

192 28 Jan 1825--Willis Casey to Simon Stallings and to secure to Whitmill Stallings and Frederick Rooks as his security for a $20 note to Abel Rogerson...small bay horse, 3 feather beds and furniture, work stand, looking glass, 9 chairs, 2 tables, 4 trunks, 3 iron pots, 1 teakettle, 1 dutch oven, 1 fry pan, 1 spider, 2 tubs, 2 pails, 1 pr. silver ladles, all household and kitchen furniture, 1 sow and 9 pigs...

T.W. Stallings

W. Casey
Simon Stallings
Whitmill Stallings
Frederick Rooks

194 17 Feb 1835--John O. Hunter to Tilly W. Carr...$1.00 and to make safe to John C. Gordon and Joseph Gordon as his security for $800 note to Joseph Coffield...Negroes George, Frank and Venus...
John O. Hunter
Joseph Gordon
Nathan Riddick
John C. Gordon

195 10 Sep 1834--William W. Stedman to Noah Harrell...1 bay mule as security for $50...
Samuel R. Harrell
Wm.W.Stedman

195 25 Nov 1834--Whereas: a marriage contract having been agreed upon between Simon Stallings and Fruzy Taylor with Whitmill Stallings to serve as trustee...$1.00 to hold in trust the following property to insure said Fruzy will have freedon of choices, for her sole and exclusive use and she may direct by her will assignment of said property and she shall not be liable for any debts of said Simon...land bounded agreeable to will of Robert Taylor, dec., Negro Jenny and her child, Andrew, 4 feather beds and furniture, 1 buffet and furniture, 1 walnut table, ½ doz. windsor chairs, 1 chest, 2 trunks, all household and kitchen furniture, loom and gear, 1 gig and harness, cart and all farm utensils, 1 mare, 3 head cattle, 3 sows and pigs, 15 head hogs...
Jno. Mitchell
Jos.A. Fairless

Fruzy Taylor
Simon Stallings
Whit. Stallings

198 14 Feb 1835--John Everitt and wife, Armety, of Nansemond to David Dunsford, Jun. $250.56...98½ acres beginning at black gum in Beaverdam Swamp in Riddick Gatling's line SW to a sassafras stump, a corner of Mrs. Hoskins SW to a white oak in William Gatlings line SW to a gum in Deep Branch down branch to Miles Parker's line and along his line NE to Beaverdam Swamp...

Feb Court 1835

John Everett
Armety Everett

199 17 Dec 1834--Thomas, Dempsey, William, Elizabeth and Nancy Gomer of Nansemond to George W. Smith...$255...171 acres beginning at a pine, William Moore and Jesse Arline's corner NE to Arline's field, to a pine, Hardy Parker's corner SE to a sassafras, Smith's corner, and with his line by Old Path SE to center of 2 gums and a pine in Jethro Williams line, on his line to said Moores...

                                    Thomas(x)Gomer   William(x)Gomer
                                    Dempsey(x)Gomer Elizabeth(x)Gomer
Caleb Savage   Nancy(x)Gomer

200 15 Aug 1834--James R. Riddick, sheriff, to Elbert H. Riddick...$95...34 acres sold by court writs against Abram Morgan brought by John A. Roberts, Thomas P. Morgan, Seth R. Morgan, John C. Gordon and Jesse Wiggens for debts of $2746...land adjoins David Riddick, Celia Pruden and others...
                                                                     J.R. Riddick
Job R. Hawl
John L. Granbury

200 1 Apr 1835--James R. Riddick, sheriff, to Timothy Walton...$1.00 ...land of Elisha Walton, adjoining Willis Walton, Henry King and others, sold by court levy for $35 plus $3.92 in court costs...
John Walton   J.R. Riddick

202 1 Nov 1834--William E. Pugh, clerk and master of court, to Thomas B. Hunter...$2400...515 acres adjoining lands of Robert Riddick, John Granbury and Risop Rawls on main road from Gatesville to Sunbury; land belonging to John Riddick, dec. and sold by court petition by his heirs at law...Thomas B. Hunter and wife, Elizabeth, William Eley and wife, Sarah, and Mary Ann Riddick, infant, by her guardian, George Costen...
                                                                William E. Pugh
C.R. Kinney

203 15 Apr 1835--William E. Pugh, Whitmill Stallings and Jethro Riddick are bound to state of North Carolina for $10,000 whereas said Pugh is appointed clerk and master of Court of Equity for County of Gates...
                                                                Wm.E. Pugh
                                                                Whitt Stallings
Asa Hill   Jet.H. Riddick

204 11 Sep 1834--William L. Boothe to William W. Cowper...$150...33 acres beginning at red oak in edge of road near corner of Boothes fence, a corner of Booths and John Riddick N and then W by a line of marked trees to a gum in white oak along branch to road to town of Suffolk...
                                                                Wm.L.Boothe
Jno. Riddick
Robert Lee

206 29 Dec 1834--Sarah Savage to James Savage...$1.00...90 acres left to her for life and after her death to said James...
Jesse M. Savage   Sarah(x)Savage
John Savage

207 2 Sep 1834--Willie Riddick, trustee, to Jesse Wiggens...$325 170 acres, residence of Abram Morgan, part of which was conveyed to him by Noah B. Benton; whereas said Abram is indebted to Ann Wiggens for $1330...
                                                               W. Riddick
H. Gilliam
H.G. Williams

208 27 Oct 1834--Exum Jenkins of Nansemond is bound to Thomas Saunders and William W. Cowper for $5000 to set aside as his part of estate of Barsheba Sears Negroes Nat, Jakey, Drew, Matilda, Carey and Abraham; whereas by consent of said Saunders and Cowper, who are entitled to same share...
H. Gilliam
                Exum Jenkins

208 16 Apr 1835--Allen Briggs to Josiah Briggs...$200...50 acres formerly belonging to Daniel Pearce and adjoining land of Isaac Hunter's heirs and Hardy Eason heirs, and 1 sorrell horse...
Jacob I. Harvey   Allen Briggs
James Briggs

209 17 May 1835--William Parker to James Morgan...$1.00 and to make safe to David Benton $200 note...Negro woman, Tamer, and 3 children, Milley, Bob and Reaney...
Jno. Wiggens   William Parker
David O. Duke

210 2 Feb 1835--Simmons Jones to James Jones...$44...19 acres beginning at a cypress corner of said James, NE to post oak corner on Isaac Pipkins line and down swamp...
               Simmons(x)Jones
John F. Parker
Henry Hays

211 9 Feb 1835--James Riddick, sheriff, to William H. Harrell... $71...110 acres, ¼ of Rice Tract, belonging to James R. Creecy, and sold by court writ issued from Chowan County Nov term 1834 at instance of president and directors of State Bank of North Carolina at Edenton for notes of $300 and $11,322.72 including interest and costs. Land adjoins William Reed, Abram Hurdle and said Harrell
Job R. Hall   J.R. Riddick
John Granbury

212 15 Aug 1834--James R. Riddick to Seth R. Morgan...$551...106 acres belonging to Abram Morgan sold by court writs from John A. Roberts, Thomas P. Morgan, Seth R. Morgan, John C. Gordon and Jesse Wiggens for notes of $2746.19. Land adjoins Joseph Benton, Seth R. Morgan and Jesse Wiggens.
Whitt Stallings   J.R. Riddick
A.W. Parker

213 5 Nov 1834--James R. Riddick to Harrison Ellis...$250...two tracts of land belonging to Josiah Ellis and Willis Parker, sold by court writ at instance of John Hofler against them for $301.50. Tract of 20 acres is plantation whereon said Josiah lives and 2nd tract of 90 acres adjoins first tract, David Benton, Tilly W. Carr and others...   J.R. Riddick
Jas. T. Freeman
Jet. H. Riddick

214 1 Jan 1835--John Brothers to James Mathias...$500...150 acres formerly belonging to his father, John Brothers, beginning at avenue in Col. Josiah Riddicks line and along his line to run of Mills Swamp N to dividing line between Marmaduke and said John Brothers corner and along Arnolds line...
John O. Hunter   John Brothers
William Arnold

215 21 Jan 1835--Gilbert G. Saunders to Exum Jenkins...$132.81
212½ acres beginning at white oak near road in Jenkins line SW
to maple to a pine called Acamons Corner, now a corner of said
Jenkins SE to a dead pine stump in corner of Ann Speight's and
said Jenkins to a small dogwood, a corner of James Williams, then
NE to a persimmon tree, corner on Jason Saunders...
Drew M. Saunders   G.G. Saunders
John B. Jenkins

216 3 Nov 1834--Hardy H.C. Jones to Zachariah Boon...$30...10
acres beginning at red oak corner on James Sumners SW to a stake
on John Jones line then NW to branch...
Harrison Hare   H.H.C. Jones

217 8 Oct 1834--Richard Cross to Richard Hinton...$100...41½ acres
whereon said Cross resides, beginning at white oak, a corner tree
in Elizabeth Hofflers line, along her line to a pine, a corner tree
in Nathan Pearces line, along his line to main road that leads to
Gatesville, to Hollow Bridge and across road to Holley Tree Branch
and along run...
Thos. E. Powell   Richard Cross
James Costen

218 12 Feb 1835--Richard Hinton to Nathan Pearce...$125...41½ acres
described in above deed and whereon said Hinton now resides...
James Smith   Richard Hinton
Kedah Hinton

218 14 Oct 1834--Jonathan Williams to Dempsey Parker...$230...150
acres beginning at a corner post oak in Parkers and Ann N. Harvey's
line running N along line of marked trees to run of Knotty Pine
Swamp, up course to a water oak, a corner of Miles Parker and Henry
Williams then S to Mrs. Harvey's line...
                                              Jonathan Williams
William Sears
Mary(x)Parker

219 19 Apr 1834--Ezekiel Trotman to Nathan Riddick...$123...27 acres
beginning on side of road and running S along Riddick's line to middle of Catren Creek Swamp W down swamp to Riddicks line and NW to
causeway and along line E...
Jesse R. Kee   Ezekiel Trotman
Esther(x)Riddick

220 29 Jan 1834--Nathan Riddick to Jesse R. Kee...gift of 50 acres
of land known as Brinkley Land beginning at a pine stump on side of
road, corner of Bushrod Riddick's line along road W to fork of road
to Drew Trotmans, along his line S to run of swamp to Jethro H. Riddicks E to Joseph Hurdles...
Jason Riddick   Nathan Riddick
Drew Trotman

221 18 Dec 1834--Nathan Riddick to Jethro H. Riddick and Whitmill
Stallings...$200...12 acres beginning at end of causeway on main
road nearly N along line of marked trees to red oak corner in James
Brinkley's line along his line to Milton Easons S to road and a 10
acre tract beginning in Eason's line N and then running E...
Jason Riddick   Nathan Riddick
Jesse R. Kee

222 7 Jan 1835--Edward R. Hunter to Andrew Eason...$800...300 acres beginning at black gum, a corner tree in Figgs line on SE side of Honey Pot Swamp at place called The Old Flax Hole, running by line of marked trees NE to sweet gum in Miles Parker's line on his line W to a pine, Norfleet's corner in Parkers Path and along path to a post oak at head of branch, down branch to 3 oak saplings intended for a corner to Figgs line and up SE side of swamp...
Bn.B.Ballard
Jet.H.Riddick
              E.R. Hunter

223 27 Aug 1834--Jesse Eason to Joseph Eason...$405...87 acres, ½ of tract whereon his father, Soloman Eason, lived and which he gave to said Jesse in his will, beginning at corner tree in Abraham Hurdle's line to Hardy Easons heirs line, to Charles Easons line to main desert S nearly opposite house; and 10 acre tract, his ¼ part of tract known as Old Woman or Thomas Easons pocosin, adjoining Hardy Eason, Samuel Green and others...
Jet.H.Riddick   Jesse Eason
J. Riddick

224 30 Oct 1834--Timothy Walton to Andrew Baker...$300...50 acres beginning at Muddy Cross at road leading from Sandy Cross and down Edenton road to Mrs. Cullens line, along line of marked trees to swamp and back to road...
James Baker   Tim. Walton
Daniel Hobbs

224 26 Nov 1834--Louisa R. Barnes and Joseph J. Barnes, with Henry Gilliam as trustee, to James Williams...$300...tract of land devised to Louisa by her father, Abraham Cross, and more fully described in his will and was duly recorded with Henry Gilliam as trustee before marriage contract between them...
             Jos.J.Barnes
             Louisa R. Barnes
Jno. Riddick   H. Gilliam

226 21 Feb 1798 (probated Aug Ct 1834)--James Griffen and Mary Darden to Jethro Sumner...$500...mulatto girl Cherry, which did belong to estate of John Darden, dec.
Ben. Wiggens   James Griffen
Thiresa(x)Ellis   Mary(x)Darden
Joseph Hare
  In obedience to commission Barnes Goodman, justice, caused Joseph Hare(he being old and infirm as to be unable to attend court) to come before him to prove execution of bill of said and said Joseph being duly sworn made oath he witnessed bill of sale...
B. Goodman, J.P.   Joseph(x)Hare

227 30 Aug 1834--Charles A. Carter to William Sears...$30...all kitchen and household furniture, 1 feather bed and furniture, 1 dest, 2 pine tables, 1 doz. sitting chairs, 2 iron pots, 1 dutch oven, 1 skillet and frying pan and 12 head hogs...
James Sears   Charles A. Carter
Jas. Simpson

227 27 Dec 1834--James Freeman and Martha Moore of Madison County, Tn. appoint Richard Willeford, esq. of Bertie as their lawful att-

orney to call on Joseph Freeman, administrator of John Freeman, dec. late of Gates, for equal shares of said John Freeman's estate and to perform all matters thereof...
                Jas. Freeman
D. Sparkman   Martha Moore
Levi Beeman

228 18 Feb 1835--Wright Hays of Halifax to Henry L. Blount...$300 2 3/4 acres beginning at corner of Methodist E. Church on Honey Pot Street W to next corner of church yard then S to H. Gilliams line W, another corner of Gilliams and back to Honey Pot Street...
Reuben Lassiter   W. Hays
Elijah Harrell

228 28 Oct 1834--Job R. Hall and wife, Emma, to Richard Odom...$9 44 acres bounded by land of Elisha H. Bond and said Odom...
Abm. Smith   Job R. Hall
John Sparkman   Emily Hall
Wm. L. Boothe and Abraham W. Parker, esq. attested that said Emily signed freely...

229 12 Apr 1834--John B. Gatling of Edenton to Richard Odom...$9 his 1/7 part of land in Great Pocosin, adjoining land of said Odom and Elisha Bond, which fell to him and his brothers and sisters in death of Mildred Bond, formerly Mildred Barnes...
Jas. Pruden   John B. Gatling
Etheldred Cross

230 21 Nov 1834--James Baker to Calvin R. Brinkley...$300...137 acres adjoining lands of Henry King, Willis Walton and others, which he bought of Elisha Walton, who drew it in division of his father's estate...
                James Baker
Wynns Baker
Levy(x)Sumner

231 7 Nov 1834--Nancy Riddick to William Gatling...$150...75 acres called Flax Island beginning at old pine stump on river side running John Rochells line along his line to river to John Odoms line to Miles Benton's line...
Riddick Gatling   Nancy(x)Riddick
Whit'l Stallings

231 30 Sep 1834--Nathan Riddick to Lemuel Cleaves...$50...29 acres adjoining lands of Williams Cleaves, Daniel Fields and others; it being part of a tract formerly belonging to Jesse Hudgins...
Levi Beeman   Nathan Riddick
W.W. Stedman Jr.

232 18 Feb 1834--William W. Cowper to Exum Lewis...$250...87 acres beginning on W side of road near Lewis house, corner of Jos. Gatling's line NW and then SE to road and along a line of marked trees NE to main run of Hackly Swamp and down swamp NW...
Peter Piland   Wm.W. Cowper
Wm.H. Goodman

233 1 Aug 1835--William Cowper to Joshua M. Harrell of Nansemond... $1.00 and to secure to Robert W. Bowden of Norfolk note of $638.86

three tracts of land, 400, 260 and 50 acres in Great Dismal Swamp, the first two purchased by John Cowper, father of said William, from James Gordon 3 Jan 1805 and the latter by John Cowper, grandfather of said William, from Jno. Small...
Open Ct.
Wm. Cowper

234 21 Feb 1835--William W. Stedman to John C. Gordon...$1.00 and to make safe to Joseph Gordon two notes $860 and $324 and as his security for a $50 note to Wilthy Riddick and a $65.34 note to Miles Briggs...two tracts of land; the first of 184 acres formerly belonged to Noah B. Hinton and was given by deed of gift from Holaday Walton to said Stedman, adjoining lands of John Granbury heirs, John Powell and others; second tract of 128 acres was bought by said Stedman from John Hofler and is on N side of Bayles Swamp adjoining lands of William Brothers heirs, John Small and Ellis heirs...
Thomas Rice
Henry Riddick
Wm.W. Stedman

236 28 Jul 1835--John Lovet to William E. Pugh...$1.00 and to secure to William G. Daughtry two notes of $400 each...1 acre in town of Gatesville on E side of street running N and S and bounded on N by Asa Hill's lot and Thomas Saunders, on S by lot of John Mathews and on W by street...
John (x) Lovet
W.G. Daughtry
Ro. Riddick
Wm. E. Pugh

237 29 Aug 1835--Clement Hill to Reuben Lassiter...$1.00 and to secure to James T. Freeman a note for $234.36...150 acres, including whereon he lives and the Davis Tract...
C. Hill
John Hinton
Jas. T. Freeman
John W. Hinton
R. Lassiter

238 17 Feb 1834--James Boyce of Mesway in County of Montgomery to Thomas Jones...$25...50 acres that his grandmother, Elizabeth Burges, gave him joining land of Isaac Pipkin, Dempsey Goodman and Robert Rogers...
Burwell Griffith
James Boyce

239 16 Feb 1835--H.H.C. Jones to H.T. Smith of Southampton, Va. $12.50...111 acres, the Duke Tract...
Open Court
H.H.C.Jones

239 29 Feb 1834--Thomas R. Costen to Timothy G. Trotman of Chowan $600...170 acres beginning at main road N along Harrell and Costen lines to John Saunders line SE to W. Stallings E to Amos Hobbs and John Mitchell, along Mitchells line NE to road and W; land he purchased of William W. Hays...
Jacob Cullens
Thomas R. Costen
Andrew Harrell

240 14 Feb 1835--Thomas Saunders to Robert Simons...$100...45 acres bounded by Hance Hofler, formerly known as Minchew Tract and purchased of Henry Gilliam, trustee for Richard Cross and known by name of Amos Lassiter Tract...
David Parker
T. Saunders
Wm.W. Cowper

241 9 Sep 1834--Jacob Eason of Chowan to Willis Bunch...$150...88 acres beginning at pine stump, corner of Eason, John Felton and others, along Eason's line to sweet gum in Bull Branch, along branch to Reuben Nixons to Levy Sumners to a pine, corner of Jesse Hobbs to Boyce's line, to Bunch's line...
J.T. Benton					Jacob Eason
Shadrack Felton

242 31 Jan 1835--Jeptha Fowlkes and William G. Daughtry, trustees of deeds executed to them by William Petty, to Benbury Walton...$60 land formerly belonging to Kedar Green and wife and conveyed by them to said Petty...
H. Gilliam					J. Fowlkes
Simmonds Roundtree				W.G. Daughtry

243 31 Mar 1835--Benbury Walton to Abram Pearce...$125...95 acres adjoining Enoch Pearce and others...
N. Nixon					Benbury Walton
Thos. R. Costen

243 31 Mar 1835--Kedar Green and wife, Judith, to Abram Pearce... $6...6 acres adjoining land of Frederick Jones and others...
						Kedar(x)Green
B. Walton					Judith(x)Green
Seth W. Roundtree

244 28 Feb 1835--Nancy Bond to John W. Bond...$20...20 acres in Deep Gut Branch adjoining land of Kedar Lassiter and others...
Henry(x)Bond					Nancy(x)Bond
Benbury Walton

244 20 Mar 1835--John Bond to Thomas Hollon...$20...20 acres in Deep Branch adjoining land of Kedar Lassiter...
B. Walton					J.W. Bond
J. Fowlkes

245 20 Dec 1834--Harrison Ellis to James Morgan...$1.00 and to make safe to Humphrey Parker as his security for note to David Benton for $257.90...2 tracts of land of 20 and 90 acres adjoining land of David Benton, T.W. Carr and others, which he purchased of James R. Riddick, sheriff...
Joshua Jones					Harrison(x)Ellis
John Barnes

246 24 Mar 1835--John Arnold to Alfred Ballard in return for payment of a note of $77 to John P. Benton...47 acres bounded on N and W by said Benton, S by Seth Benton and E by T.W. Carr...
Wm.W. Powell					John Arnold
Jno. Wiggens

246 5 Mar 1835--Quinton H. Trotman to Jesse R. Kee...$1.00 and to make safe to Jet.H. Riddick $250 note...horse called Packett, bridle and saddle, 1 single gig and harness, 1 mahogny table and 2 ends, 3 feather beds and furniture, candle stick and dressing table, 1 walnut and 1 pine table, 1 bureau, 1 pine chest and all his library...
Bushrod Riddick					Quinton H. Trotman
Martha H. Sutton
Nathan Riddick

247 27 Nov 1834--Charles Carter to William Sears...$25...Negro girl

Mary, with relinquishment of two sons, Ira and Lewis Carter, and witnessed by Abraham W. Parker 29 May 1830 (Book 14 p. 296) and since that time has rented her...

James Simpson
John Allen

Charles Carter
Lewis (x) Carter

248 27 Mar 1835--David Rooks to William Sears...$219.40...50 acres beginning at pine stump near Sears Mill Race up Bear Garden Branch to corner of Isaac Pipkins NE to Sears Mill Pond...

John Willey
Belver Sears

David (x) Rooks

249 17 Mar 1835--John Riddick to William Wills Cowper...$250...40 acres beginning at white oak on road leading to Winton and to mouth of Jack's Branch, up branch to road to a pine corner in said Cowpers line SE...being ridge of land on which Abrm. Blades lives...

John B. Baker
Wm. L. Boothe

Jno. Riddick

250 31 Mar 1835--Jordon Williams and wife, Christian, to William W. Cowper...$25...20 acres adjoining Isaac Pipkin, Pryor Savage, Eff Lewis, Whitmill Stallings and said Cowper; it being land that descended to said Christian Lewis, wife of said Williams, at death of her father, Luton Lewis...

W.G. Daughtry

Jordon Williams
Christian Willi

251 20 Mar 1835--Jethro Willey relinquishes all rights in deed of trust given to him by Levi Creecy to secure to Dempsey S. Goodman as his security for debts, which have now been paid...

H. Willey

Jethro Willey

251 4 Jan 1833--David Outlaw to James Costen...$400...Negro, Harry.

R. Rawls

David Outlaw

251 8 Oct 1835--William E. Pugh, Lassiter Riddick and James R. Riddick are bound to the state of North Carolina for ten thousand pounds whereas said Pugh is appointed clerk and master in equity for the County of Gates...

Rufus K. Speed

252 7 Jul 1834--Cynthia Brinkley and Calvin R. Brinkley to Leah Riddick...$101.50...Negro girl, Harriett...

Henry L. Spivey
Nathan Ward

Cynthia (x) Brin
Calvin R. Brink

253 25 Mar 1835--Moses Wilkins to William W. Powell...$1.00 and to make safe to John M. Haslett note of $54.08...75 acres adjoining land of Barnes Goodman, William Parker and William Benton...

Simon Walters
Lewis J. Hurdle

Moses (x) Wilki

254 1 Jun 1835--William W. Stedman to Henry Gilliam and Joseph Gordon...$1.00 and to secure $500 note for which they are his security 3 tracts of land: 29 acres whereon he lives adjoining Richard H. Ballard and others, another 128 acres that he purchased at sale and belonging to John Hofler, adjoining land of John C. Gordon,

John Small, dec. and others and last tract of 160 acres lately belonging to Holloday Walton, adjoining lands of Abraham Riddick, John Gwin and others...
                                                     Wm.W.Stedman
James A. Harrell   H. Gilliam
Jacob J. Harvey

255 2 Sep 1834--Jesse Wiggens and Risop Rawls, trustees of Abram Morgan, to Allen Daughtry...$301...3 tracts of 305 acres and including the Gregory Tract whereon he lived, joining the Duke Tract on N and E and on main run of Bennetts Creek and adjoining heirs of Micajah Riddick, dec. and formerly belonging to Jane Gregory, and was purchased by late Dr. Richard B. Gregory, dec. from Noah Hinton, Wm. S. Barnes and said Abraham Morgan...to secure debts of said Morgan to Nancy Wiggens for $731.79, John Savage for $443.62, Charles Fowler, Josiah Coffield real plantiff, for $563.33 1/3, estate of William Hinton, dec. $356.50 and Jethro Willey for $95.25...
                                              Jesse Wiggens
H. Gilliam
Henry R. Pugh   R. Rawls

257 25 Feb 1835--Jacob Powell to Wiley P. Jones...$240...123 acres bought of Charles and Josiah Briggs, joining lands of William Miller, Robert Riddick, Soloman Small and others...
                                              Jacob Powell
Jos. Gordon
Wm. W. Speight

257 18 May 1835--William E. Pugh, CME, to Isaac Pipkin...$555.55...160 acres...by petition of Benjamin Barnes; Etheldred Cross and wife, Charity; Job R. Hall and wife, Emily; James Pruden and wife, Martha; John B. Gatling; William Strode and wife, Eliza; Richard B. Gatling by his guardian, John D. Pipkin; Mary Jane Gatling by her guardian, Lassiter Riddick; and Harriett B. Gatling by her guardian, James Pruden...land adjoins lands of Isaac Pipkin, William Goodman and others and which lands were in part devised to said John by will of his father and balance is one undivided fifth part descending to above petitioners by death of Margaret Darden...
                                              Wm.E. Pugh
H. Gilliam

258 31 Mar 1835--Henry Gilliam relinquishes all rights in land of John D. Pipkin for which he was security in note of $600 made to John Roberts and which said Pipkin has paid...500 acres adjoining Ann N. Harvey, John B. Baker and others...
John Willey   H. Gilliam

259 3 Apr 1835--John D. Pipkin to Isaac Pipkin...$2000...500 acres adjoining Ann N. Harvey, John B. Baker and others and which was conveyed to him by Benjamin Wynn and wife...
John Saunders   Jno. D. Pipkin

259 28 Nov 1834--Samuel S. Bond to James Costen Sr...$15.00...10 acres joining said Costen, heirs of William Bond, dec.; it being land said Samuel heired from his father, Richard Bond...
Bn.B.Ballard   S.S. Bond

260 25 Mar 1835--Timothy Rogers to Elizabeth Lee...$20...10 acres beginning at pine at corner on said Rogers, NE to corner of heirs of Lewis Eure, dec. to an oak stump to a sweet gum, a corner on

John Langston's and SW...
John Langston
Isaac Williams   Timothy (x) Roger

261 24 Dec 1834--William Brown to John Brown...$61.25...24½ acres beginning at white oak in W.G. Daughtry's line SE to corner of said Daughtry and N to branch a corner of P. Savage...
Jesse Brown   William Brown
Briant Brothers

261 1 Apr 1835--James Figg to John Figg...$250...80 acres beginning at a maple a corner tree on Honey Pot Swamp to Honey Pot Road near bridge along road E to foot of Figgs Path and N to a dividing line between said Figgs and then W...
                                                  James Figg
Robert Rogers
John Matthews

262 16 Mar 1834--Levi Creecy to James Arline...$550...224 acres beginning at white oak a corner on Hardy Williams on Mills Swamp NE to a pine and SE to post oak stump to a black gum to a small pine corner on Hillory Willeys and S. Parkers and SE to a branch in Henry G. Williams line and down road to land of heirs of Dempsey Williams, dec. NW to Mills Swamp...
                                                  Levi Creecy
Jethro Willey
H. Willey

263 2 Apr 1835--James Arline to Joshua Levesay...$550...224 acres same as described above...
                                                  James Arline
James Costen
Mary Ann Costen

263 10 Jan 1836--Charles Eason to Joseph Gordon...$1.00 and to secure note to Josiah Blanchard for $110 and one to John C. Gordon guardian to Henry Lassiter's heirs for $160 and for which said Gordon and Abraham Hurdle were his security...37½ acres it being two tracts of land, one 25 acre tract whereon he lives and the other in Great Marsh, adjoining lands of heirs of Frederick Eason, dec. it being 3 shares in division of said Frederick Eason; all his stock of cattle, horses, hogs, corn and fodder and his household and kitchen furniture...
                                                  Charles Eason
Jacob J. Harvey
Richard B. Baker

266 20 Oct 1835--William Hudgins to William E. Pugh...$1.00 and to secure notes of $440 to Joseph Riddick and $100 to James R. Riddick...190 acres adjoining Benjamin Saunders, James Benton, David Riddick and Willis F. Riddick and his stock of cattle and hogs and household and kitchen furniture and farm utensils...
                                                  W. Hudgins
                                                  J.R. Riddick
A.W. Parker   Wm.E. Pugh

267 18 May 1835--William E. Pugh to Frederick Jones...$106.25... 110 acres sold by petition to court by Docton Hays and wife, Penelope, Priscilla Bond, Wright Hays, Asa Hays, Robert Hare and William Hare by their guardian, James Boothe...land adjoins lands of

Frederick Jones, James Lassiter and others and which land descended to said petitioners by death of Christian Hare as tenants in common...

                  Wm. E. Pugh
H.R. Pugh

267 13 Apr 1835--Jesse Mathias to Joseph Mathias...$1000...two tracts of land; the first of 130 acres begins at fork of Marsh Road running NE and adjoining land of Elisha Brinkley, dec. heirs, E to lands of Riddick Jones, formerly called The Ridge Land, purchased from Kedar Ellis, then S to land of Col. J. Riddick and W to Jones line and then N; second tract of 150 acres is at foot of Orapeak Swamp adjoining lands of Col. Josiah Riddick on N, William Riddick, dec. heirs and R.H. Ballards on S and which said Mathias purchased of James Brinkley, which said James heired from his father, David Brinkley, dec...

                  Jesse Mathias
Dempsey Vann
Jas. A. Ballard

268 3 Apr 1835--Hardy H.C. Jones to Miles Howell...$135...90½ acres beginning at a gum corner on said Jones and Howell, NE to heirs of Lewis Eure, dec. SE to corner of Eure and Speights...
Myles Parker   H.H.C. Jones

269 24 Oct 1834--Elisha Umphlet to Abraham Pruden...$200...200 acres joining Etheldred Cross, heirs of John Beeman, Abraham Crafford and others; being land purchased by said Umphlet of John R. Norfleet and wife, Harriett, which is considered or named The Curl Tract...
                  Elisha Umphlet
John Eure
William H. Savage

270 15 May 1835--Robert P. Hays to George Polson...$140...75 acres adjoining lands of John Hoffler, Zaccra Hays, Willis R. Hays and others, known as Benjamin Hays land, beginning at a popular a corner in John Hoflers line E to black gum in Willis R. Hays line S to run of Bennetts Creek to cypress corner of said Zaccra and NW.
                  Robert P. Hays
Lassiter Riddick
Robert B. Parker

271 31 Mar 1834--Levi Rogers, executor of will of Mills R. Fields, dec., who departed this life sometime in 1834, to comply with will sells to Timothy Hays...for $36.52...50 acres beginning at a cypress in fork of Little Hawtree Branch running SW to run of branch to a large pine, a corner tree near blacksmith shop, nearly N to Alston's Road and NE to the cross path to Hays path and S to a black oak at head of other prong of said Hawtree Branch; it being tract purchased by said Fields from James Brady and Jesse Parker.
Jethro Willey   Levi Rogers
James Arline

271 14 Feb 1834--James Boyce of Montgomery Co., Mo. to Richard Odom $33...150 acres beginning at pine stump on edge of Reedy Branch, a corner of Burwell Griffith and Abraham Cross running Cross line to a corner white oak of Jacob Odoms and Lassiter Riddicks...
                  James Boyce
Etheldred Cross
Elisha Williams

272 17 Mar 2835--Henry Stallings to Edward Hobbs...good will gift of land whereon said Hobbs lives, that is to say not being able to comply with terms of deed of gift from said Edward to him registered in Book 15 p. 89 and 90 14 Oct 1834...
                                                         Henry Stallings
John Mitchell
John (x)Moran Jr.

273 12 Sep 1834--John Lewis to Nathan Cullins...$100...50 acres beginning at white oak a corner of said Lewis and Susan Pilands, down road toward edge of Sarum Creek road and to corner of Peter Piland, James Goodwins, Abram W. Parker and others...
Wm. L. Boothe   John Lewis

274 12 Sep 1834--William G. Daughtry to John Lovett...$800...2 acres in Gatesville N of Asa Hill's lot, E of land of Thomas Saunders, S of lot of John Mathews and W of main street...
Ro. Riddick   W.G. Daughtry

274 24 Jul 1832--John Hinton Sr. to William Hinton...$22.50...10 acres swamp land on S side of road leading from Edenton to Gatesville and beginning at a gum in middle of swamp and across swamp...
Jet. H. Riddick   Joseph Eason
I. Riddick

276 3 Oct 1834--Abraham Hurdle to Jesse Eason...$290...85 acres beginning at Hollow Bridge in Joseph Riddick's line N across field to pine saplin across road to W side a corner tree of Hardy Eason, dec. and W to Riddicks and then S...
                                                    Abraham Hurdle
Jethro H. Riddick
Abner Eason

277 13 Sep 1833--Samuel Brown to Henry Gilliam...$75...75 acres beginning at a popular, a corner tree in John Gatling's line running SE by line of marked trees to corner tree in Jethro Reed's line and along his line to red oak in line of Bond heirs and along line to Deep Branch and running along branch to black gum on side of Bennetts Creek NW to run of creek and SW to Gatlings line...
                                                  Samuel (B) Brown
Benjamin Brown
Miles Brown

278 2 Dec 1834--Lemuel Benton to John Benton...$200...80 acres bounded by land of Wiley Riddick, Jesse Benton, John Pruden and William Parker...
Henry (x) Benton   Lemuel Benton

278 26 Feb 1835--Moses D. Hare to Hardy Williams...$250...100 acres adjoining lands of Levi Creecy, Hillory Willey, Jonathan Williams and Robert Rogers; being land sold to said Hare by said Williams...
Wm. W. Cowper   Moses D. (x) Hare

279 23 Feb 1835--William Gatling to James Williams of Hertford...$160...75 acres beginning on N side of Notaway River running Rochels line of marked trees to Cyprean Cross line to Richard Odom's line to a corner pine and along Odom's line to Isaac Pipkins and along Pipkins to Notaway River and down river...
Rich'd Odom   William Gatling
Drew M. Saunders

280 16 Mar 1835--Cyprean R. Cross of Talladega Co., Ala. to James Williams of Hertford...$150...250 acres beginning at mouth of Beef Gut on Chowan River adjoining lands of Clement Rochel and along his line to corner pine of said Williams, formerly Gatling's, and Richard Odoms and along Odom's line to Asa Odom's heirs, along a line of marked trees to corner gum in Mirey Branch to Abraham Smith's corner to juniper on river pocosin and up pocosin to a corner pine, formerly Odoms and Skinners corner and along Skinners line to pine on Chowan River at or near fishery, which was called the Old Indian Field...
Rich'd Odom
Abrm. Smith
               Cyprean R. Cross

281 15 Aug 2835--Samuel Harrell to Michael Williams...$40...25 acres at place called Little Islands beginning at a pine on S side of Stallings Old Field in said Harrells line along line of marked trees to run of outside swamp...
Abm. Smith
Thomas Hoggard
               Samuel Harrell

281 13 Nov 1834--John Taylor to Abraham Riddick of Upper Parish of Nansemond...$100...25 acres whereon said Taylor lives and which he purchased of Henry Hare, orphan of John Hare, dec., adjoining Demsey Knight and others...
               John Taylor
Dempsey Knight
William (x)Brinkley

282 12 Sep 1833--James Benton Jr. to Jacob Speight and wife...lease for 15 years on 1 acre beginning at corner of Abraham Morgans and John Matthews line on S side of main road running from Bentons Creek to Gatesville...for 1 pack of Indian corn yearly...
William Hudgens   James Benton

283 16 Nov 1835--William W. Stedman, Henry Gilliam, Joseph Gordon and Abel Rogerson are bound for $4000 whereas said Stedman is clerk of court of Pleas and Quarter Sessions for Gates County...
               Wm.W. Stedman
               H. Gilliam
               Jos. Gordon
John C. Gordon   Abel Rogerson

283 22 Jun 1835--Andrew P. Matthews to John C. Gordon...$62...62 acres swamp land allotted to James P. Small in division of his father, Moses H. Small's land, and bounded on both sides and one end by land of said Gordon...
               Andrew P. Matthews
Mary E. Gordon
Patience B. Gordon

284 27 Oct 1835--Benbury Walton to George W. Reed...$4000...650 acres beginning in Cabin Branch on road leading from Gatesville to Edenton down run of branch on line of Henry Bond to Indian Swamp, down run of swamp to mouth of Schoolhouse Branch up branch to Isaac and Richard Hofler's line to Hinton's path along path to John Walton's corner across Gum Pond E to Old Field N to Mill Race and up Indian Swamp to Patience Branch to main road from Gatesville to Ed-

enton; includes mill and all fixtures and excluding family grave-
yard of 22 and 60 feet. If said Reed dies before his wife, Sarah
E., with reason that she sold her land in Perquimans County for
$2750 and applied to purchase of said land, she should have land...
Will. Reed   Benbury Walton
R.K. Speed

285 29 Aug 1835--Edward Parker to Jordon Parker...$85...24 acres
adjoining land of Kedar Taylor on N, Tilly W. Carr on W, David
Benton on S and said Jordon on E and is said Edward's part of
tract belonging to heirs of Alfred Parker, dec....
John Riddick   Edward Parker
James Morgan

285 10 Nov 1835--Jesse Wiggens to Allen Daughtry...$100...10½
acres beginning at white oak in said Wiggens line NE to new road
N to said Daughtry's line SW to red oak stump and SE to a small
pine...
                                                          Jesse Wiggens
Open Court

287 2 Nov 1835--Benbury Walton to James Parker...$680...Negro
woman Sophia, 25, and child slave, Soloman...
Jas. T. Freeman   Benbury Walton

287 10 Nov 1835--Allen Daughtry to Jesse Wiggens...$100...12½
acres beginning at Wiggens own corner SE to run of branch John
Duke's former line and SW...
                                                          Allen Daughtry
Open Court

287 5 Nov 1834--Nancy Riddick to Riddick Gatling...$100...100
acres on Sand Banks beginning on Speights Old Mill Run on line of
Henry Hare running his line W to Chowan River and up river to line
of heirs of Frances Speight and E to Old Mill Run...
                                                          Nancy (x) Riddi
Whit'l Stallings
William Gatling

288 27 Oct 1835--Robert Rogers to Blake Brady...$300...109 acres
beginning at a corner white oak SE to a gum in Mills Swamp, up run
of swamp to white oak James Jones corner thence E to the fence binding on said path of branch then SE...
Elisha Hayes   Robert Rogers
John E. Rawls

288 12 Oct 1835--John R. Norfleet to Thomas R. Costen...$2800...
371¼ acres beginning at road at George Costen's corner down his
line of marked trees to 6-ft. ditch, down ditch to white oak corner of said George's line in Willis F. Riddick's line SE along
Riddicks line and then NE to persimmon in Harris place and along
Riddick line to Bennetts Creek and down run of creek to main road
and up road...
Richard H. Parker   John R. Norflee
Riddick (x) Arnold

289 12 Oct 1835--William L. Boothe to William W. Cowper...$80...
50 acres adjoining lands of Benjamin Wynns, James Brown and other
and which was devised to Mary Cullens as her dower by her first

husband, John Lewis, dec...
Jno. Riddick
Wm.L. Boothe

290 7 Nov 1835--William L. Boothe to William W. Cowper...$50...
20 acres beginning at or in run of White Oak Branch on road leading from Mrs. Ann Harvey's to Wynns Ferry, down run of branch to black gum in Cowper's line S to Sarum Creek and across road...
Jno. Riddick
Wm. L. Boothe

290 25 Aug 1835--Charles Jones to James Jones...$200...150 acres whereon he lives adjoining Humphrey Parker, Jacob P. Jones, James Morgan and others...
Charles Jones
James Morgan
Washington Jones

291 7 Nov 1835--James Woodward to Thomas Rice...$100...50 acres bought from Robert Riddick adjoining land of said Woodward, Mary Goodman, said Riddick and Andrew Harrell on public road...
Jos. Gordon
Jacob J. Harvey
James Woodward

292 18 May 1835--William E. Pugh, clerk and master of court of Equity for Gates County, to Thomas Hinton...$51...2 3/4 acres sold by court petition made by Noah Hinton, Thomas Hinton, John Alphin and wife, Leah, Seth Nowell and wife, Mary, Sarah Hinton by her guardian, James Boothe, Leah Hinton by her guardian, John Walton, John, Elizabeth and Louisa Lewis by their guardian, Noah Hinton, tenants in common...land adjoins William Hays, Thomas Hinton and James Boothe...
Open Court
Wm.E. Pugh, CME

293 12 Jun 1835--Easton Blanchard to Henry Bond...$150...60 acres beginning at a gum in run of Cabin Branch on side of main road, adjoining Joseph Sutton's line up branch to Robert Blanchard's line to Henry Bond's line...
J.W. Bond
B. Brothers
Easton Blanchard

294 15 Oct 1835--William E. Pugh, CME for Gates County, to Drew M. Saunders...$65...114 acres adjoining lands of William Speight, heirs of Lewis Eure and lands of Gilbert G. Saunders...sold by court petition made by Drew M. Saunders, Gilbert G. Saunders, Robert Saunders, John Saunders, John Anthony March and wife, Mary; Jesse, Thomas, James and Benjamin Saunders...
Open Court
Wm. E. Pugh

294 14 Oct 1835--William Faulk and wife, Elizabeth; Mary Hare, Pheraby Stanton; John Hare, Harrison Hare, Jesse Hare and wife, Marsha; Anna Hare and Harrison Hare as guardian for Mary and Jane Hare, all of Nansemond; James Pulle and wife, Ruth of Northampton; William Harris and wife, Eliza, of Southampton...to Elijah Hare...$60... their interest in two undivided tracts belonging to estate of Henry Hare, dec. and deeded to him by Abigail Goodman by Soloman K. Goodman, her agent...first tract of 57 acres on Sumerton Creek begins at small sourwood, a corner of Jesse Wiggens, and running NW to creek to Jethro Sumners corner tree and SW. Second tract of 109 acres is on Sand Banks adjoining lands of Miles Parker, Jethro

Sumners and others beginning at a pine and running S...
          William Harriss   William Faulk
          Eliza Harris   Elizabeth Faulk
          James Pulle   Mary Hare
          Ruth Pulle   Pheraby Stanton
          Jesse Hare   John Hare
          Marsha Hare   Harrison Hare
                             Ann Hare

296 14 Oct 1835--Edward Howell of Nansemond to David Howell Sr...
$150...117 acres near Wainsak (Wain Oak) Ferry beginning in Somerton Creek in state line W along line to short leaf pine, corner for Dempsey and Edward Howell, S along line of marked trees to a pine stump on Wain Oak Road up road to foot of path called Henry Jones path and along path to Somerton Creek...
Open Court   Edw. Howell

296 17 Aug 1835--Lewis Green to Margaret Green...$30...50 acres beginning at outside pocosin in Mills Eure's line along his line to Jethro Teabouts to Jason Roundtrees to corner gum of William Goodman's in Little Causeway to Mills Eure's line...
                                                    Lewis (x)Green
Kicheon Taylor
Samuel Green

298 8 Dec 1834--Brittian Smith to Charney Umphlet...$200 18 acres beginning at mulberry tree on road, a corner tree, down road to red oak Dempsey Parker's line, another red oak on Beeman's road and along road to Little Cypress Swamp and down run of swamp to land of Joseph Smith's heirs, along run to gum to William Savage's line of marked trees...
                                                    Brittian(x)Smith
John Sparkman
John Eure

299 1 Jun 1834--Peggy Matthews to loving granddaughter, Margaret E. Matthews...1 teester bedstead and feather bed...
                                                    Peggy (x)Matthews
Pleasant Perry
James D. Perry

299 25 Aug 1835--James Jones and wife, Absala, to Andrew Matthews $130...32 acres beginning at a small dogwood near where said Matthews now lives in line belonging to heirs of Benjamin Jones, dec. and along line of marked trees W to John R. Barr's line to a gum in swamp and then S...land which was allotted to Absala in division of land belonging to heirs of Abraham Benton, dec...
James Morgan   James (x) Jones
T. Saunders   Absala (x) Jones

300 20 Jan 1834--Timothy Hays to Riddick Cross...$125...20 acres beginning at Hollow Bridge in road leading from Gatesville to Sunsbury Post Office and near Richard Hays dwelling house, thence to pine tree, to persimmon tree, to post oak, to John Walton's line to maple in Flat Branch and along branch to Joseph Hare's line...
                                                    Timothy Hays
Joseph R. Hays
Richard Hays

300 15 Feb 1836--William G. Daughtry, James R. Riddick, Joseph Riddick, John Gatling, William H. Goodman and Abel Rogerson are bound for 10,000 pounds to state of North Carolina whereas said Daughtry has been appointed clerk of county court of Gates...
                               Jno. Gatling   W.G. Daughtry
                               Abel Rogerson J.R. Riddick
                               Wm. H. Goodman Jo. Riddick

300 19 May 1835--Division of estate of Mills R. Fields, dec. which was surveyed and contains 492 acres adjoining lands of Daniel Williams, Blake Baker, Mildred Kittrell, James Boothe, Fisher Felton and others as follows: Survey No 1--Richard Fields...246 acres valued at $615, the house lot and beginning at sweet gum corner on Daniel Williams and Blake Bakers SE to land of heirs of James Matthews, to sweet gum a corner of Aaron Pearce SW to new course made between two lots to a small branch. No. 2--Lemuel K. Fields...246 acres valued at $615, beginning at a maple a corner SW to James Boothe, NW to red oak of George Kittrells along line of marked trees to a corner of heirs of George Kittrell, dec. SE to a black gum in Watering Hole Branch to corner of Daniel Williams and to dividing line SE to a bay and along line of marked trees...
                                      H. Willey
Simon Walters, alternate   J. Williams
                                      Levi Rogers
                                      Isaac Williams

303 24 Sep 1835--Division of land of the late Thomas Bond as follows: Survey No. 1--Archibald Jones in right of wife, Easter... 80 acres valued at $320, beginning at elm in branch running NE across plantation along line of marked trees NW to pine stump and white oak corner of David Parkers, SE to branch to Indian Swamp corner of James Parkers. No. 2--Mary Bond...80 acres valued at $160, beginning at corner of Suttons and Bonds and running NW to post oak corner of Benbury Waltons and along a line of marked trees... Said Jones to pay said Mary $80...
                                     David Parker
Isaac Williams, surveyor   Jethro Blanchard
Kedar Hinton, alternate commissioner Noah Hinton
Nathan Pearce, alternate commissioner

305 25 Nov 1835--Division of land of John Granbury, dec. containing 636 acres adjoining lands of Thomas Twine, Jesse Wiggens and others as follows: Survey No. 1--George Granbury...290 acres beginning at gum stump at run of Cypress Swamp along Mrs. Yeates line NW to corner on Allen Daughtry's and Seth Morgans to dividing line of No. 2, a branch and down run of Cypress Swamp. No. 2--John Granbury...340 acres beginning at run of Cypress and junction of dividing line branch NE to Thomas Twines to Briggs corner NW to white oak, Powell and Walton's corner to a pine at Ellis corner to sweet gum, Col. Jesse Wiggens corner to run of dividing line branch and down run. Unequal in quanity but adjudged to be equal in value...
                                     Noah Harrell
Wm. M. Jones, county surveyor   Jesse Wiggens
Thomas Twine, alternate   R. Rawls

305 15 Feb 1836--Division of estate of William Hinton, dec. containing 553¼ acres as follows: House Tract division of 438 acres between...No. 1--Dianna Hinton...land beginning at road leading to Parkers Landing at an oak bush corner on John Hinton's running his line SE to black gum to dead pine NW to between barn and dwelling house to run of swamp and down run to John Roberts line and SE to road leading to Gatesville thence NE down road to fork. No. 2-- Mary Hinton...land beginning at dead pine at John Hinton's line SE to sowwood to pine NE to road and NW up road toward John Waltons to run of branch, cornering on Roundtrees to black gum and SE. No. 4--Richard Hinton...land beginning in run of swamp at black gum NW to a pine to John Roberts Mill Pond thence SE to run of swamp. No. 5--Sarah Hinton...land beginning at pine Q. Roundtrees corner NW to run of Roberts Mill Pond up run of pond to road NW to small pine corner on Powells, NE to large white oak corner on John Waltons SE to stake corner of Waltons and Roundtrees and SW. No. 6 is part of No. 1 drawn by Diana Hinton and begins in run of swamp NW along line of marked trees to run of Roberts Mill Pond and up swamp. No. 3--Louisa Hinton...land is separate from others and begins in road leading to Gatesville SE down road to Parkers Landing to pine corner on Clement Hills SW to John Roberts then NW along Roberts line to road. No. 1 pays No. 4 $98.87½ and No. 3 pays No. 2 $25.87½, No. 5 $26.87½ and No. 4 $1.00...

Alternate commissioners:
John Walton
James Boothe
Allen Smith, co. surv.

John Roberts
H. Gilliam
Tim. Walton

307 1 Apr 1836--Abraham Hurdle to niece, Nancy Hurdle, gift of love and affection...Negro girl, Mary, and cow and calf...
J. Riddick
Jesse Eason

Abraham(x)Hurdle

307 6 Apr 1836--John White and wife, Mary, to Kedar Powell...$35... 14 acres of undivided land binding on land of William Hinton, dec. heirs, Jonas Hinton and others; which fell to them by death of Jacob Powell, dec...
Wm. E. Pugh
John Walton

John (x)White
Mary (x)White

308 26 Oct 1835--Nathan Ward to Cooke and Hatton of Town of Portsmouth, Va....$1000...mortgage on 70 acres beginning at cross roads along public road to Jethro H. Riddick's line to causeway and up causeway to Isaiah Riddicks line to road and across road to Abner Easons line to Joseph Riddicks line to Joel B. Hurdles line to Henry S. Spivey's line to public road and with road...
James Boyce
Joel B. Hurdle

Nathan Ward

309 3 Dec. 1835--Frances Ann Cotter to Jacob N. Parker of Chowan whereas: marriage about to be solemnized between said Frances Ann and Hillory H. Eure of Chowan and said Frances Ann is possessed of Negro slaves and personal estate...to insure her freedom of choices of said estate...for $1.00...deed in trust to said Parker 3 slaves Boys Tom and Ceasar and Girl Harriett, double gig, 1

bedstead and bed and furniture. In case, her death before said Hillory said Parker is to pay annual profits for support of any children...
                                                              Frances Ann Cotter
Baker F. Welch   H.H. Eure
Wm. H. Elliott   Jacob N. Parker

311 17 Nov 1835--James R. Riddick, sheriff, to Jason Saunders... $39.30...50 acres whereas: Drew M. Saunders, Jason Saunders, John B. Baker and E.L. Neal placed a court levy on land of David Rooks for debt of $40.79...adjoining lands of Isaac Pipkin, William Sears and others...
                                                                J.R. Riddick
Kindred Parker
John S. Roberts

312 22 Dec 1835--Jason Saunders to Sarah Rooks...$41.50...30 acres beginning at a pine stump at old bridge below Sears Mill up run to Isaac Pipkin's line along his line to a corner of William Sears to a dogwood thence to a white oak to Bear Garden Branch and down branch; land was bought at sheriff's sale...
                                                              Jason Saunders
Kindred Parker
John Saunders

313 21 Sep 1835--Richard H. Fields to Henry Willey...$1.00 and to make safe to Daniel Williams a note of $60...½ of tract of land where Mills R. Fields, dec. formerly lived, adjoining lands of Blake Baker, Daniel Williams and others...
                                                 Richard H. Fields
J. Willey

315 12 May 1835--John Matthews to Riddick Matthews...$400...mortgage on 1 acre in Gatesville adjoining lands of Thomas Saunders on N and E and main road leading to Suffolk and running road as far as plank fence encloses and adjoining grounds where his shop stands.
                                                Riddick Matthews
H. Gilliam   John Matthews
Robert B. Parker

316 11 Apr 1836--Thomas W. Stallings to Henry Gilliam...$1.00 and for payment of bond of $199.40 given 2 Feb 1836...80 acres whereon said Stallings lives...
                                              Thomas W. Stallings
John B. Harrell   Henry Gilliam

317 2 May 1836--William F. Bennett to Richard H. Parker...$1.00 and to secure several notes for which James M., Willis F. and Elizabeth Riddick are bound as follows: Mary B. Roberts of Edenton $700, Noah Harrell $83.53, Henry and John Bond $69.55 and $75.10, Hardy D. Parker $57, David Riddick $35 and John Kerr $978.45...200 acres adjoining lands of James M. Riddick and Isaac R. Hunter, Negroes Marcus, Lucas, Margaret and child, Harrison, horse, gigg and harness, household and kitchen furniture, stock of hogs and cattle and farm utensils...
                                              Wm.F. Bennett
                                              Rich'd H. Parker
                                              James M. Riddick
Wm. E. Pugh   W.F. Riddick
Wm.(x)Brothers

319 14 Apr 1836--Henry A. Skinner and wife, Mary, of Edenton in Chowan County to William H. Harrell...$150...one undivided fourth part of 456 acres; being tract devised by David Rice, dec. to his grandson, William Creecy, and upon death of William descended to his brother, James, and his three sisters. Land is bounded by lands formerly belonging to Benjamin Gordon, dec. now in occupancy of William Reed and wife, lands of Willis W. Harrell, lands of Holliday Walton, lands of Andrew R. Harrell and lands of William H. Harrell...
                Henry A. Skinner
John R. Gilliam   Mary Skinner
John M. Dick, judge of suprene court, confirmed said Mary signed freely

320 5 Mar 1836--James Trevathan to son, Henry, gift of two tracts of land and to insure he pay James debts...first tract of 10 3/4 acres is where said James lives adjoining John Walton, Noah Hinton, Nathaniel Jones and heirs of Charles Smith, and being his first purchase; second tract of 12¼ acres adjoins first tract. Also 2 feather beds, bedsteads and furniture, 2 chests, 2 tables, 1 loom and gear, pewter and crockery ware, 1 steer, 1 cow, 2 sows and pigs and stock of bees...
                James(x)Trevath
John Walton
John(x)Trevathan

320 26 Mar 1836--John Walton to Henry Trevathan...$1.00...release of land described above and which was conveyed to him by deed of trust by James Trevathan 11 Mar 1830 to satisfy debts...
Open Court   John Walton

321 28 Sep 1835--Marmaduke Norfleet to Willis F. Riddick...$1000 160 acres which he purchased of Edward R. Hunter bounded on N by James Murdaugh's land, E and S by John R. Norfleet and others and on W by public road...
                Marmaduke Norfl
W. Riddick
William F. Bennett

322 9 Mar 1833--Hardy Williams to Robert Rogers...$175...55 acres beginning at corner red oak in said Robert and Henry Hays line N to a line of marked trees to a pine stump or post oak a corner, running E to run of Ann Harvey's Mill Pond and down run to Henry Hays line...
                Hardy(x)William
Charles Vann
James Parker

323 15 Feb 1836--John B. Griffin of Guilford County to Joseph Riddick...$60...50 acres known by name The Griffen Place, which was given to him by his grandmother, Thamer Briggs, dec. in her will and which adjoins lands of William Harrell, heirs of Ezekiel Trotman, dec., Pheraba Trotman and others...
Abel Rogerson   John B. Griffen
H. Gilliam

324 6 Feb 1836--George W. Granbury to John J. Granbury...$1450 290 acres beginning at run of Cypress Swamp along Rachael Yeates line NW to several saplins, corner of Col. Jesse Wiggens, with his

line NE to black gum then NW to a corner of said Wiggens and
Allen Daughtry, by said Daughtry and Seth Morgan's line and
along Wiggens other tract NE to a maple corner of said Wiggens
and along dividing line branch to run of Cypress Swamp...
                George W. Granbury
Open Court

324 3 Dec 1855--Martha Horton of Darlington County, S.C. and
John Odom to James C. Smith of Nansemond...$120...83 acres adjoining land of said Smith, Samuel Cross and others; it being
land given by the late Benjamin Odom, dec. in his will to his
daughter, said Martha, and a part of which was sold three or
four years ago for taxes and which said John purchased...
                Martha(x)Horton
James Arline   John W. Odom
W.K. Moore

325 4 Feb 1836--Jesse and John Benton to Wiley Riddick...$350...
262 acres known by name Chinquapin Ridge, land drawn by Jesse
Benton, Lemuel Benton, Charles Jones in right of wife, Elizabeth,
and heirs of Jethro Benton, dec. and begins at corner of David
Parkers heirs and Robert Wilson and Lot No. 4 Margaret Bentons NE
to white oak to a pine corner of said David and William Parkers
heirs, SE to a white oak and NE to a cypress, corner on William
Parkers and Jesse Wiggens, dec. in main run of Bennetts Creek and
down run to Wileys at entrance of small branch and up branch SW
to a corner of John Prudens SW to Lot No. 4 of Margaret Bentons...
Elbert H. Riddick   Jesse(x)Benton
David F. Felton   John Benton

327 27 Sep 1834--Nathan Riddick to daughter, Esther...48½ acres,
part of land known by name of John Hill land on E side of tract
binding on Joseph T. Hurdle and James Brinkley to main road...
                Nathan Riddick
Jesse R. Kee
Jason Riddick

328 15 Mar 1835--Jesse Arline to Richard Austin...$5.50...2 acres
beginning at black gum near Austins residence S binding on his
land and along a branch binding on James Boothe and said Arline...
James Arline   Jesse Arline
John W. Odom

329 2 Dec 1835--Brittian O. Barr to Wright Barr...$85...28 acres
beginning at a pine in James Jones line E to a pine to a white oak
to a corner pine in Jones line E to Brinkley's line and S to William Barr's line...
                Britton O. Barr
Abraham Benton

329 10 Feb 1836--John Granbury to Jesse Wiggens...$780...130
acres beginning at a black gum running NW to corner of Col. Jesse
Wiggens and Allen Daughtry by said Daughtry and Seth Morgan's line
NE to a maple of said Wiggens and SW...
                John J. Granbury
Open court

329 28 Jan 1836--Joseph Gordon, trustee of Charles Eason, to
Jesse Eason...$160...Lots No. 2 and 3 in division of said Jesse's
father containing 25 acres...   Joseph Gordon
I.S. Harrell
J. Riddick

330 13 Feb 1836--Thomas Eason and Joseph Gordon to Jesse Eason...
$130...25 acres, tracts drawn by William and Hardy Eason in division of their father's estate...
                   Thomas(x)Eason
H. Gilliam   Jos. Gordon

331 13 Jan 1835--Andrew Eason to Abner Eason...$350..100 3/4 acres...two tracts; the first whereon he lives adjoining lands of Nathan Ward, Joseph Riddick and Isiah Riddick and second tract is all the land his father, Solloman Eason, dec. gave him in his will out of the Gregory high land adjoining land of Abner Eason and others...   Andrew Eason

Jos Gordon
James Briggs

331 26 Oct 1835--Dempsey Parker to William L. Boothe...$42...88 acres beginning at a red oak, a corner tree on lands of Harrison Vann heirs, nearly SE along the old road commonly known as Hugh's Road to a post oak a corner tree between said land and lands of Daniel Fields and Jonathan William Jr., along Fields line of marked trees to Allen Smith's line to a red oak a corner tree, then along said Smith's line to black gum, a corner adjoining lands of Andrew Eason, formerly owned by John O. Hunter NW along a line of marked trees to land belonging to Vann heirs...
John Williams   Dempsey(x)Parker
James Simpson

332 10 Feb 1836--Hardy H.C. Jones to Miles Howell...$490...200 acres beginning at a stake a corner on Zach Boons, then NW along line of marked trees to a water oak on Boon's and James Sumner, NE to forked maple a corner on Sumners, Harrison Hare and heirs of Henry Jones, dec. E to red oak, NW to a branch pine, a corner on said Hare and Elijah Hare and heirs of Lewis Eure, dec. to a lightwood stake, a corner on said Howell's S to black gum and W to John Jones or James Williams...
Timothy (x)Howell   Hardy H.C.Jones
Enoch Britt

333 24 Dec 1835--Kedar Ellis to Benjamin Franklin...$40...30 acres bounded on E by land of Riddick Jones, S by land of John Jones, SE by land of Col. J. Riddick and running to the Sumner Mill Swamp and E binding on said Riddick's land and public road...
Titan K. Rudolph   Kedar(x)Ellis
Abraham(x)Meltear

334 2 Mar 1835--Bray and Euriah Eure to Reuben Piland...$75...
20 acres beginning at a spruce pine, a corner of Martha Taylors and Boon Eures and others to run of Mire Branch, down branch to Cypress Swamp, up swamp to a gum a corner of David Lewis, out of swamp to a pine then a line of marked trees to a pine at side of path down lane and across branch...
Thomas Hoggard   Bray(x)Eure
Wiley Carter   Uriah Eure

334 28 Jan 1836--Malachi Cuff to Henry Willey...$40...10 acres beginning at a red oak corner on Nisum Cuffs and James Boothe,dec. heirs, along Boothe's path to a white oak, a corner and along a

line of sliped trees to a gum in Frogburrow Branch, a corner on
said Boothe's heirs and along edge of branch...
H.G. Williams   Malachi(x)Cuff
James Parker

335 1 Feb 1836--Burwell Griffith of Hertford to Thomas Saunders...
$825...Negro man Jacob 22 years old...
Richard Odom   Burwell Griffith
Rodon Odom

336 10 Dec 1836--William G. Daughtry to John Brown...$700...150
acres including two tracts; first begins at white oak on main road
leading from Somerton to Gatesville, a corner tree in William
Brown's line SE on his line thence NE to a pine, a corner tree in
Pryor Savage's line to Honey Po Swamp road, on road to branch in
line of heirs of Willis Parker, up branch to road nearly opposite
John Brown's house; second begins at black gum by line of marked
trees to an oak, a corner tree between above tract and John Brown
and running NE...
                                                       W.G. Daughtry
D. Parker
H. Gilliam

336 25 Mar 1835--Elisha H. Bond to Nathaniel Eure...$65...73 acres
beginning at sweet gum corner on said Eures SE along line of marked
trees NE to corner of Elisha H. Bond and Eff Lewis and NW to a branch, a corner on James Williams and along his line...
William W. Cowper   Elisha H. Bond
Jethro Willey

337 1 Oct 1835--William E. Pugh, clerk and master of court of equity, to Lassiter Riddick...$37.50...50 acres belonging to Marg-
aret and Christian Lawrence, infants and sold by court petition
made by their next friend, Treacy Laurence, for sale. Land adjoins land of James B. Riddick, Lassiter Riddick and Jethro Howell...   Wm.E. Pugh
Open Court

338 20 Oct 1835--Christian Cullens to Timothy Walton...$400...
160 acres on Catherine Creek, whereon she lives, beginning at
a stake in Nathan Nixons line on N side of plantation and running SW to edge of swamp on Nixons line to fork of creek, down run
to mouth of Deep Branch, Powell's corner, up Powell's line to edge
of branch and SE to white oak where Old Schoolhouse formerly stood
and then NW and through plantation...
N. Nixon   Christian(x)Cullens
Sarah W. Nixon

339 27 Nov 1835--Jethro H. Riddick, constable, to Christian Cullens...
$267...property of Nathan Cullens sold by court order in judge-
ments against Whitmill Stallings, executor of Nathan Cullen, dec.
in favor of Thomas Harrell, Benbury Walton for use of Jacob N.
Parker, John Winslow for Joseph Gordon and Kedar Felton for Elizabeth Hinton...totaling $267. Said Christian bought the follow-
ing: Negro Omar and children, Sillar, Harriett and Goodman $15,

Negroes Cherry $5, Peter $15, Belton $15 and Daniel $151, sideboard $6, table $8, 3 feather beds $40 and 1 doz. Windsor chairs $12...
Jet.H.Riddick
Abel Rogerson
James Brinkley

340 4 May 1835--Nancy, Sophia, Jordon, Benjamin, Allen and Sarah, heirs of Mills Williams, dec. to James R. Riddick...$150...6 lots of land they drew in division of his estate containing 150 acres adjoining Joshua Allen, said Riddick and others...

                                        Benjamin Williams Ann Williams
Allen Smith   Allen Williams   Elizabeth(x)Wil
William Cleaves   Sarah(x)Williams Sophia(x)Willia
                                                                   Jordon(x)Willia

341 9 May 1835--Lovina Williams to James R. Riddick...$16.67...35 acres, Lot No. 7, in the division of her father, Mills Williams, dec. land, adjoining lands of Joshua Allen and Benjamin Williams...
Archibald R. Jones   Lovina Williams
Saroe Smith

342 24 Oct 1834--Job R. Hall to John S. Roberts...$525...110 acres adjoining lands of Lassiter Riddick, James Brown and Pryor Savage and known as James C. Riddick tract beginning at red oak on side of Honey Pot Road to a corner tree in land of Lassiter Riddick, formerly land of Daniel Southall, to pine stump, corner in James Browns land on his line to land of Pryor Savage, formerly Benjamin Williams, and to white oak, corner of said Savage, formerly land of Timothy Walton, esq. and E...
                                                                         Job R. Hall
J.R. Riddick
Jonas Croplin

343 6 Nov 1835--Thomas Rice to Richard H. Parker...$120...7½ acres bounded by land of E.R. Hunter and said Parker, being part of tract formerly belonging to Aaron Speight...
Andrew Harrell   Thomas Rice
Willis F. Riddick

344 14 Nov 1835--Margaret Ann Ballard to Jordon Parker...$180... 60 acres bounded on N by Thicket Road, E by lands of Soloman Ellis, S by pocosin and W by Parkers land; being part of tract set off to Margaret in division of land of Thomas Parkers plantation...
                                                          Margaret A. Balla
Jordon Parker
T.W. Carr

345 1 Aug 1832--Randolph Sherard of Edgecomb, agent for Levi W. Parker, of Pickens County, Ala. to Abram Parker...$110...100 acres beginning at a corner water oak in branch, a corner of Mills Eures and others, running Eure's line of marked trees E to Dempsey Eure's line to a corner white oak of Benjamin Wynns, along Wynns line of marked trees N to John Sparkmans and down Sparkman's

line S...
John Sparkman   Levi W. Parker
Kindred Parker

346 19 Mar 1835--Thomas Hoggard to Abram W. Parker...$600...150
acres beginning at persimmon tree on road leading to courthouse
in said Parkers line SW to red oak on side of road to Sarum Creek
SW along Parkers line to corner hickory in Boon Eure's line along
his line SW to corner pine in Martha Taylor's line, up branch to
cedar stump in Reuben Parker's line NE to a corner hickory NE to
a popular SE to a maple to holly in Lickingroot Branch and up run
of branch to road leading to courthouse; it being part of Nathan
Cullen's patent in 1807 and conveyed to said Hoggard by Arthur
Smith and wife, Rachael 6 Sep 1825...
Wm. L. Boothe   Thomas Hoggard
Lassiter Riddick

347 14 Dec 1833--Samuel Eure, trustee for Dempsey Eure, to Abram
W. Parker...$160...200 acres adjoining land of said Parker, Mills
Eure, Elisha Harrell, John Beeman's heirs, Dempsey Sparkman, Ben-
jamin Wynn and James Brown; it being land whereon said Dempsey Eure
now lives and which he placed in trust 10 Sep 1832 to secure debt...
Peter Eure   Sam'l Eure
J. Willey

348 21 Nov 1835--Robert R. Smith to Josiah Perry...$275...Negro man,
Jacob, bought by James M. Griffin and ran away from him at Somer-
ton...
                                                               Ro.R. Smith
Caleb Perry

348 1 Feb 1836--Brittan Smith to Dempsey Parker...$20...6¼ acres
of undivided land beginning at corner pine in Hawtree Branch, a
corner of Reuben Parkers, dec., along Parkers line to Penny Car-
ters line, down her line to run of Little Cypress up run to mouth
of Hawtree Branch...
                                                               Britton(x)Smith
Elisha Parker
Hillory Taylor

349 17 Jun 1835-Louisa Brinkley, Henry Brinkley, Christian Yeates,
Ammon, Isaac, Jerry, Louisa Parker and Timothy (heirs of Richard
Brinkley) to John O. Hunter...$50...SW quarter Sec. 4 Township 1,
N in Range 3, territory of Arkansas...160 acres; it being land set
apart by the United States for their brother, Richard Brinkley,
as per a patent signed by Andrew Jackson at Washington 28 Sep 1830.
                              Louisa(x)Parker   Lewis(x)Brinkley
                              Ammon(x)Brinkley   Henry(x)Brinkley
                              Timothy(x)Brinkley Isaac(x)Brinkley
                                                 Jerry Brinkley

350 1 Apr 1830--Jethro Brinkley to Josiah Riddick of Nansemond
$47.02...1 young horse, 1 feather bed, 2 sows and 15 pigs...
Jno. O. Hunter   Jethro Brinkley

350 May Ct. 1836--Nathan Riddick to Peter B. Minton...land placed
in trust by Henry S. Spivey...
                                                               Nathan Riddick
Open court

Page

1 16 Feb 1836--Jesse Brown and wife, Elizabeth, to Mills Sparkman...$150...their interest in 300 acre plantation belonging to the heirs of Abraham Beeman, Esq., dec., bounded by lands of Dempsey Sparkman, Dempsey Parker, Abram W. Parker, Charney Humphlet and William L. Boothe...
                                            Jesse Brown
Wm.L. Boothe   Elizabeth Brown

1 16 Feb 1836--Riddick B. Eure and wife, Nancy, of Halifax to Mills Sparkman...$200...their interest in tract of land adjoining lands of Dempsey Sparkman, Dempsey Parker, Abram W. Parker, Charney Humphflet, heirs of Reuben Parker, dec., Elisha Harrell and William L. Boothe; it being tract that Abram Beeman, Esq. died in possession of and well known as the Esquire Beeman plantation containing 300 acres...
                                            Riddick B. Eure
William L. Boothe   Nancy Eure

2 16 Feb 1836--Dempsey Sparkman and wife, Margaret, to Mills Sparkman...$150...their interest in tract of land adjoining lands of said Mills, Dempsey Parker, Abram W. Parker, Charney Humphlett, heirs of Reuben Parker, dec., Elisha Harrell and William L. Boothe, it being same tract that Abraham Beeman, Esq. died possess of and containing 300 acres...
                                            D. Sparkman
Wm.L. Boothe   Margaret Sparkma

3 16 Feb 1836--Felisha Freeman to Mills Sparkman...$150...interest in tract of land adjoining lands of Dempsey Sparkman, Demsey Parker, Abram W. Parker, Charney Humphlet, heirs of Reuben Parker, dec., Elisha Harrell and William L. Boothe and well-known by name of Abram Beeman, dec. plantation containing 300 acres...
Wm. L. Boothe   Felisha Freeman

3 26 Feb 1835--Elizabeth Parker and Peninah Parker to Mills Sparkman $60...60 acres beginning at a pine stump below the foot of Fort Island bridge in edge of outside pocosin thence running up said pocosin to said Sparkman's line, along his line to a corner in a pond, down pond and Sparkman's line to Mills Eure's and along his line...
                                            Elizabeth(x)Par
John F. Parker   Peninah(x)Parke
Kindred Parker

5 18 Jan 1836--Martha S. Bagley and husband, Thomas, to Easton Blanchard...$280.88...88 acres on Watery Swamp at end of said Martha's ditch, a corner of Joseph Brooks, thence running down swamp to a gum, a corner tree SW to a pine, a corner tree in Samuel Brown's line, along his line to a pine, a corner of said Joseph, E by a line of marked trees to a red oak at end of ditch and down ditch...
                                            Martha Bagley
Jet. H. Riddick   Thomas(x)Bagley
Joseph Brooks

6 16 Jan 1836--Ann E. Lassiter and husband, John, to George Brooks

$145...88 acres on Watery Swamp beginning at a sweet gum, a corner tree on Margaret C. Brooks, thence SW along her line to a pine, another corner in Brown's line NW along Brown's line to a water oak NE by line of marked trees to a sweet gum, a corner of Henry Hoflers and up swamp...
                                                Ann E.(x)Lassiter
Henry E. Blanchard   John(x)Lassiter
Henry Hofler
Easton Blanchard

7 Feb. Ct. 1836--James R. Riddick, sheriff, to Zachariah Hays...$14.11...land of Thomas Davis, adjoining lands of Elijah Harrell, Robert Hays, Zachariah Hays and others and sold by court levy placed on said Davis land in Nov. Ct. 1828...
                                           Jas. R. Riddick, sheriff
Timothy Hayes
Willis R. Hayes

7 29 Nov 1834--Robert P. Hays to Zachariah Hays...$35...25 acres adjoining land of Elijah Harrell, the Davis Tract and others...
                                                      Robert P. Hays
Timothy Hays
J.R. Riddick

7 5 Dec 1835--Elisha Umphlet to Dempsey Parker...$15...6 acres of undivided land beginning at a pine in Hawtree Branch, a corner of Reuben Parker, dec. and along Parker's line to Penny Carter's line and down her line to run of Little Cypress up run to mouth of Hawtree Branch and up branch...
                                         Elisha Umphlet
A.W. Parker
Nathan Smith

9 1 Jan 1835--John Walton to Kedar Hinton...$88.75...17 acres W side of main road that leads from Gatesville to Sunsbury beginning at a post oak on side of road; it being a corner tree of said Hinton and Bond Menchew, dec. heirs, along road W to white oak, a corner now between said Walton and Hinton NW along line of newly marked trees to a sweet gum, a corner tree in Thomas Ellinors line NE to a pine between said Hinton and Ellinor SE along old dividing line between said Walton and Hinton...
Thos. R. Costen   J. Walton
Sam'l R. Harrell

9 20 Feb 1835--Harrell and Costen to Reuben Lassiter...$54.19...5 acres bounded by land of Henry Gilliam, Catherine Creek and known by name Old Town Tract...
                                              Harrell & Costen
P.B. Minton
Jet. H. Riddick

10 25 Mar 1836--James Mathias to James Morgan...$1.00 and to make safe to Humphrey Parker as his security for $200 note payable to David Benton...100 acres, all his land on S side of road that leads to house where he lives then W to Mill Pond...
                                              James Mathias
Jordon Parker
Edward Parker

10 14 Apr 1836--Daniel S. Hobbs to Burwell Brothers...$1469.00...Negroes Joshua and Sally...
                                              Daniel S. Hobbs
John Shepperd

11 21 Mar 1835--Wesley W. Speight to Miles Brown...$1.00 and to
make safe to Samuel Brown as his security for bond payable to
David Parker and said Samuel for $81...6 Sep 1833...40½ acres
bounded by lands of Samuel Brown, Jethro Blanchard and Timothy
Spivey; it being land whereon he lives and which he purchased
of Samuel Brown...
Benjamin Brown   Wesley W. Speight
Henry Hofler   Samuel (B) Brown
                                         Miles Brown

12 24 May 1836--Andrew Baker to James Baker...$1.00 and to
a note payable to John Walton, guardian for Leah Hinton, for
$310.50 24 May 1836 and one to David Parker for $110 19 Dec.
1835...50 acres at Mudy Cross and on which said Andrew has his
store and which he purchased of Timothy Walton...
John Walton   Andrew Baker
Benbury Walton   James Baker

12 24 Sep 1835--John O. Hunter and William Arnold to James Mathias
$420...150 acres bounded on N by land of Jason Franklin and Abra-
ham Riddick, on S by dividing line between Marmaduke and his bro-
ther, John, E and W by line of marked trees to run of Mills Swamp
E by Arnold's line running N and on W by run of swamp...
Henry Pearce   John O. Hunter
Simons H. Jones   William Arnold

14 15 Aug 1836--James Mathias to David Parker...$1.00 and to in-
sure payment of debt of $477.46...300 acre Brick House Plantation
adjoining lands of Jason Franklin and Abram Riddick on Orapeak
Swamp and 100 acres called the Parker Place adjoining lands of
James Morgan and Humphrey Parker and Negroes Dave, Charity, Isaac,
Robert and Peninah...
                                         James Mathias
Henry Boothe   D. Parker

15 1 Oct 1836--Isaac Hofler to David Parker...$5.00 and to hold
in trust for payment of notes of $83 and $29 to James Parker tract
of land bounded by lands of Henry Bond, George W. Reed and Docton
Hays and which was devised to him by James Hofler. Also, his crop
of peas and potatoes now growing, stock of horses, cattle and hogs,
cart and wheels, farm utensils and household and kitchen furniture
to hold in trust until 1 Jan 1837...
                                         Isaac Hofler
                                         D. Parker
W.G. Daughtry, clerk   J.H. Parker

16 7 Jan 1836--Daniel Hobbs and Burwell Brothers to Absalom Blanchard...$1.00 and to make safe a deed of trust to Abel Rogerson
and James Baker for becoming security for two notes: $969.66 due
14 Oct 1836 and payable to Burwell Brothers and $700 payable to
Julia Hutson...two tract of land; 121 acres beginning at main road
binding on Timothy Walton and running main road to Muddy Cross,
along road to Bagleys Swamp, it being land given by David Hobbs to
said Daniel and 30 acres bounded by main road on E and by T. Walton and heirs of Walton Freeman, dec. and Negroes Joshua and Sally,
also, given to him by David Hobbs...
                                         Daniel S. Hobbs
                                         Burwell Brothers
                                         Abel Rogerson
John B. Hunter   James Baker
William Goodman   Absalom Blanchard

17 18 May 1836--Bryant Brothers and wife, Mary, to Ezekiel T. and Elizabeth G. Jones...18 3/4 acres, adjoining land of said Brothers, and beginning in fork of road running up main road from Gatesville, by Pryor Savage's NW up road opposite some small oak suckers, corner of John Brown's land, that tract which he bought of William G. Daughtry, along Brown's line of marked trees NE to a black gum, a corner of said Browns, standing in branch near where the corner pine stood which is blown up, thence down branch to Honey Pot Road; is said Brothers and wife's part in her right set apart to heirs of Willis Parker in division of Robert Parker's land divided 29 Oct 1798 and is No. 1...
Lassiter Riddick   Briant Brothers
Pryer Savage   Mary (x)Brothers

18 18 May 1836--Ezekiel T. Jones and wife, Elizabeth G., to Thomas Saunders...$250...50 acres on both sides of Honey Pot Road, beginning in fork of road up main road from Gatesville by Pryor Savage's NW to oak suckers, corner of John Brown's line of marked trees NE to black gum, a corner of said Brown's in branch near where corner pine stood which was blown up, and down branch to Honey Pot Road and across road and down branch; is land set apart to heirs of Willis Parker in division of Robert Parker's land 29 Oct 1798 and is No. 1...
Wm. E. Pugh   Ezekiel T. Jones
Pryor Savage   Elizabeth G. Jones

20 16 May 1836--John Lewis and wife, Rachael, to Mills Sparkman...$200...their interest in plantation of Abraham Beeman, Esq., dec. bounded by lands of Demsey Sparkman, William L. Boothe, Dempsey Parker, Charney Umphlet and others containing 300 acres; excepting the life right of Mrs. Lucretia Beeman, who has a dower on part of land...
                                              John Lewis
Wm. L. Boothe   Rachael Lewis

21 17 May 1836--Andrew Doughtie and wife, Barsheba, to Miles Brown...$30...100 acres, their interest in tract formerly belonging to Abyslla Blanchard, adjoining land of Miles Brown, Benjamin Brown and others...
                                              Andrew(x)Doughty
H. Gilliam   Barsheba(x)Doughty
Tim. Walton

22 9 Mar 1836--Willis F. Riddick to Thomas R. Costen...$591.25... tract of land purchased of Marmaduke Norfleet, beginning at a white oak tree between said Costen, George Costen and said Riddick, down said Thomas line to a maple, another corner and along line to a persimmon tree in branch in Harris Plantation, down branch to a cypress and to run of Bear Creek, thence corner at run of creek SW up branch to a black gum, thence binding James Murdaugh's line to a white oak, a corner tree, thence NW to Wild Cat Branch and up branch to foot of 6-ft. ditch and up ditch...
Eli Worrell   Willis F. Riddick
William(x)Brothers

22 11 Apr 1836--Levi Beeman to George Costen...$1500...187 acres on S side of main road that leads to plantation where Humphrey Hudgins formerly lived, beginning at fork of road near John Matthews, binding on road S to a pine, a corner tree of said Matthews

E and S to a corner black gum to a ditch and N to a beach, a corner of Josiah Hudgins heirs, E along his line to main road...
Thos. R. Costen   Levi Beeman
Andrew Johnson

23 24 Feb 1836--Isaac Pipkin to William B. Wynn of Hertford...$300...100 acres beginning in James Williams line to Samuel Feltons to main road leading from Winton to Suffolk up road to Richard Odom's and along his line to Asa Hill's line thence along his line to Riddick Gatlings to said Williams; being land conveyed to said Isaac by Isaac Pipkin Sr...
     Isaac Pipkin Sr.
I.W. Harrell

24 27 Feb 1836--James R. Riddick, sheriff, to Pryor Savage...$15.31 land where William Brown lives, sold by court levy brought by Jeptha Fowlkes; adjoins land of John Brown, said Savage and others...
John Willey   J.R. Riddick
B. Goodman

25 26 Oct 1835--Henry S. Spivey to Peter B. Minton...$500...two 50 acre tracts; the first beginning at Sandy Cross running S to Jacob Nixon's line along his line to Joel B. Hurdle's line, to Nathan Wards and second tract is bounded on W by lands of Kedar Riddick, N by land of Reuben Nixon, E by land of Mills Riddick and on S by land of John Nixon...
     Henry S. Spivey
A. Blanchard
William Blanchard

26 26 Feb 1836--John Hinton to Hance Hofler...$500...133 acres beginning at a gum of Willis Bond's corner, binding on said Bond's line to a pine stump on side of John Roberts Mill Pond, up run to a dam across branch to John Felton line up branch to a gum, a corner between said Feltons, Jonas Hinton and said Hance running a line of marked trees S to heirs of Jacob Powell and said Hance and W...
     John Hinton
H. Gilliam
Pryor Savage

26 15 Aug 1833--Jethro Lassiter to James T. Freeman...$90...28 3/4 acres bounded on S by swamp of James Baker, on SW by Dempsey Bond and on NW by lands of William Roundtree and Jacob N. Parker and on SE by land of Susannah Lassiter...
     Jethro(x)Lassiter
W. Baker
Henry Jocelin

26 5 Apr 1836--John Matthews to Fletcher Haslett...$500...1 acre in Gatesville adjoining land of Henry Gilliam and John S. Roberts and lying on road leading from Gatesville to Winton...
     John Matthews
H. Gilliam
Jno. H. Haslett

27 29 Sep 1835--George M. Mullen to Richard Odom, Esq...$800... Negro slave, Miley, and her three children; and Peggy and Daniel...
Isaac Pipkin Sr.   George M. Mullen

27 14 May 1836--Easton Blanchard to Joseph Brooks...$91...29 acres beginning in Watery Swamp at end of Blanchard's ditch, a corner of said Joseph's, running down swamp to an ash on said swamp, by line of marked trees to red oak in Benjamin Brown's line...
Jethro Blanchard   Easton Blanchard
Henry E. Blanchard

28 12 May 1833--James R. Riddick, sheriff, to William Hudgins...
$4.75 for taxes on 49 acres belonging to Seth P. and Samuel R.
Morgan and listed by Samuel R. and Abram Morgan Sr., and former-
ly belonging to Seth Morgan Sr...
Wm. E. Pugh   J.R. Riddick
Jno. R. Gilliam

29 7 Apr 1836--George Brooks to Jethro Blanchard...$200...88 acres
beginning at a sweet gum, a corner tree on Margaret C. Brooks' line
in Watery Swamp, nearly SW along her line to a pine, a corner in
Brown's line NW to a water oak to a sweet gum on Henry Hofler's...
                                                     George Brooks
Henry E. Blanchard
Joseph Brooks
Frederick Blanchard

29 12 Jan 1831--Ira Carter to James Williams...$75...his right in
a Negro girl belonging to said Ira and wife, Ludy, and Charles
Carter...
                                                     Ira(x)Carter
Burrell Eure   Charles(x)Carter
John(x)Eure   Ludy(x)Carter

29 22 Dec 1834--Sarah Smith (widow of late Richard Smith, dec.),
Dorotha Smith, James Rogers and wife, Millicent, and Thomas Smith,
all heirs of said Richard, to Mary Powell...$1.00...gift of Negro
girl, Catey, 8 years old. Said Mary is also heir of said Richard...
                                                     Thomas Smith
                                                     Saroe Smith
                                                     James Rogers
                                                     Emily(x)Smith
                                                     Dorotha Smith

30 1 May 1836--Moses Hurdle of Chowan to Christian Twine...$300...
125 acres, formerly tract of Jacob Eason, beginning at Cabin Swamp
at William King's line running S along line of marked trees to a
ditch in field where said Jacob did live, along ditch to Felton's
line...   Moses(x)Hurdle
Joseph R. Eason
James M. Riddick

31 11 Mar 1836--Marmaduke Ellis of Halifax, Joseph R. Billups and
wife, Mary, of Perquimans and Robert Newsome of Nansemond to John
Benton Jr...$100...50 acres near Hollow Bridge on N side of Baylis
Swamp in a small branch in Charles Briggs, dec. line, down swamp
near edge to James Powell's line, N along his line to John C. Gor-
don's W to Briggs and S...   Marmaduke Ellis
Joseph Gordon   Joseph R. Billups
Nath'l Griffin   Mary R.(x)Billups
Humphrey Parker   Robert Newsome

31 13 Feb 1836--James Powell to Joseph Speight...$196...39½ acres
adjoining lands of James Gwinn, John Powell and others...
                                                     James Powell
John C. Gordon
John J. Granbury

31 13 Feb 1836--Joseph Speight to Robert Hill...$200...50 acres
beginning at post oak in Richard H. Parker's line and cornering
on said Hill, along Parker's line to forked water oak, a corner
on Whitmill Hill W along line of marked trees to high water mark

of Bennetts Creek, up creek and E...
                                        Joseph(x)Speigh
R. Rawls
John Rawls

32 20 Feb 1836--Joseph Gordon to Robert Hill...$1200...184 acres formerly belonging to Holoday Walton and given by said Walton to his son-in-law, William W. Stedman, by deed of gift and bought by said Gordon under deed of trust, adjoining lands of Jacob Powell, John Granbury, John Powell, Abraham Riddick and others...
                                        Jos. Gordon
Jacob J. Harvey
James Briggs

33 18 May 1835--Nancy Bond to Samuel Stuard Bond...$175...78 acres on W side of road beginning at white oak, a corner of John Figgs, along his line to a post oak, a corner tree, NE to a pine and sweet gum, both choped, thence along William Cleaves line SE to main road to a black gum, a corner of Joseph Riddicks...
                                        Nancy Bond
Ezekiel T. Jones
Penelope(x)Blanchard

33 20 Aug 1835--James R. Riddick, sheriff, to Benjamin Saunders... $849...190 acres and $62...20 acres, both tracts of Abraham Morgan Sr. and sold by court writs at instance of John A. Roberts and Seth R. Morgan against said Abraham for $1641.73. Land begins at pine between James Benton and land formerly belonging to Seth Morgan, dec. along line of marked trees to run of creek, up creek to Wiley Riddick's line, along his line across road to a large pine a corner tree, S to red oak at side of road...
                                        James R. Riddick
Open Ct.

35 14 Oct 1835--Jethro Sumner and wife, Nancy, to James Russell, all of Nansemond...$80...96 acres adjoining lands of Miles Parker and heirs of Ira Odom...
                                        Jethro Sumner
Miles Howell   Ann Sumner

35 1 Dec 1835--John Copeland to James Russell, both of Nansemond... $500...333 acres beginning at a pine in head of Flat Cypress Swamp, formerly head of Speights Mill Pond, cornering on Willis Cross, along his line to river pocosin and to Chowan River...
Miles Howell   John Copeland
Dempsey Langston
Exum Jenkins

36 1 Mar 1836--Benjamin Saunders to James Saunders...$350...two pieces of land...first of 200 acres joins John A. March, Elizabeth Lee and others and second tract of 180 acres joins Etheldred Boyt's heirs, Miles Parker and others...
                                        Benja. Saunders
Drew M. Saunders
Francis Duke

37 10 May 1836--Jemimy Thornton of Pasquotank to Jesse Eason... $13.50...25 acres, 1/6 of tract left by will of Abraham Hurdle to be equally divided between his children; it is a part of the Hunter Tract on W side of main road leading from Sandy Cross to Suffol

joining lands of Josiah Briggs, Joseph Riddick and others...
Abner Eason   Jemimy(x)Thornton
J. Riddick

37 18 Mar 1835--James Figg to Nancy Bond...$200...78 acres beginning at white oak on road, a corner of John Figg's line, along his line NE to pine and sweet gum, both chop'd trees, along William Cleaves line SE to main road to black gum, a corner of Joseph Riddicks...
                                                      James Figg
John Figg
T. Saunders

38 1 Feb 1836--Burwell Griffith of Hertford to Richard Odom...$400 350 acres beginning at a corner pine of James Williams, formerly Abraham Cross, dec. running Williams line to Mirey Swamp, up swamp to a corner cypress in Asa Odom's line to forked black gum in Gum Swamp and down swamp; it being land Richard and Roden Odom sold to said Griffith...
                                                      Burrell Griffith
T. Saunders
Rodon Odom

38 12 May 1836--John Arnold to John P. Benton...$90...45 acres on E side of main road leading from Wiggens Crossroads to Elm Swamp; it being all land allotted to said Arnold from his father's estate.
                                                      John Arnold
John Wiggens
Brian Hare

39 16 May 1836--Daniel Hobbs to Abram Spivey...$50...50 acres beginning in road leading to Suffolk, running a straight line from road to a pine and persimmon tree to Overton's line, formerly known as the Hill Tract, running along road from Muddy Cross to Gatesville Courthouse, up Spivey's line whereon he now lives to the Virginia road; it being part of tract where said Hobbs now lives...
                                                      Daniel L. Hobbs
Whit' Stallings
James Boyce

40 24 Mar 1836--Moses R. Harrell of Nansemond to John Wiggens... $200...38 acres of a 152 acre tract and ½ of widows dower, tract of land sold to Edward Knight by Thomas, Humphrey and William Parker beginning at a popular in branch called Folly Branch, a corner tree of Jethro Sumners and Jesse Wiggens and binding on said Wiggens to James Bentons, on his line to John Parkers, dec. line and leaving his line and binding on lands of William Arnold, dec. line to John Hares and along Hare's line to said Sumners and along his line...
                                                      M.R. Harrell
James Mathias   Daley(x)Harrell
David(x)Brinkley

41 24 Mar 1836--John Knight of Nansemond to John Wiggens...$200... 38 acres out of 152 acre tract and ½ of dower rights, land which was transferred to him by Thomas, Humphrey and William Parker, beginning at a popular in Folly Branch, a corner tree of Jethro Sumners and Jesse Wiggens, E on Wiggens line to James Benton's, bindon his line to John Parkers, dec. line and leaving his line and

binding on lands of William Arnold, dec. to John Hare's and along
Hare's line to said Sumners and along his line...
                                                    John Knight
M.R. Harrell
Dempsey(x)Peel

42 14 May 1836--Jesse Mathias to Riddick Jones...$500...30 acres
adjoining lands of Jesse Mathias, Dempsey Vann and others, Negroes
Anna and three children Jacob and Hanna, all stock, cart and wheels
and all household; it being all property conveyed to him by said
Jones and wife in 1829...   Jesse Mathias
Dempsey Vann
Joseph Mathias

42 18 May 1835--Willis R. Hays to James Evans...$32.50...10½ acres
adjoining lands of James R. Riddick, Joseph Riddick and others,
known as the Benjamin Hayes Land, beginning in road at pine stump
and running SW along road, SE to a pine and N...
Lassiter Riddick   Willis Hays
Wm. W. Stedman

43 12 Oct 1835--William Taylor of Chowan to Starky Eure...$75...
70 acres formerly belonging to Joseph Taylor, dec. adjoining land
of Noah Roundtree, Daniel Eure, James T. Freeman and Riddick Trotman; it being land given to him by his father...
                                                    William Taylor
Simon Stallings
Jno. Mitchell

43 25 Jan 1836--Abraham Pruden to J. Riddick Eure...$25...100
acres beginning at a corner gum in George Harrell's along his
line to Richard Odom's thence to Bray Parker's line along Bray's
line of marked trees across ridge to a corner in the run of the
outside swamp, up run of swamp to Wynn's Ferry road and down road...
                                                    Abraham Pruden
Thomas Hoggard
Samuel Harrell

43 21 Jan 1835--Thomas Hoggard to Bray Eure...$75...29 acres be-
ginning at a spruce pine, a corner tree on Mills Eure's line, a-
long line of marked trees to a post oak, a corner tree, along Hoggard's line to a dogwood to a pine, to a hickory, to Long Branch,
along Bray Eure's line and across cornfield to a stob in Mills
Eure's line...   Thomas Hoggard
Wiley Carter
Boon Eure

44 29 Sep 1834--Moses Hill to Joseph Hurdle...$140...40 acres
beginning at a sycamore on Jacob Nixon's line to Hurdle's line
and along it to William King's and along Kings to main road and
along road...   Moses(x)Hill
Jacob Nixon
Abraham Hurdle

44 2 Nov 1835--Benbury Walton to John Walton...$100...20 acres on
N side of Indian Swamp beginning at run in main road leading from
Gatesville to Edenton E to run of Patience Branch, SE to Indian
Swamp to Walton's line W up run...
                                                    Benbury Walton
George W. Reed
Wm.(x) Matthews

45 22 Nov 1836--John B. Baker to James Riddick...$1.00 and to make safe to John Gatling and Joseph Gordon as his security for the following notes: John Roberts $4301.02, Joseph Riddick $500, Henry Bond $660, Abraham W. Parker $147.78...deed in trust, land whereon he lives and called Quarter Plantation joining Kicheon Norfleet and others, shingle swamp and all shingles on hand and Negroes Stephen, Delilah, Clinton, Phillis, Ellin, Cathera, Harriett, Olive and Cherry...
                Jno.B.Baker
T. Saunders   Jos. Gordon
M. Norfleet   Jno. Gatling

46 11 Jun 1836--William Daniel to Henry Gilliam...50¢ and to secure to him a note for $30 to Thomas Twine and for which he is bound...75 acres adjoining lands of Mary Nurney, John Gatling and others and the tract he purchased of said Gilliam, who bought it from Samuel Brown...
               William Daniel
J.W. Bond   H. Gilliam
Jas. C. Riddick

49 17 May 1836--Elisha H. Bond to Nathaniel Eure...$99.20...91½ acres beginning in road at a pine running NW to red oak corner on Richard Odoms and said Eure's, thence NE and then NW to a black gum, corner of said Eure and Eff Lewis and SE...
              Elisha H. Bond
H. Gilliam   Mills Roberts
Henry Bond

49 23 Feb 1836--Riddick B. Eure to Elisha Parker...$212.50...129 acres beginning in Sarum Creek road in Deep Branch at Tinson Y. Eure's, down run of branch to run of Coles Creek, up creek to white gum, Samuel Eure's corner, thence a straight line W to post oak near corner of Old Field N to a maple in Miles and Nathaniel Cullens line and along Cullens line W to road...
Levi Eure   Riddick B. Eure

49 15 Aug 1836--Robert Hill to Joseph Hill...$125...30 acres beginning at peach tree in the opening fixed by them as a corner and beginning an E course along a line of marked trees to a post oak, a corner in Doctor Richard H. Parker's line, thence along his line S to a white oak, a corner on Whitmill Hill's and along Hill's line to a pine and N...
               Robert(x)HillJr.
R. Rawls
Whitmill Hill

49 18 Mar 1836--Abel Rogerson to Jess Hobbs...$15...8 acres adjoining land of John Mitchell and Thomas J. Miller and binding on main road...
               Abel Rogerson
Daniel S. Ward
William Hurdle

49 18 Mar 1836--Riddick Smith to Henry Costen...$155...Negro girl, Harriett...
               Riddick(x)Smith
William Jones

50 1 Jul 1836--William Goodman to Jethro D. Goodman...$500...420 acres beginning at a white oak, corner of Exum Jenkins, running line

of marked trees SE to Anne Speight's corner, binding on Speights and Joseph Freeman to Burwell Griffith's corner, along his line SW to a white oak, a corner of Abraham W. Parker, thence along Parker's line to an elm, binding on said Parkers to a corner on Sand Banks and running a line of marked trees to a pine, Willis Cross and James Russell's corner...

                    William Goodman

Hardy Cross

50 19 Apr 1836--Burwell Brothers to Daniel Hobbs...$660...27 acres where Brothers formerly lived and purchased of Andrew Baker, adjoining lands of Timothy Walton and Walton Freeman...

                    Burwell Brothers

John Sheppard

51 2 Jul 1836--James Johnson and wife, Margaret, of Nansemond to Miles Parker...$110...152 acres belonging to estate of Edward Knight, dec. adjoining lands of John P. Benton, Seth Benton and others...

                    James Johnson

James Morgan   Margaret(x)Johns
Edward(x)Pearce

Abraham W. Parker and Wm. L. Boothe testified said Margaret signed deed freely.

52 26 Jun 1836--Jesse Porter and wife, Sabra, of Nansemond and Amos, William and Humphrey Parker to Miles and Abram Parker... $100...their right in 50 acres belonging to John Parker, dec., adjoining lands of John Arnold...

                    Jesse Porter

John Hare   Sabra(x)Porter
Henry Brinkley   Amos(x)Parker
                    William(x)Parker
                    Humphrey(x)Parke

52 3 Aug 1836--Jonathan Williams to Miles Parker...$150...41 acres beginning at a water oak in Henry G. Williams running S binding on Dempsey Parkers to a white oak in Kicheon Norfleet's corner, binding on said Norfleets E to a pine of said Miles, thence N to said Henry G. and W...

                    Jonathan(x)Willi

Wm.W. Cowper
Nath'l Doughtie

53 8 Sep 1835--Willis F. Riddick to Marmaduke Norfleet...$1000... lot or piece of land in Gatesville called The Grove beginning at middle of branch at fork of Honey Pot Road, leading to Bennetts Creek bridge, down road to a post near the Brick-Hole opposite a line of red oaks nearly opposite the corner of Jesse Brown's lot, straight line of James Garrett's heirs and line of Willis Parker heirs...

                    Willis F. Riddic

Wm. F. Bennett
W. Riddick

54 24 Dec 1835--Kedar Ellis to Benjamin Franklin...$100...Negro boy Reuben...

                    Kedar(x)Ellis

Titan K. Rudulph
Abraham(x)Meltear
Elizabeth Duke
Jas. A. Ballard

54 16 Jan 1836--Thomas R. Costen to Samuel R. Harrell...$280...
land on N side of road leading to Gatesville beginning at school
house running NE to Bennetts Creek down run E to bridge and up
road by Noah Harrells...
                Thomas R. Costen
Allen Smith
Noah Harrell

55 23 May 1836--Elisha H. Bond to Henry Bond...$225...142 acres
beginning at an oak a corner of Richard Odom's line, along his
line SW to a black gum corner of said Odoms NW to a red oak, corner of Odoms and Jesse Vann then NE to a black gum corner of said
Vann and Dred Cross SE and then SW...
                Elisha H.Bond
George W. Reed
J.W. Bond

56 25 Oc6 1834--Paul Jones to Job R. Hall...$400...100 acres bounded
on N by main road beginning at Henry Green, dec. line and running
road to Hardy Eason, dec. land on S by a branch belonging to Thomas
Riddick, on E by Henry Green, dec. land and on W by Hardy Eason,
dec. land...
                Paul(x)Jones
Jet. H. Riddick
Thomas Riddick

57 30 Apr 1836--David Benton to Joseph Benton...$301...Negro womam
Tamer and her child, Reaney...
                David(x)Benton
James Morgan
Abraham Benton

57 2 Jan 1836--George Freeman and Henry Gilliam to Archibald
Jones...$235...70 acres whereon said George lives, adjoining land
of Frederick Pearce, Reuben Hinton and others...
                George Freeman
J.W. Bond   H. Gilliam

57 2 Mar 1836--Abraham Pruden and Thomas Hoggard to James Williams
of Hertford...$200...200 acres adjoining lands of Etheldred Cross,
Asa Odom, Abraham Crafford and others...reference Abraham Cross
land was willed to Harriett Cross and conveyed by her husband,
John Norfleet to Elisha Umphlet...
                Abraham Pruden
                Thos. Hoggard
John Sparkman
Rodon Odom

58 15 Aug 1836--Charlotte Green to Job R. Hall...$12.50...her
interest in dower land laid off to her by court of land of her
late husband, Henry Green, dec...
                Charlotte(x)Green
Jos. Gordon
Jet. H. Riddick

58 1 Nov 1835--David Dunsford to John Dunsford...$95...36½ acres
beginning at sweet gum at run of Beaverdam Swamp SE along lane to
Mrs. Hoskins line NE to swamp...
                David(x)Dunsford
J.R. Riddick
R.K. Speed

59 2 Aug 1836--J.R. Riddick, sheriff, to Amos Hobbs...$1.90...27½
acres...sold for taxes due for 1833. Land listed by Jacob Hobbs
and adjoins land of Jesse Hobbs, Milton Eason and others...
Jet. H. Riddick   J.R. Riddick
John C. Gordon

60 18 Jul 1836--Burwell Griffith of Hertford to Dempsey Griffith, Pleasant Gatling, Nancy Saunders and Martha Griffith his interest in tract of land where he lately lived and crop now growing on it adjoining lands of James Williams Sr., Willis Cross and Etheldred Cross. Contains 500 acres...
                     Burwell Griffit
John A. Anderson
Thos. Maget

61 18 Jul 1836--Burwell Grifith of Hertford to his beloved children: Dempsey Griffith, Pleasant (wife of James Gatling), Nancy (wife of Jason Saunders) and Martha Griffith ...Negro man Jack and all stock of cattle except 1 yoke of steers and 2 cows and calves given to John Griffith, 2 cows and 2 calves given to Dempsey Griffith and 2 cows and calves given to Martha Griffith; out of which they are to pay Cintha, wife of Jesse Vann and Elizabeth, wife of James Brady, and Peggy Waren $15 ($5 each)...
                     Burwell Griffi
John A. Anderson
Thos. Maget

62 18 Jul 1836--John Griffith to Dempsey Griffith, Pleasant Gatling, Nancy Saunders and Martha Griffith...25¢...1/5 part of 500 acre tract whereon his father lately lived adjoining land of James Williams Sr, heirs of Jacob Odom, lands of Etheldred Cross, Willis Cross and others...
                     John S. Griffit
John A. Anderson
Thos. Maget

63 15 Mar 1836--Jesse and Joseph Mathias to Abraham Riddick of Upper Parish of Nansemond...$130...lands in the Marsh, which is expressed in old former deed from James Brinkley, N side of White Oak Spring Marsh, adjoining land of heirs of William Riddick, Col. Josiah Riddick, Mills Riddick, Miles Brinkley, dec. and is land given by David Brinkley, dec. by will...
Dempsey Knight   Jesse Mathias
Dempsey Vann   Joseph Mathias
Benjamin Brinkley

63 15 Aug 1836--William Hudgins to Thomas Eason...$216...12½ acres beginning at a sweet gum at road S and then SE to a post oak, a corner of James R. Riddick's line, NW to main road and along road...
                     William Hudgins
Etheldred Mathias
James Benton

64 4 Jan 1836--Nathaniel Cullens to Miles Cullens...$50...28 acres adjoining land of William W. Cowper and others and is land where he now lives...
                     Nath'l Cullens
Wm. L. Boothe

64 19 Nov 1835--Job Blanchard to Hardy Jones...$65...12 acres binding on lands of Henry Bond, separated by a branch from land of Mary Hudgins, and main road opposite Methodist Meeting House...
                     Job(x)Blanchard
Benjamin Brown
Thomas Blanchard

65 29 Aug 1836--Thomas Holland to Archibald R. Jones...$1.00 and to make safe to Ezekiel T. Jones a note of $16.57 signed by said Holland and William Hudgins...20 acres adjoining Frederick Jones, Kedar Lassiter and James Lassiter...
Frederick Jones   Thomas(x)Holland
Charles Eason

66 12 Feb 1836--Miles Briggs to James Copeland...$1.00 and to make safe to Richard H. Ballard his security for debt of $37 to Mary Benton...1 gray mare and 5 cattle...
                                             Miles Briggs
Robert H. Ballard
John Brothers

66 21 Nov 1836--James Costen Jr. to Peter B. Minton...$700...150 acres beginning at a water oak on the Virginia Road N to land of Thomas or William Harrell, down Harrell's line to Bagley's Swamp, which is Timothy Walton's line up swamp to said Waltons and Walton Freeman's line...
                                             James Costen Jr.
Henry Costen
James A. Harrell

66 5 Nov 1836--Timothy Walton to Nathan Nixon...$575...140 acres beginning at Jacob Cullens corner on said Nixon's line W to creek swamp down side of swamp as to take all high land, to Charles Powell's line to said Cullens...
                                             Tim. Walton
John G. Walton
Nathaniel Jones

67 21 Nov 1836--Nathan Nixon to Zachariah Nixon of Perquimans...$575...140 acres on Catherine Creek swamp beginning at a pine stake at Nathaniel Cullen's corner in Nixon's line W to swamp to Charles Powells and to said Cullens...
                                             Nathan Nixon
Samuel Nixon
Reuben Nixon Jr.

68 23 Sep 1836--T.W. Carr releases Negroes George, Frank and Venus to John O. Hunter who placed them in a deed of trust to secure $800 note to Josiah Coffield for which John C. and Joseph Gordon were security...
                                             T.W. Carr
John C. Gordon

68 3 Sep 1836--Richard H. Field to Daniel Williams...$400...246 acres beginning at a sweet gum on Daniel Williams and Blake Baker's SE to a popular corner, to a black gum then NE to another black gum, SE to a corner of heirs of James Matthews, dec to a corner of Aaron Pearce's SW to a maple, a new corner between Richard H. and Lemuel K. Fields, to a branch...
                                             Richard John H. Fields
Henry Willey
Jethro Willey

69 20 Sep 1836--Robert Rogers to William Lee...$200...71 acres beginning in Lee's line at a small spruce pine corner on Edward Howell's thence N along his line of marked trees to Howell's line to run of Beach Swamp, up run to James Barnes line and along his line S to said Lee's line and W...
                                             Robert Rogers
William Cross
Hardy Cross

70 17 Jan 1837--Seth Piland to Mills Piland...$230...75½ acres, a part of land of George Piland, beginning at a cypress on E side of Coles Creek, William Piland's corner, up Long Branch to a sweet gum in William's line, up run of branch to a popular, James Goodwin's corner, up branch to black gum in Goodwin's line to Pryor Savage's corner and along his line to a pine on Great Thicket Ridge, the corner of Seth Piland's land, along Cherry Sparkman's dower line to a black gum, Mills Piland's corner to E side of Coles Creek and down creek...
                                                    Seth Piland
Arodi Draper
Hillory Taylor

72 17 Jan 1837--Joseph Gordon to Isaac L. Harrell (page 71 is missing with amount, etc.) 525 acres 100 yards from Gordon's new dwelling house, including 180 acres of desert patent land parallel with James Harrell's desert land W up run of Mills Swamp against mouth of Bull Ridge Branch and up branch to Andrew R. Harrell's line to John Alpin's line, to Moses Spivey's, to public road...
                                                    Jos. Gordon
Wm. H. Harrell
Jacob J. Harvey

72 16 Feb 1837--William Robins to Henry Bond...$60...50 acres whereon he lives adjoining Isaac Hyatt, Noah Roundtree and James T. Freeman's. Also 1 horse, stock of hogs and feather bed...
                                                    Wm. W. Robins
Joseph Sutton

73 4 May 1837--Thomas I. Miller to Henry Gilliam...$1.00 and to secure debt of $650 to John C. Gordon...179 acres, including saw and grist mill, adjoining lands of John Mitchell, Timothy G. Trotman and heirs of Robert Taylor...
                                                    Thos. I. Miller
Asa G. Hofler   H. Gilliam

73 5 Apr 1837--William W. Cowper, Henry Gilliam and William G. Daughtry are bound to state of North Carolina for $5000 whereas said Cowper has been appointed clerk and master for county of Gates...
                                                    Wm.W. Cowper
                                                    H. Gilliam
John Walton, P.R.   W.G. Daughtry

73 15 Oct 1836--Samuel Felton to David F. Felton...$100...40 acres allotted to him in division of his father's estate and is Lot No. 10, beginning at a cypress in NW branch then NE to a maple in David Riddicks to a new road leading from Haslett's shop to James Riddick's up road to middle of swamp and up swamp...
Elbert H. Riddick   Samuel Felton
David Riddick

74 28 Apr 1836--John S. Roberts to John W. Bond...$100...¼ acre beginning at Jesse I. Cox's corner on Honey Pot Street SW to a post on Parker's lane then S to corner of John Matthews E to Honey Pot Street and N...
                                                    John S. Roberts

Briant Brothers
Asa Hill

75 23 Sep 1836--John B. Baker to Lassiter Riddick...$136.53...
41 acres beginning at a sweet gum at said Lassiter's corner down
his fence to Simon Roundtrees, by line of marked trees to road,
which leads from Bakers to Honey Pot...
Rich'd I. Gregory   John B. Baker
W.J. Baker

76 11 Nov 1836--Julia Lawrence to Lassiter Riddick...$17.62½...
23½ acres adjoining lands of Jethro Howell, Julia Lawrence and
said Riddick, beginning at a maple, a corner of Howell and Riddicks NE to a water oak, corner of Howell and Lawrence, SE to
said Riddick's line (formerly Henry Lawrence's land) and SW...
Lem. Riddick   Julia(x)Lawrence
Jethro Howell

77 23 Aug 1836--William Arnold to James A. Ballard of Nansemond...
$500...103 acres beginning at a red oak at foot of avenue running
main road to Suffolk joining land of Col. Josiah Riddick and James
Mathias W to a small red oak down avenue N by a line of marked
trees to Jason Franklin's line E to main road and up road S...
James Morgan   William Arnold
Wm. H. McGuire

79 5 Jan 1837--William E. Pugh to James R. Riddick...$1.00 and
for consideration of payment of debts for which James R. and
Lassiter Riddick, Mills Roberts, John Lovett and William G. Daughtry are security as follows: Nancy Parker $126.51, John Roberts
$350 and Thomas Saunders $380...Negroes Jim and Peter, his office
in Gatesville;   all books...deed in trust...
                                                Wm. E. Pugh
                                                Mills Roberts
                                                J.R. Riddick

79 25 May 1836--Jethro Eure to Jethro Eure Jr...gift of land on
W side of road leading immediately from Sarum Creek Landing to
Suffolk, after his death and that of his wife, Mildred..1 horse
1 gun 1 bed and furniture 1 cow and calf and 1 sow and pigs...
Tinson Y. Eure   Jethro(x)Eure
Purnal King
William Carter

80 15 Nov 1836--Jethro Blanchard to Currie Blanchard...$300...
88 acres in Watery Swamp beginning at a sweet gum, a corner tree
in Margaret Brooks line nearly W along her line to a pine, another
corner in Brown's line NW to a water oak NE by a line of marked
trees to a sweet gum, a corner in Henry Hofler's line and up swamp.
Henry E. Blanchard   Jethro Blanchard
Robert Blanchard

81 4 Nov 1836--William H. Goodman to Lemuel Smith of Nansemond...
$85...50 acres near Manneys Ferry and bounded by lands of Henry
Jones heirs, Miles Parker and Elijah Hare...
John Goomer   Wm.H. Goodman

81 23 Sep 1836--John B. Baker to John Worrell...$190.25...55 acres
beginning at a pine stump corner on Pryor Savages, along said

Worrell's line to William Brooks line and on his line to road leading from Bakers to Gatesville, down road to Pryor Savage and almost SW to Savage's field...

                                                        John B. Baker

Richard I. Gregory
Wm. J. Baker

82 6 Jan 1836--John C. Gordon to James Powell...$505...128 acres, which was placed in a deed of trust to him to pay Wm. W. Stedman; it being a tract said Stedman bought at a trust sale and lately belonging to John Hofler, adjoining heirs of John Small, dec. and William Brothers, dec...

                                                     John C. Gordon

John O. Hunter

82 16 Aug 1836--Riddick Trotman to John White...$285...27 acres beginning at Catherine Creek Swamp, adjoining land of Jacob N. Parker E to Joseph Taylor's NE to land belonging to Mills Stallings, on his line W to creek...

                                                   Riddick Trotman

N. Nixon
E. Trotman

83 26 Aug 1836--James Goodman of Nansemond to Charles Jones...$437.50 180 acres beginning at a black oak near main road in William Cross line, running line of marked trees to a popular standing in the branch, a corner tree of Edwin Cross and Mary Willey, thence running said Cross line to James Rogers line, along Rogers line to main road and down road...

                                               James Goodman

Jethro Willey
H. Willey

84 29 Sep 1836--Shadrack Stallings and wife, Nancy, to Frederick Jones...$40...plantation on which said Jones now lives, adjoining land of George Costen, Thomas Riddick, Thomas Hunter, John Hunter and others...

                                       Shadrack(x)Stalli
Bn.B. Ballard   Nancy(x)Stallings
Jesse White

              Riddick Gatling testified that said
        Nancy signed deed freely after private examination.

84 29 Sep 1836--Ann Walton, Milicent Powell and William Walton to Frederick Jones...$40...their interest in plantation on which said Jones lives, adjoining lands of George Costen, Thomas Riddick, Timothy Hunter, John Hunter and others...

                                     Ann(x)Walton
Bn.B. Ballard   Milicent(x)Powell
Jesse White   William(x)Walton

85 27 Oct 1834--Abraham Pruden to Bray Eure...$10...interest in land of Peter Harrell, dec. so far as the right of Andrew Johnson in said land so far as he is entitled to his wife's interest in said land...

                                     Abraham Pruden

Henry Speight
Thomas Hoggard

85 29 Feb 1836--Bray Parker to Nannah Humphflet...$30...30 or 40 acres adjoining land of Samuel Harrell and others and known as the Stallings Tract and said Bray defends the right George M. Mullen may warrant in tract...

                                          Bray Parker

Wm. L. Boothe

85 4 Feb 1835--Abraham Pruden and wife, Martha, to Jason Roundtree...$29...15½ acres beginning at a juniper on side of big
pocosin by a line of marked trees to a black gum on side of
Long Branch, thence along Mills Eure's line to a pine, a corner
on side of pocosin...
Thomas Hoggard   Abraham Pruden
Wm. H. Savage   Martha(x)Pruden

        Lemuel Riddick and Abram W. Parker
        testified said Martha signed freely after
        private examination.

86 28 Sep 1836--John Wiggens to Dempsey Peel...$148...40 acres
beginning at large pine corner on John V. Sumner on his line to
a sweet gum corner on John Wiggens to a small post oak corner on
Seth Bentons thence his line to Garrett Knight's corner thence a
straight line of marked trees...
                                                       John Wiggens
James Morgan
John Benton

86 24 Nov 1836--John B. Baker appointed James R. Riddick to convey
any real or personal estate named in deed of trust...
Rich'd M. Harvey   Jno. B. Baker
Wm. J. Baker

86 26 Aug 1836--Charles Jones to Jethro Willey...$1.00 and to make
safe to James Goodman as security for the payment of a $339.50
note...tract of land adjoining lands of William Cross, Hillory
Willey, Edwin Cross, James Rogers and others... Charles Jones
                                                               Jethro Willey
Hardy Cross   James Goodman

87 28 Jun 1837--John H. Felton to David Parker...$1.00 and to
make safe a note of $970.50 to him...150 acre plantation whereon
he lives adjoining lands of John Roberts, John Hare's heirs,
Jonas Hinton and others; being land devised to him by death of
his father. Also, Negroes Beck, Lizza, Cassandra and Bob...
                                                           John H. Felton
Robert Simons   David Parker

87 4 Nov 1836--John B. Baker and John Worrell to Pryor Savage...
$3.50...tract beginning at a gum in Savage and Bakers corner near
Halfway Run Swamp W on Savages tract 70 yards N and 70 yard to
a sweet gum E on ditch and back 70 yards...
                                                       John B. Baker
Rich'd M. Harvey   John(x)Worrell
Wm. J. Baker
Wm. B. Harvey

92 16 Jan 1837--Richard H. Parker, trustee of William F. Bennett,
to said Bennett...$1.00...having sold sufficient to condition of
said trust leaving a surplus...1 horse, gig and harness, household and kitchen furniture, all his stock of hogs and cattle,
farm utensils and title to land he owns in right of his wife, adjoining lands of James M. Riddick and others...
Jos. Gordon   Rich'd H. Parker

92 22 Oct 1836--John B. Baker to William W. Cowper...$200...
80 acres beginning at a holly on road leading from Winton to
Suffolk near Mrs. Nancy Gatling's, John Riddick's corner on his

line of tract said Riddick purchased of Arthur Gatling, to a large
white oak in branch at crossing place, a new path on Baker's patent
line, to Exum Lewis line, to a line of marked trees on road near
Lewis house to main road; it being a part of land formerly belonging to Miles Gatling, dec....
                   J.B. Baker
Jos. Gordon
Wm. J. Baker

92 14 Jan 1836--Mary Cullen to William W. Cowper...$50...100 acres
bounded by John Riddick, Benjamin Wynns, James Brown and others.
Land known as White Oak and laid off to said Mary as her dower
rights in lands of first husband, John Lewis...
                   Mary(x)Cullens
Wm. L. Boothe

92 3 Mar 1836--Thomas R. Costen and Isaac S. Harrell, merchants
trading under firm of Costen & Harrell, release to Abel Rogerson
the following property, which was conveyed to them in a deed of
trust by Jeremiah Rogerson of Perquimans 11 Jan 1835: 550 acres
adjoining land of Reuben Nixon, Kedar Felton, Abraham Hurdle and
Willis Riddick and slaves Celia, Rose, Amos, Jack, Sam, Charles,
Ritty and Jenny...
                   Thomas R. Coste:
Jet. H. Riddick   I.S. Harrell

93 5 Sep 1836--Henry Willey releases to Richard H. Field all rights
of real estate conveyed to him as trustee 21 Sep 1835 to secure to
Daniel Williams a note of $60; the note having been paid...
J. Willey   Henry Willey
Nathan Nixon

93 8 Feb 1837--Daniel H. Fields to William A. Matthews...$200...
217 acres beginning at a red oak and running E binding on Allen
Smith's to a black gum, corner between Smith and John Cuff, N to
Pugh's land then W to Kicheon Norfleets, to William Booths and S...
Jesse S. Matthews   Daniel H.(x)Fie:
John M. Matthews

93 3 Nov 1836--John J. Crawford of Hertford to Simon and Charles
Walters...$180...175 acres beginning in road leading from Wynns
Ferry at Gum Swamp near Mrs. Landing's residence down swamp bind-
ing on Richard Odom's to Mills Eures and along his line to Oda
Boss' line, down her line to Rachael Landing and others, to road
at or near Black Fishing Hole...
                   John J. Crawfor
Allen Smith
Thomas Hoggard

94 20 Aug 1836--Mary Franklin of Nansemond to Edward Jones...$72.50
50 acres beginning at a forked maple binding on Gallberry Pocosin
nearly E and adjoining land of Thomas Twine, binding on his land
to George Brooks, along his line N to Watery Swamp thence E adjoining lands of said Jones...
                   Mary Franklin
Thomas(x)Lassiter
Jam. A. Ballard

94 26 Jun 1836--Jesse Wiggens, administrator of William Parker, dec
to Miles Briggs...$182...Negro girl Milley and boy Bob...
                   Jesse Wiggens
James Morgan

95 20 Feb 1837--James Savage, executor of John Matthews, dec. to
Soloman Roundtree...$258.50...4 acres in town of Gatesville adjoining lands of Henry Gilliam, Jesse Brown and others...
H. Gilliam   James Savage
Matt Jordon

96 20 Feb 1837--Riddick Hunter to Willis W. Harrell...$400...85
acres, part of a tract whereon said Hunter lives; all that part
on S and W side of public road, beginning at Hollow Bridge on a
prong of Hunters Mill Swamp and along road to said Harrells dwelling house, where his father lived, down road joining Joseph Harrells
heirs, to run of Hunter's Mill Swamp NW to a prong and up run...
Ben.B. Ballard   Riddick Hunter
Jos. Gordon

96 1 Nov 1836--Isaac S. Harrell to James A. Harrell...$250...100
acre tract formerly belonging to John G. Liles on N side of Horsepool Swamp beginning in a branch in John Alpin's line along a line
of marked trees to said Isaac's land S to swamp, up swamp to high
water, to mouth of Bull Ridge Branch then up branch to Andrew Harrels E to said Alpins...
                                                     I.S. Harrell
Jos. Gordon
Wm. B. Harrell

97 14 Jan 1836--William Cleaves to Joseph and James R. Riddick...
$2000...750 acres known by name Cypress Pond, beginning at a pine
near John Cuff's fence, a corner, thence a line of marked trees SE
to a post oak binding on Lemuel Cleaves, dec. land, thence SW to
a black gum on W side of new road to Joseph Riddick's line to James
R. Riddick's, formerly Mathew M. Dye's corner, to a sweet gum on
S side of Honey Pot Road, down road to Allen's line, along his
line to Thomas Smith's to John Matthews, to John Cuff's reserving
¼ acre(being graveyard where said Cleaves' son, Lemuel,) was buried...
Allen Smith   William Cleaves
Wm. E. Pugh

98 21 Feb 1837--Henry Gilliam to Joseph Riddick, Esq...$26...26½
acres belonging to the parish, adjoining land of William Cleaves
(formerly) and said Riddick and sold by a commission appointed by
court...   H. Gilliam
John F. Parker   J. Riddick

99 31 Oct 1836--Riddick Trotman to Ezekiel Trotman...$150...
land beginning in mouth of Poley Bridge Branch W to a gum, a corner tree, N binding on land of Hance Hofler, E bordering on land
of said Ezekiel, to a cypress on Catherine Creek...
Milton Eason   Riddick Trotman
Elisha Blanchard

100 11 Aug 1837--John Lovett to Henry Gilliam...$5.00...household,
kitchen furniture, hold in trust to secure notes, secured by said
Gilliam, William G. Daughtry and Abel Rogerson, to John Roberts
for $100, John Willey for $154, Exum Jenkins for $200, Wilie
Riddick for $684, David Parker for $200, Prior Savage for $160,

and Henry Willey for $100. Also, 1 horse and gig, 4 beds and furniture, 2 dozen windsor chairs, 4 tables, 2 end tables, 1 sideboard and 1 clock and all goods on hand...

             John Lovett
             H. Gilliam
D. Parker   W.G. Daughtry
Robert H. Ballard   Abel Rogerson

101 11 Aug 1837--Nathaniel Jones to David Parker...$1.00...50 acres whereon he lives adjoining lands of Henry Trevathan, James Hare, Riddick Smith, Robert Jordon and Reuben Hinton, to hold in trust. Also 3 beds and furniture, 1 stear, 8 shoats, 1 sow and 5 pigs, 3 sheep, 4 hogsheads, 1 loom and gear, household and kitchen furniture, 1 cart and wheels and crop growing...$100 note...
             Nathaniel(N)Jones
Robert Simons   D. Parker

101 3 Aug 1837--William Robins to James H. Parker...$1.00...50 acres adjoining James T. Freeman, Noah Roundtree, Isaac Hyatt and others; land devised to him by his father...to hold in trust for $110 note...
             Wm.(x)Robins
D. Parker   James H. Parker

102 4 Apr 1837--James R. Riddick, attorney for John B. Baker, to John C. Gordon...$3330...666 acres known as Quarter Plantation, adjoining lands of Kicheon Norfleet, Ann Harvey, Isaac Pipkin and others...
             J.R. Riddick
Jet. H. Riddick
Whit'l Stallings

102 10 Nov 1836--John C. Gordon, executor of Nancy Granbury, dec. to Mills Riddick...$176...300 acres of desert land adjoining lands of Joseph Gordon, Mills Riddick, George E. Harvey and others. Mills Riddick is from Nansemond...
             John C. Gordon
Wm. H. McGuire

103 2 Feb 1837--James Hare to James H. Parker...$75...25 acres beginning at a pine in said Parker's line near his fence and John Walton's corner, binding on Walton's line, to water oak, a corner between Walton and Parker, to Noah Hinton's lane and from his house to Edenton road and up lane; land devised to said Hare by death of his father...
             James Hare
James Smith
D. Parker

104 19 Nov 1836--Joshua Jones and wife, Margaret, to John Wiggens...$12...1/6 part of tract containing 75 acres, which James Wiggens died possessed of and adjoining land of Wilie Riddick, David Benton and others...
             Joshua Jones
             Margaret Jones
James Morgan
John Barnes

106 23 Aug 1837--William Mathias to John G. Wilson of Murfreesborough in County of Hertford...deed of trust for 2 notes of $500 each...his undivided 2/3 of schooner or vesel known as Two Sisters

with her furniture, tackle and apparel and certificate of registration No. 105, of which said Mathias is at present master. Said vesel was built at Blue Hill, state of Main, 1825 as appears by certificate of enrolment # 270 granted at port of Boston and port of Charleston 22 Sep 1834. Has 1 deck 2 masts is 61 ft 9 in breadth 7 ft 7 in in delpth and measures 72 and 38/75 tons, has square stern, no galleries and schooner has been registered at Edenton...
Robert H. Ballard   William Mathias

107 6 Nov 1821--Joseph Riddick, sheriff, to James Parker of Nansemond land of William Brinkley adjoining Thomas Parker and others, sold by court writ at instance of John Roberts for $110.25 debts...
Open Court   J. Riddick

107 10 Jun 1836--Moses D. Hare, Esther Hare and Burwell Hare to Elijah Harrell...$11.00...21½ acres beginning on Bennetts Creek running E and then W back to swamp, N to a pine, corner tree, then E; land formerly belonging to their mother, Elizabeth Davis, but when she died was Elizabeth Hare...
                                                 Moses D.(x)Hare
Wm.W. Cowper   Esther(x)Hare
Henry S. Blount   Burwell(x)Hare

107 4 Feb 1837--Riddick Smith and Pleasant Smith, widow of Charles Smith, dec. to James Hare...$70...25 acres, being part of tract whereon said Charles died and which he gave to his son Riddick, reserving ½ of plantation to his wife, Pleasant, with exception of graveyard; beginning at a water oak in Nathaniel Jones line S to a corner pine near Trevathans, binding on his line to a stake, where used to stand a plum tree, to Walton's corner on his line W to white oak in Old Nichols line...
James Smith   Riddick(x)Smith
Willis B. Smith   Pleasant(x)Smith

109 4 Jan 1837--John Jones to Riddick Smith...$450...100 acres, including three tracts: one Dempsey Jones gave to John Jones in will, one John purchased of Mills Riddick and formerly owned by Marmaduke Smith and called the Polson Tract and one John purchased of James Smith and Riddick Smith and formerly owned by said Charles; land begins at white oak in Henry Gilliams line, formerly line of John Lewis, SE to Cypress Branch at Boothe's corner, along his line to Old Mill Branch up branch to Nathaniel Jones corner NE to William Jones corner and by a line of marked trees...   John Jones
James Smith
William P. Jones

110 30 Aug 1837--William E. Pugh, attorney for John O. Hunter, to James R. Riddick...$1.00 and to cover $550 note given to Joseph Riddick, Esq., Negroes placed in trust Venus,28 and two children...   Wm. E. Pugh
Henry L. Blount   J.R. Riddick

111 3 Sep 1836--Elisha Benton to Joseph Benton...$30...31 acres, two parcels of land beginning at Bryant Hares line at the road, along his line to run of Bennetts Creek to Joseph Bentons line and up road, the second joins David Benton and others...
Benja Saunders   Elisha(x)Benton
Abraham Benton

112 8 Feb 1837--Seth R. Morgan to Abram Benton...$16.50...3 acres beginning at a red oak, a corner of Joseph Bentons, with his line SW to a pine, a corner on Seth Morgans, across to line of Seth Benton's heirs...
Allen Daughtry   Seth R. Morgan
Joseph Benton

112 24 Oct 1836--Peter B. Minton to John Shepperd...$150...1 acre lot beginning at stake at Sandy Cross, along main road S to side of store house, across field to Burwell Brother's line N to road leading to Chappel and NW...
Abner Eason   P.B. Minton
Bushrod Riddick

112 23 Nov 1836--Joseph Gordon to Mary Brinkley...$125...Negro woman, Chloe, belonging to estate of Miles Brinkley, dec...
Owen(x)Brinkley   Jos. Gordon
Joseph G. Granbury

112 5 Jul 1836--Mary Goodman to her beloved grandson, William Israel Noah Twine...Negroes Joe, Martiller, Albert and John, being the same which his father, Thomas Twine, have now in his possession and if he should die before lawful age same should go to his father.
Kichen (x) Howell   Mary(x)Goodman

113 22 Nov 1836--Jacob T. Johnson, Willis Evans and wife, Mary, Leah Johnson, Samuel Evans and wife, Nancy, to Elizabeth Marshall and her son, Samuel Lassiter...gift of life lease of land on Deep Gut Branch, bounded by land of Enoch Pearce, Kedar Lassiter and Abner Pearce...   J.T. Johnson   Leah(x)Johnson
                                 Willis(x)Evans   Samuel(x)Evans
John H. Felton   Mary(x)Evans   Nancy(x)Evans

114 24 Dec 1836--Jesse Wiggens to Joseph Benton...$300...60 acres beginning at a maple corner on John Granbury, NE to a sweet gum, NW to a pine stump and white oak to a corner on Abram Bentons and Seth Morgans and SE...
                                                      Jesse Wiggens
Abraham Benton

114 Feb Ct. 1837--Whitmill Stallings, administrator of William Blanchard, to Henry Bond...$464.25...Negro woman Esther and child, Trease...to comply with court order...
                                                      Whit'l Stallings
Nathan Riddick

115 29 Dec 1836--Odah Boss of Bertie to William Landing of Hertford...$75...50 acres beginning at a gum on edge of river pocosin N to Landings line to back line of Crawfords, E to Mills Eure and up his line to river; formerly belonging to William Crawford and conveyed to Odah Crawford, now Odah Boss...
                                                      Odah Crawford
Rex(x)Parker
William J. Sutton

116 30 Dec 1836--William Landing to Henry Eure...$75...50 acres described in the above deed...
I.W. Harrell   Wm.(x)Landing
Dempsey Eure

116 16 Feb 1837--Edwin Cross to Jonathan Williams...$25...24
acres beginning at a pine, a corner on John Cross heirs NE and
then SW to said Williams fence, along fence to a bay, Hillory
Willeys and NW...
                                                                            Edwin Cross
Jethro Willey
James Savage

117 7 Oct 1836--John W. Bond to Henry L. Blount...$200...¼ acre
beginning at Jesse J. Cox's corner on Honey Pot Street SW to a
post on Parker's line to corner of John Matthews to Honey Pot
Street and N...
Henry Bond   J.W. Bond
Willis J. Riddick

118 25 Apr 1836--Isaac Pipkin Sr. to Gilbert G. Saunders...$270...
90 acres which formerly belonged to Josiah Sumner, bounded by Henry
Carter, Jason Saunders, heirs of Henry Jones and others...
William Gatling   Isaac Pipkin Sr.
D.M. Saunders

120 2 Jan 1837--John W. Hay and William Jones to James Smith...$6
1 acre between Smith's house and road, beginning at a post oak
thence to a forked white oak at corner of said Smiths to a cherry
tree to main road...
                                                           Wm. P. Jones
Willis B. Smith   John W. Hay
James Hare

122 19 Sep 1836--Burwell Brothers, administrator of James Baker,
Jr., dec., to Abraham Spivey, by virtue of deed of trust executed
by Andrew Baker to James Baker Jr....$302...50 acres beginning
at Muddy Cross at road leading from Sandy Cross down Edenton road
to Timothy Walton's line to road...
                                                    Burwell Brothers
N. Nixon
John Walton

123 1 Aug 1835--Charney Umphflett to Britton Smith...$93...30
acre plantation where Smith now lives beginning at a red oak, a
corner of Dempsey Eure's line, N to a corner of Asa Hill's, NW
to corner of Richard Odoms and said Hills and SW...
Abraham Smith   Charney(x)Umphlett
Sam'l Harrell

124 1 Dec 1836--John Gatling to Willis Daniel...$150...100 acres
called John Hill Tract, beginning at run of Bennetts Creek on S
side binding on Theophelus Hunter's line to Willis Woodley's line
to Samuel Brown's and along his line to creek and down creek...
A.B. Booker   Jno. Gatling

125 12 May 1837--Wiley Perry Jones to Joseph Gordon...$1.00 and
to make safe to said Gordon and Jacob Powell as his security for
the following notes: $137.04 to John C. Gordon, guardian to Henry
Lassiter's heirs and a judgment of $30 obtained against him by
said Gordon; $151.48 to Joseph Gordon and witnessed by James Wood-
ward and two of $100 and $16 given to Joseph Riddick...tract of
land containing 123 acres he bought of Jacob Powell, formerly
belonging to Soloman Briggs, dec. and joining Robert Riddick and
another tract of 74 acres he bought of Abm. Harrell joining land

of William Miller and others and a third tract of 5 acres, where
he now lives...
                                            Wiley P.(x)Jones
D. Parker   Jos Gordon

126 16 Sep 1836--William Cleaves to William Boothe...$800...
149 acres, the J. Hudgins Tract, beginning at foot of Allen
Smith's lane, down his lane to Honey Pot Swamp, down swamp
to John Figg's corner thence along his line to Joseph Riddicks
line to Joseph and James R. Riddick's line to new road by a black
gum and up road...   William Cleaves
John Matthews
Calvin Cleaves
Joshua Allen

127 20 Sep 1837--Isaac Hofler to David Parker...$1.00 and to se-
cure notes of $28, $5.60, $50 and $25 to said Parker...plantation
whereon said Hofler resides, bounded by land of Henry Bond, George
W. Reed, Docton Hayes and others, containing 50 acres. Also crop
of corn, peas and potatoes, all stock, household and kitchen furniture, 1 mare and colt, cart and wheels and farm utensil to hold
in trust with commission of 5% and $2.00...
                                            Isaac Hofler
James H. Parker   D. Parker

127 22 Jul 1837--Jeremiah Rogerson of Perquimans to Abel Rogerson...$1000...550 acres in Perquimans County, adjoining lands of
Reuben Nixon, Kedar Felton, John White and others and interest
in Negroes Celer, Rose, Amos, Jack, Sam, Charles, Rilly and Jerry;
it being plantation whereon the late Jesse Rogerson lived...
                                            Jeremiah Rogerso
J. Riddick   H. Gilliam
Asa Hill   Joseph Hurdle

127 7 Sep 1837--William E. Pugh to James R. Riddick...$1.00 and
to insure to William G. Daughtry a debt of $104. 60 and a note
to Joseph Riddick for $440...to hold in trust Negro boys Jim,
18 and Peter ...
                                            Wm. E. Pugh
                                            W.G. Daughtry
H.M. Daughtry   J.R. Riddick

127 14 Oct 1837--Thomas I. Miller to Robert T. Paine of Edenton
to secure notes of $2400 and $500 owed to Merchants Bank of Newbern and signed by Thomas J. Charlton, Charles C. Taber and
Charles Creecy...50 acres of land in Gates County he purchased of
Edward Hobbs, and where Hobbs now lives, adjoining land of John
Mitchell and Perry and John Kelly; stock of dry goods, hardware
and groceries, household and kitchen furniture, 2 beds and bedsteads, candlestand, 3 bureaus, 1 pair cross and irons, tongs
and shovel, 3 pair iron dogirons, looking glass, small table,
2 small stands, sideboard, glass and crockery ware, pots, kettles,
tubs, pails, 10 kitchen knives and forks, 2 carpets, 3 looking
glasses, 1 rocking chair, horse cart, ploughs and gear, hoes,
spades and all husbandry, cow, saddle and bridle...
Richard M. Pearson, judge   Thos. I. Miller
John Walton, PRC   Robt. T. Paine

128 4 Mar 1837--John W. Odom to Richard Austin...$76...38 acres adjoining land of William K. Moore, Jesse Arline and said Austin...
Open Court   John W. Odom

128 7 Mar 1837--Richard Austin, administrator of Richard Austin, dec., to James C. Smith of Nansemond...$150...62 acres bounded on N by Virginia line, S by Beach Swamp, W by land of said Smith and E by swamp; it being land said Austin died seized of and bought at public sale by said Smith...   Richard(x)Austin
William J. Smith

128 11 Apr 1836--John W. Bond to Thomas A. Jordon...$400...½ of two parcels of land in Gatesville, containing 2 acres, being lot where said Bond has retail store and other lot on Bennetts Creek which he holds with Benbury Walton...
H. Gilliam   J.W. Bond
Asa Hill

128 16 May 1836--Benbury Walton to Thomas A. Jordon...$300...½ of lot in Gatesville which he and John W. Bond purchased of John Roberts and on which store and warehouse stand; another lot known as The Landing (or Wharf) on Bennetts Creek bounded on E by land of Thomas Saunders, N and W by land of Henry Gilliam and on S by creek...   Benbury Walton
Jesse Brown
Wm. L. Boothe

129 15 Feb 1836--John Walton to Abraham Morgan...$2.00...balance of the following left over after discharge of debts: 2 tracts of land, The Gregory and Barnes Tracts, and Negroes Sam, Robin, Hardy, Harrison, Chaney, Agga, James Madison, Mary, Sophia, Malviney, Mourning, Armsted and Ailey. Sold were Granville, Haywood, Jim, Washington, Jim Arnold, Austin, Warren, Big Ned, Almod, Abigail, Lucy and children, Sam and Mary...
Open Court   John Walton

130 3 Apr 1837--William Harrell to Joseph Riddick...$66...30 acres beginning at a small sassafras on side of ditch in Riddicks line E to Nathan Riddicks, along his line to heirs of Ezekiel Trotman, dec...   William Harrell
John Walton
John Riddick

130 1 Nov 1834--William E. Pugh, clerk for court of equity, $50... land belonging to Edward, James and Mary Riddick, infants, sold by petition made to court by their next friend, John Riddick, 3 undivided 4th parts of 290-a. tract of land, which descended to them by death of their father, John Riddick...
Open Court May 1837   Wm. E. Pugh

131 21 May 1836--William E. Pugh to Rufus K. Speed...$30...778 acres beginning at marked cypress on Bennetts Creek, corner tree of 500-acre tract bought by H.R. Pugh from Abel Rogerson, and known as Pintard's Upper Corner, W through Juniper Swamp to Chowan River 300 yards below mouth of Cow Creek or Beef Creek down river to Bennetts Creek...   Wm.E. Pugh
Open Court

132 3 Apr 1837--David Parker to Henry Riddick...$600...Negro man, Davy, belonging to James Mathias and placed in deed of trust to said Parker...

David Parker
Aug. Moore   James Mathias

132 11 May 1831--J.R. Riddick to James Carter...$306...Negro man, Reuben, property of Alexander Carter, dec. and in hands of Penelope Carter, his executrix...to satisfy a court execution at instance of Henry Carter for $176.16...
T. Saunders   J.R. Riddick

133 27 Mar 1837--William G. Daughtry to William C. Brooks of Pasquotank...$912...Negro boy, Garrison, property of William Brooks, dec...
T. Saunders   W.G. Daughtry

133 27 Mar 1837--Catherine Brooks to William C. Brooks of Pasquotank...$912...Negro boy, Nathan, formerly property of William Brooks, dec...
                                                         Catherine Brooks
Elisha Harrell

133 6 Mar 1837--Leah Ward to Whitmill Stallings...$250...100 acres on S side of Catherine Creek Swamp joining land of William Hobbs, said Stalling and others and whereon he lives; being land Mrs. Ward purchased at public sale of estate of James Roundtree, dec., which he died possessed of...

Quinton H. Trotman   Leah(x)Ward
Eliza Ward

134 29 Apr 1837--Soloman Roundtree to William Mathias of Norfolk $320...4 acres in Gatesville adjoining lands of Jesse Brown, Henry Gilliam and Pryor Savage...
                                                         Soloman Roundtree
W.G. Daughtry
John Lovett

135 1 Dec 1836--Celia M. Pruden to Elbert H. Riddick...$200...52 acres and was Lot. No. 5, given to her in division of her father's real estate, beginning at a pine stump that was a corner tree of David Riddick and others, by a line of marked trees to Seth Bentons, dec. to a red oak, formerly a corner between said Benton and Abram Morgans and now is Elbert Riddicks...
John Williams   Celia M. Pruden
David Riddick

136 17 Feb 1836--Abram W. Parker to Dempsey Parker...$200...$\frac{1}{2}$ of 200 acre plantation he purchased of Dempsey Eure and sold to him by Samuel Eure, Jr. as trustee, adjoining lands of Dempsey Sparkman, William L. Boothe, Mills Eure, Elisha Harrell, James Brown, Benjamin Wynns and said Abram...
Wm.L. Boothe   Abram W. Parker
Elisha Parker

136 4 F3b 1837--Archibald R. Jones to Robert Jordon...$250...70 acres binding on lands of Nathaniel Jones, Reuben Hinton and Docton Hays...
Easton Blanchard   Archibald R.Jones
Joseph Brooks

137 25 Apr 1837--James R. Riddick, sheriff, to Kedar Powell...
$26...James Powell's right in real estate of Jacob Powell, dec.
sold by court order to satisfy attachments of $123.36 and $26.50
brought by Kedar Powell and Hance Hofler against said James...
Open Court   J.R. Riddick

138 22 Feb 1836--Jonas Hinton to Kedar Powell...$20...land be-
ginning at pine on new road in dividing line NW to a maple, S
to Jacob Powell, dec. land and E to road and N along road...
John Walton   Jonas Hinton
John Hinton

138 19 Nov 1836--Bray and Euriah Eure to Jesse Piland...$7.00...
15 acres beginning at a pine in Sarum Creek road, corner tree be-
tween Reuben Piland and said land, down edge of marsh to Reuben
Harrell's line to branch and up branch...
A.W. Parker   Bray(x)Eure
Washington Harrell   Uriah(x)Eure

139 16 May 1837--James Savage, executor of will of John Matthews, dec. to Allen Daughtry...$400.50...1 acre lot in Gatesville
beginning at a stump in edge of street, between Thomas Saunders
and William G. Daughtry's tavern, to John Lovett's line to street...
Wm.L. Boothe   James Savage
S.W. Worrell

139 2 Oct 1837--Henry Gilliam, Hardy D. Parker and Dempsey Sparkman are bound to state of North Carolina for $4,000; Henry Gilliam
having been elected clerk of Superior Court of Law for Gates County.
                                                        H. Gilliam
                                                        H.D. Parker
H.M. Daughtry   D. Sparkman

140 22 Aug 1837--William G. Daughtry, John Gatling, Joseph Riddick and Riddick Gatling are bound to state of North Carolina for
$10,000; said Daughtry having been elected clerk of court of Pleas
and Quarters Session for Gates County...
                                                        W.G. Daughtry
                                                        Jno. Gatling
                                                        J. Riddick
                                                        R. Gatling

140 3 May 1837--Stuart S. Bond and wife, Dorothy, to James Rogers
of Nansemond...$44.93...½ of 50-acre parcel of land, which is un-
divided; the same having been left in will of Richard Smith, dec.
to be sold and proceeds paid to his daughters, Dorothy and Millicent Smith...   S.S. Bond
H. Gilliam

141 9 Mar 1835--Isaac S. Harrell and Thomas R. Costen to Peter
B. Minton...$2250...land known as Mintonville beginning on E side
of main road running along Mill Pond to John Saunders, along his
line to Timothy G. Trotmans, to John Mitchells, then along his line
to Robert Taylor's, to Mill Swamp; Also, wharf and ½ acres at Old
Town bounded by James Howard; grist mill with 2 acres known as
Walton's Mill; in all 179 acres and was purchased from said Minton
in 1832...   I.S. Harrell
                                                        Thos. R. Costen
H. Gilliam
Jason Riddick
Ephriam Bunch

142 1 May 1837--Thomas I. Miller to Drew Welch and Asa Hofler...
$2000...179½ acres adjoining John Mitchell, Timothy G. Trotman
and Robert Taylor, dec. heirs; includes 2 acres and saw and Grist
Mill...
                                                                                Thos.I.Miller
H. Gilliam

142 15 May 1837--H. Gilliam releases above 179½ acres to Thomas
I. Miller, placed in deed of trust to secure $656.79 bond...
James Costen Jr.   H. Gilliam

143 8 Feb 1836--Elisha Walton to Willis Walton...$105...42 acres
heired from his brother, Asa, and father, Henry, joining land of
Willis and Daniel Walton...
                                                   Elisha Walton
Wynns Baker
James Baker

143 21 Nov 1836--Daniel Cuff to Keziah Cuff...$82...41 acres beginning at water oak, corner of Henry Willey's, N to corner of Miles Parkers, to Kicheon Norfleet's and back to Parkers...
William Hudgins   Daniel Cuff
Jesse L. Matthews

144 3 Jan 1837--Seth Spivey to William Spivey...$3 per acre...15 acres beginning at gum in Miles Welch's Mill Pond, E to water oak to red oak in Henry Gilliam's line NW to Nathaniel Taylors called Old Mill Neck...
                                                 Seth Spivey
Zachariah Nixon
Thos. W. Stallings

145 23 Feb 1837--Julia Lawrence to Abram Rabey...$2.25...1½ acres on dividing line of Jethro Howell and said Rabey, adjoining said Howell, Lassiter Riddick and others...
                                       Julia(x)Lawrence
Simmonds Roundtree
John(x)Felton

145 25 Mar 1837--Asa Hill to Micajah Reed...$50...½ acre in Gatesville, line between Hill and Reed, up main road to back of lot...
Jesse Brown   Asa Hill
William Humphreys

146 22 Feb 1837--Thomas A. Small to James Morgan...$1.00 and to secure to Humphrey Parker $100 debt to David Benton...99-acre plantation whereon he lives, adjoining John C. Gordon and others...
Jordon Parker   Thomas A. Small
Edward Parker

147 23 Oct 1837--Quinton Roundtree to John Walton...$1.00 and to secure to John Roberts debt of $159.80...100 acres devised to him by his father, Thomas Roundtree, bounded by John Walton, John Hinton and William Hinton, dec. heirs...
                                       Quinton(x)Roundtr
Willis I. Riddick   John Walton

148 1 Dec 1837--John B. Baker to James C. Riddick...$1.00 and to secure to Lassiter and James R. Riddick debt of $2569.71 to John Roberts...tract of land where he lives and Negroes Stephen, Delia, Clinton, Phillis, Ellen, Orphey, Parthenia, Harriett, Olive and Buron...
                                       Jno.B. Baker
                                       Lassiter Riddick
                                       J.R. Riddick
Mills Roberts   Jas.C.Riddick

149 17 May 1836--Elisha H. Bond to Riddick Gatling...$153...144½ acres beginning on road at a pine running Isaac Williams line SE to corner of James Williams and Sears, to a chinquepin oak at Johnson's path to a post oak in William Goodman's line NE and then NW to road. Land was conveyed by deed of trust to Mills Roberts, who is now paid...
                Elisha H. Bond
H. Gilliam   Mills Roberts
Henry Bond

150 31 Oct 1836--James Pruden, guardian of Richard B. Gatling, orphan of Etheldred B. Gatling, dec., to Riddick Gatling...$250 Negro Tom, 55, belonging to said Richard B...
                Jas. Pruden
Isaac Pipkin Sr.

150 21 Jun 1837--John O. Hunter of Yazo_ Co. Miss. appoints William E. Pugh, his attorney, to convey all his negroes to his sister, Artamesia G. Jones, to witness: Venus and children, Sally and Frank, and to Samuel W. Carr of Yellow bushey (Yalobusha) all his Negroes in Mississippi: George, Frank and Luzina, and pay estate of Edwin Mathias, dec. $600...
                Jno. O. Hunter
James M. Bunton, judge
Yazoo County

151 1 Aug 1837--Benjamin Saunders to Willis F. Riddick...$175... 43 3/4 acres on N side of Middle Swamp and E side of main road leading over swamp by Middle Swamp Baptist Meeting House, adjoining land of said Riddick, Saunders and James Benton, beginning at large gum in main run of swamp NW to Bentons, SW to road and up swamp; land obtained from Wm. E. Pugh, trustee of Wm. Hudgins.
B. Goodman   Benja. Saunders
H.D. Parker

151 20 Feb 1837--James R. Riddick to Joseph Riddick...$1250... 750 acres called Cypress Pond beginning at black gum near new road, corner of William Boothes, along line to said Josephs, formerly James Brown's, to Stuart Bond's, across Honey Pot Road, thence Job R. Halls line to corner of Thomas Easons, formerly Hudgins, to Nath'l Allen's line, to John Cuff's...
Jet.H.Riddick   J.R. Riddick
Allen Smith

152 26 May 1837--William E. Pugh to Benjamin Saunders...$725 190 acres conveyed to him by deed of trust by William Hudgins 20 Oct 1835 and adjoining land of said Saunders, James Benton, David Riddick and Willis F. Riddick...
                Wm.E.Pugh
Jas. M. Riddick
Elbert H. Riddick

153 18 Aug 1837--John Parker of Nansemond to Abram Parker...$90 75 acres commencing at Bay Branch and running W along road to Benjamin Savage's line then S along line to red oak, E to Bay Branch and winding along branch NE...
                John Parker
John Savage
Richard Parker

154 11 Jan 1836--William H. Goodman to William Sears...$420...180 3/4 acres beginning at a black gum, a corner of Dempsey S. Goodman's,

running line of marked trees on his line to main run of Peters Swamp, down swamp to mouth of Poley Branch, up main run to said Sears line leading from South Quay to Gatesville, across road and up branch and binding on said Sears...
John Willey   Wm.H. Goodman
Dempsey Parker

155 10 Feb 1837--Archibald R. Jones to Frederick Jones...$100...
57 acres binding on land of Joshua Allen, Thomas Smith and John Smith...
Henry R. Blanchard   Archibald R.Jon
Jethro Blanchard

155 10 Feb 1837--Frederick Jones to Archibald R. Jones...$300...
160 acres binding on land of Nathan Pearce, James Lassiter, Kedar Lassiter and David Parker...
Henry E. Blanchard   Frederick Jones
Jethro Blanchard

156 16 May 1836--Miles Briggs to Jethro Briggs...$20...50 acres formerly belonging to Kedar Briggs, and given to him by his father, Soloman Briggs, in his will and conveyed to said Miles by said Kedar 16 Jun 1833...   Miles Briggs
R. Rawls

156 24 Jul 1837--John Jones of Chowan to Riddick Jones...$50...
25 acres bounded on S by lands of Mary Mathias, W by lands of Josiah Riddick, N. by Benj. Franklin and E by Riddick Jones...
Dempsey Vann   John(x)Jones
Joseph Mathias

157 8 Jul 1837--Mary Brinkley to Riddick Brinkley...deed of gift Negro woman Cloey, 5 head cattle, 20 head hogs, 1 feather bed and furniture, cart and wheels, sett silver spoons, 6 windsor chairs, 2 pine tables, 2 iron pots, 3 wash tubs, 3 pails, 4 trays, 2 Dutch ovens, gridiron, trunk, 2 chests, 1 case, 4 jugs, 2 hogsheads, 4 weed hoes, 2 axes, 2 dishes and 4 bowls...
Dempsey Vann   Mary(x)Brinkley
Joseph Mathias

157 1 Aug 1837--Kedar Taylor to Joshua Jones...$45...10 acres beginning at rosemary pine running SE to a red oak thence NE to a gum in branch up Barnes line and SW...
James Morgan   Kedar Taylor
William Arnold

158 5 May 1837--Joseph Riddick to Thomas Eason...$1.00...½ acre land, in trust, beginning at sweet gum on side of road adjoining Eason's line SW to white oak and NW to road...
                                                           Jo. Riddick
Anson Williams
James Parker

159 1 Jan 1837--Thomas Hoggard to Lewis Green...$250...171 acres beginning at a corner of Gatling's in flat woods along Elisha Umphflet's line to a post oak by side of marsh, across marsh to outside swamp to corner of John Sparkmans, up line of marked trees

and across Sand Banks to flat woods...
Abraham Pruden   Thomas Hoggard
Samuel Green

159 1 Mar 1837--Willis Walton to Jeremiah White...$400...45 acres
beginning in Catherine Creek Swamp running to a branch, up branch
to Calvin Brinkley's line to a holly, along his line to Asa Walton's, dec. SE to Timothy Waltons; all land that he heired from
his father, Henry Walton, dec....
Jet.H.Riddick   Willis Walton
Elisha Walton

160 20 Aug 1837--William E. Pugh, attorney for John O. Hunter, to
Tilly W. Carr..$1 and payment of $559.43 note to Edwin Mathias,
for which Mrs. A.G. Jones was security...the following Negroes
now in Yazoo County, Miss. George, Frank and Luzina...
                                                       Wm. E. Pugh
W.F. Riddick   Artemisa G. Jones

161 27 Sep 1837--Dempsey Peal to James Morgan...$1.00 and to
make safe to John Wiggens notes of $148 ($8.67 credit) and $7.50
40 acres of land he purchased from said Wiggens adjoining lands
of Seth Benton, John V. Sumner and others...
Henry Pearce   Dempsey(x)Peal
Daniel Brinkley

161 17 Nov 1837--Joseph Speight to James Cobb of Hertford...$1.00
and payment of $203 note to Abram Riddick of Hertford...300 acres
bounded by Drew M. Saunders, G.G. Saunders, Emmy Speight and others
and 2 bedsteads and furniture, cooking and farm utensils and bay
mare...   Joseph(x)Speight
John B. Jenkins   James Cobb
J. Waddae   A. Riddick

162 19 Jan 1838--Henry S. Blount to Henry Gilliam...$1.00...deed
in trust for $1200 note to Mills Roberts, for which said Gilliam
and William W. Cowper are his security...5 acres in Gatesville
on which he resides, ½ acre where his storehouse stands and Negroes Jack and Lucy...
                                                       Henry S. Blount
                                                       H. Gilliam
Jennings A. Blount   Wm.W. Cowper

163 14 Sep 1835--Joshua M. Harrell of Nansemond to William
Bramble of the Borough of Norfolk...$250...three parcels of land
placed with him by indenture of trust by William Cowper 16 June
1834 as his security for $350 note to Bank of Virginia at Norfolk
Branch, for which said Cowper has paid $250...Land includes a
400 acre tract and a 260 acre tract purchased by John Cowper, his
father, from James Gordon 1 Jan 1805 and 50 acres in Great Dismal
Swamp which John Small conveyed to John Cowper, his grandfather,
and used as security to Wills Cowper of Nansemond for William's
note...   Jos. M. Harrell
Edw. F. Riddick
Thos. W.G. Allen
Wiley Rawls

164 25 Jun 1836--Edward Hobbs to Thomas I. Miller...$50...50 acres, including 10 acres Shadrack Stallings has in his possession, bounded on S by Warwick Swamp, E by William Perry, N by John Mitchell and Walton Hobbs and W by Elmira Ward...

William Hurdle
N. Nixon
                                                         Edward(x)Hobbs

164 17 Jan 1838--Capt. William Mathias...$1.00...appoints John Lovett as his attorney...
Orrin B. Savage
                                                     William Mathias

164 17 Jan 1838--John P. Savage...$1.00 appoints John Lovett as his attorney...
R.K. Speed
                                                     John P. Savage

165 19 Feb 1838--William Mathias, John Lovett and John P. Savage agree to the sale of the schooner, Two Sisters, commanded by said Matthias upon the following terms: Said Mathias to remain in command and to retain $50 salary from freight; each party to pay 1/3 of the expenses and each to receive 1/3 of net profit. Schooner shall be freighted with cargo purchased by said Lovett and said Mathias to receive commission of 5% upon sale...

                                                       John Lovett
                                                     William Mathias
O.B. Savage
                                                     John P. Savage

165 19 Feb 1838--William Mathias and John P. Savage are to furnish John Lovett with letters of credit upon certain mercantile houses in cities of New York, Baltimore and Norfolk for purchase of a stock of goods not to exceed $6000 to be shipped to Gatesville during next spring and said Lovett will furnish storehouse for sale, permitting him to retain 1/3 of net profit and allow him 2/3 to hire a clerk, and paying for entire stock of goods, expenses, etc.; net profits to be divided 1/3...

                                                     John Lovett
                                                   Wm. Mathias
O.B. Savage
                                                   John P. Savage

168 13 May 1837--William S. Riddick and wife, Anna Maria, of Nansemond to Willis F. Riddick...$1000...151½ acres bounded by land of said Willis on N, Bennetts Creek on E, land belonging to heirs of William S. Barnes, dec. on S and on W by main road leading from Middle Swamp by Baptist Meeting House to Gatesville.
Joshua M. Harrell   W.S. Riddick
Lem'l C. Holland   Anna Maria Riddic

Richard H. Baker, judge of general court and 1st judicial circuit in 1st district of Virginia for county of Nansemond, attested said Anna Maria signed freely. Proceedings attested to by David Campbell, governor, 23 May 1837 in Richmond

170 17 Nov 1837--Timothy Perry and wife, Lucinda, to Frederick Jones...$20...plantation where they now live adjoining lands of George Costen, Thomas Riddick, Timothy Hunter, John Hunter and others...
R. Lassiter   Timothy Perry
Jesse Piland   Lucinda Perry

171 20 Feb 1837--Edward Howell and wife, Sally, of Nansemond to
Francis Duke...$250...92 acres near residence of William Lee, Esq.,
beginning at a dead pine, corner on said Lee, purchased of Robert
Rogers, thence along a line of marked trees to Beach Swamp, thence
down said swamp to a corner on said Lee's...
Exum Jenkins   Edw'd Howell
John B. Langston   Sally Howell
John R. Lee
     Henry Gilliam and Richard Odom, county justices, testified
said Sally signed deed freely.

171 27 Dec 1836--Riddick Matthews relinquishes all rights in tract
of land in land of executor of John Mathews, dec. in consideration
of notes executed by him for payment of said land; having been re-
turned to him by executor...
                                                Riddick Matthews
Thos. Matthews
W.G. Daughtry

172 20 Mar 1837--William E. Pugh, CME, to Humphry D. Savage...$150
land owned by Henry S. Blount and wife, Sarah, and Sophia Odom,
sold by court petition filed by guardian; land in Mirey Swamp and
belonged to their father, Ira Odom...
Wm.W. Cowper   Wm.E. Pugh

173 20 Nov 1836--Division of land of Hardy Eason, dec. containing 740 3/4 acres between his heirs as follows: Lot No. 1--Sol-
oman Eason...150½ acres beginning at small pine at road running
SE to Hurdle's corner SW to small pine corner to red oak in Samuel Green's NW to holly, corner of said Greens and Hunters, NE up
swamp to Allen Briggs to Hurdle's line. Lot No. 2--Isaac Eason...
186½ acres beginning at large red oak, corner of above tract SW
to a black gum then NW to corner of Jesse Eason's to Samuel Greens
and to dividing line. Lot No. 3--Whitty Eason...99½ acres and is
part of the Stallings Tract, beginning at oak stump in road, running SW to a pine, S to run of swamp, up branch to White's corner,
NE to road leading from Mintonville to Gatesville and down road.
No. 4--James Costen...122½ acres and balance of Stallings tract,
beginning at oak stump NW up road to a pine, SW to branch corner
to Timothy Waltons, NE to road leading to Muddy Cross, and down
road SW to other road. No. 5--Robertson White...100 acres beginning at small red oak on road, corner of Job R. Hall's, SW to Walton's line to small white oak, corner at Thomas Riddick's ditch NE.
No. 6--Elisha Eason...82 acres, the Perry Tract, beginning at gum
in swamp on Kelly's running his line up branch, corner on Kelly's
and Jesse Eason's NE to large cypress to run of swamp...No. 1 to
receive from No. 3 $83.33 1/3, No. 2 to receive from No. 3 $83.33 1/3,
No. 5 to receive from No. 4 $83.33 1/3, No. 6 to receive from No.4
$83.33 1/3 and from No. 3 $100...
                                                J. Riddick
                                                Nathan Riddick
Allen Smith, Surv.   Wm.H. Harrell

174 30 Aug 1836--Division of 195 acres of land adjoining lands of
John Wiggens, Seth Benton, Miles Parker and John V. Sumners as
follows: ½ to John Wiggens, ¼ to Miles Parker and remaining ¼ to
Garrett Knight...Survey No. 1--John Wiggens...97½ acres beginning
at a popular corner on said Wiggens, SE along ditch SE to red oak

NE to a pine in Seth Benton's line to a corner of Lot No. 2. Lot No. 2--Garrett Knight, an infant...48 3/4 acres beginning at rosemary pine in John Sumner's line, a corner of Lot No. 1, SE to a red oak, NE.. Lot No. 3--Miles Parker...48 3/4 acres beginning at a pine in said Sumner's line SE to another pine, NE to a pine and gum and W to corner of said Parker's NE to corner maple stump of said Sumners...

James Morgan,
Humphrey Parker,
alternate commissioners

Jno.V. Sumner
Dempsey Knight
B. Goodman

175 20 Nov--Division of estate of James Boothe, containing 827 acres among the following heirs: Survey No. 1--John Boothe... 148½ acres beginning at large red oak at foot of R. Hinton's lane, down road SE to corner on Hintons and Hays, NW to Edenton road, down run of swamp to Bennetts Creek, Reuben Hinton's corner. Also, 20 acres of swamp land not surveyed. No. 2--Henry Boothe...178½ acres called the Foster Tract, beginning at black gum in swamp, Docton Hays line NE to John Jones, down branch NW to Mrs. Blanchard's corner SW then NW to Bennetts Creek and down creek to small island. No. 3--William Boothe...177½ acres, The Knight Tract of 53 3/4 acres and the Ellen Tract of 129¼ acres, beginning at small white oak at new road running NE to sweet gum in path to an oak stump, corner of Nisum Cuff's and John Willey's, to a large popular SE to red oak, W to Willey's. No. 4--Francis Boothe...145½ acres beginning at large popular in said Cuff's line, NE to oak stump SE to a hickory at path to a maple corner in John Williams and Lassiters NW to red oak and SW to a line of marked trees. No. 5--Martha Boothe...177 acres beginning at black oak stump, corner on Nisum Cuff's NW to a large pine, corner on Cuff's and Kittrells, NE to red oak corner of Kittrells and Fields SE to Fisher Felton's fence to hickory corner and NW...

20 Nov 1836

John Roberts   J.R. Riddick
Henry Willey   Reuben Hinton
Allen Smith,CS H. Gilliam

177 24 Oct 1834--Division of land of Benjamin Hayes, dec. to lay off to Caroline Hayes, an infant daughter, so much of lands as would have descended to her had no will been made. Said Hayes estate of 535½ acres divided as follows: Lot No. 1--Willis R. Hays...229 3/4 acres valued at $500, beginning at a pine stump on road, corner of James R. Riddick and Job Hall, along Hall's line SE to a red oak, SW to a branch to Bennetts Creek to a cypress, corner of Timothy Hays, NE and then NW to road. To pay said Caroline $9.89. Lot No. 2--Robert P. Hays...150 acres valued at $300, beginning at cypress corner of said Timothy's, NW to small branch to road and along road to an ash corner of Elijah Harrells then SE to a pine in branch. To pay Caroline $5.93. Lot No. 3--Zachariah Hayes, in right of wife, Lovinia, 43 3/4 acres valued at $88, beginning in road at a branch, corner of said Timothy's SW along road to corner of James Brown, SE to red oak, NE to a popular corner of John Hofler's in branch and down branch. To pay Caroline $1.75. No. 4--John Hofler in right of wife, Sarah, 66½ acres valued at $88, beginning at ash corner of Elijah Harrells

NW to a pine at road, corner of William G. Daughtry's, to pine corner of Robert Hayes and on James Brown, then SE to red oak and NE to Zachariah Hayes and down branch. To pay Caroline $2.63. No. 5--Caroline Hayes...45½ acres beginning at pine stump, corner of James R. Riddicks NW to water oak, corner of Lassiter Riddicks SW and then SE to corner of said Timothy and Zachariah and along road...

Isaac Williams, CS

W.G. Daughtry
J. Walton

Thomas Saunders
James Boothe
Pryor Savage

179 15 Aug 1836--Division of land of Ira Odom, 551 acres, adjoining land of Riddick Gatling, John Speight and others, as follows: Survey No. 1--Henry Blount...256 acres, including dwelling, beginning at a persimmon tree at road on John Speights, running SE down road to small oak bush and then SW to James Williams line near the path then NW to red oak corner in said Williams and Nathaniel Eures NW to cluster of sliped trees and NE. No. 2--Sophia Ann Odom...295 acres beginning in the road at a pine of Riddick Gatlings along his line SE to black gum and then SW to Eff Lewis corner to Nathaniel Eure and Eff Lewis corner and NW to road...

Allen Smith, CS
John Willey, alt. commissioner

R. Gatling
Isaac Pipkin
John Saunders
John Speight

180 15 Feb 1836--Division of estate of William Miller, dec., including 203 acres, 78 of which is affected at follows: No. 1--Martha Miller...24 3/4 acres beginning in road, corner on Reuben Millers, SE to Richard Ballards along his line N to corner and then SE. No. 2--James Miller...20¼ acres beginning in road at a stake, SE down road to Ballards line and N. No. 3--Richard Miller 23 acres beginning at stake in road, running down road and W to Wiley P. Jones and NW to Ballards and then NE. No. 4--William Miller...29 acres beginning at black gum on said Jones SW to a corner and then SE to Bassy Swamp, up swamp said Jones and NW. No. 5--Jane Miller...32 acres beginning in Jones line SE to branch corner, along branch to Luke Greens, along Bassy Swamp and NW. No. 6--Elizabeth Miller...32 acres beginning at Jones SE to run of branch along said Green's line NW to said Jones. No. 7--Moses Miller...32 acres beginning at Wiley Jones line and running to said Green's and NW...

Allen Smith, CS
Elisha Small, alternate commissioner

John C. Gordon
Miles Briggs
James Powell

181 30 Sep 1837--James A. Jones to William R. Brothers...$1.00 and to make safe to Andrew R. Harrell three notes, each for $100 tract of land he purchased of Isaac S. Harrell, adjoining James Woodward, James Davis and Robert Riddick and containing 50 acres.

Jos. Gordon
James Briggs

James A.(x)Jones
Andrew R. Harrell
Wm.R. Brothers

182 20 Jan--Division of estate of David Rice, which he devised in his will to William Creecy, and which descended to Agnes Righton, Penelope Pipkin, Mary Skinner and James R. Creecy(the said James

R. Creecy and Mary Skinner's rights having been conveyed to William H. Harrell). Survey includes 560 acres, adjoining land of heirs of Frederick Eason, Andrew Harrell and William H. Harrell, and is divided as following: Lots Nos. 1 and 2--William H. Harrell...338½ acres beginning at blackjack stump corner on John Alpin's running NW to 3-pine corner of Jesse Harrell's and SW to Willis Harrell, then SE to line of marked trees binding on Charles Eason, to corner of Abram Hurdle's on Cypress Branch, along his line N to Joseph Riddick's corner. No. 3--Misses Jane and Ann Writen...60 acres beginning at 3-pines corner on Jesse Harrell's and running SW along line of marked trees to maple corner of Willis Harrell's and along his line. No. 4--Penelope Pipkin's heirs... 161½ acres beginning at a pine corner on James Harrell's NW to corner of Andrew Harrells and along his line of marked trees to branch and down branch to Holaday Walton's and along branch and up Waltons line to causeway corner of Waltons and Willis Harrells and SE... 20 Jan 1837...

Allen Smith, co. surv.
Joseph Riddick, Esq.
Bushrod Riddick, alt. comm.

Nathan Riddick
Job R. Hall
Thomas Riddick

182 20 Jan 1837--Division of land of Henry Speight among his legal heirs as follows: Lot No. 1--John Allen...57½ acres covers house lot, beginning at water oak corner on John Everetts SE along line of marked trees to Peter Eure's line to a large pine corner of Eures and Miles Parkers, NE and then NW to path to red oak at end of lane. No. 2--Sophia Speight...50½ acres beginning at water oak on corner of said Everetts NW to large pine and SW to branch corner, SE to hickory and NW. No. 1 to pay No. 2 $12.5

Allen Smith, co. surv.

Wm. Gatling   John Willey
Henry Carter, Peter Eure
alternates   R. Gatling

183 16 Jan 1835--Division of estate of John Hare, including 100 acres valued at $250, to his children: Lot No. 1--Eliza Hare... 28 acres beginning at chinquapin oak in swamp corner of Bryan Hare's along swamp to Dempsey Knights, SW and then SE to a pine on path and NW. No. 2--Martha Hare...28 acres beginning at pine corner along Dempsey Knight's line SW to red oak, NW to path. No. 3--Nancy Hare...22 acres beginning at red oak in path SE along line of marked trees to red oak corner of Dempsey Knight and John Benton NW to pine stump and S to path then NE. No. 4--Henry Hare...22 acres beginning at pine corner NW to sweet gum on John V. Sumner's NE to path and SE...

Alternates:
John V. Sumner
John P. Benton

John C. Gordon
Barnes Goodman
Dempsey Knight

184 20 Nov 1837--Division of land of Frederick Lassiter, dec., including 47½ acres adjoining lands of Jethro Blanchard, Henry Hofler and lands formerly owned by Abram Pearce, as follows: Survey No. 1--William Marshall...9 3/4 acres beginning at dead oak at path, corner on Jethro Blanchards, running NE to a gum in run of Watery Swamp, down swamp to cypress stump in run of branch and up branch to corner on said Pearce and Blanchard's line, SE..

No. 2--Alexander Marshall...8¼ acres beginning at dead oak SE to a pine corner NE to run of Watery Swamp, down swamp and SW. No. 3--James Marshall...4 acres beginning at a pine corner on Jethro Blanchard's to small cypress in run of Watery Swamp down swamp SW. No. 4--Willis Daniel in right of wife, Elizabeth...7 acres beginning at a pine of said Blanchard's to small hickory, corner of Henry Hoflers NE to gum in Watery Swamp, corner on said Hofler and D. Gatling, down swamp SW. No. 5--Robert Marshall...8 acres beginning at a pine corner on said Blanchards NE to oak stump to Henry Hofler's corner and NW. No. 6--John Lassiter...10½ acres beginning at a pine corner on Jethro Blanchard's SW to his field then NE to said Hoflers...

Allen Smith, co. surv.
Abram Pearce, alternate commissioner

D. Parker
Henry Hofler
Jethro Blanchrd

186 20 Jan 1838--Division of estate of William Sears, including 859 3/4 acres, divided into four parts as follows: Lot No. 1--Belvadera Knight and husband, Dempsey...170½ acres, the House Tract, beginning in road at a branch corner on John Willeys, along road NW to Mill Pond, down pond to chinquapin corner of Nancy Worrells, then E to red oak at path, SE to Blake Brady's and NE to Willeys to bay in branch. No. 2--William H. Sears... 3 separate tracts; Hill Tract, 97 acres beginning at small sweet gum corner up road to Peters Swamp and down run to marked gum and SE; Jones Tract 51½ acres beginning at gum in Mills Swamp SW to corner on Benjamin Wynns, SE to Wynns and Jones corner down run of swamp and Pocosin Tract, 33 1/3 acres beginning at sweet gum on corner of William Goodmans and Whitmill Stallings NW to black gum corner on Riddick Gatlings and said Goodmans, SE to holly corner on John Lee's, SE to maple corner on Lee's and Stallings and N. No. 3--James Sears--two tracts: Collins tract of 195 acres beginning in road at run of branch, corner on John Willey's, up branch NE to corner of said Willeys and Hardy Cross, NE to black jack oak and NW to Peters Swamp and White House tract of 72 acres begins at persimmon on road running NW to Blake Bradys to gum in swamp, up swamp to a small ash, corner on Kindred Parkers and said Bradys, along Parkers line of marked trees NW to road. No.4--Belver Sears (no description). Belvadera Knight and Belver Sears to each pay William H. Sears $60.

Allen Smith, co. surv.
Robert Rogers
Dempsey S. Goodman, alternate commissioners

John Willey
Wm.H. Goodman
John Brady

187 3 Mar --Mary Speight and Julia A. Briggs, only heirs living of their father, Benjamin Briggs, dec., having arrived at lawful age, with consent of Joseph Speight, Mary's husband, agree to divide tract of land said Benjamin purchased , 1812 from Richard Briggs, as follows: part S of boundary beginning at pine in Thomas Twine's line running E to a ditch, through old field to Robert Riddick's line, to go to Mary Speight and part N of line to go to Julia Briggs, but subject to widow's dower...

Miles Briggs
Edward Briggs
1837

Mary Speight
Julia A. Briggs
Joseph(x)Speight

188 3 Mar 1837--Phereba Trotman to John Hollowell of Perquimans...$205...80 acres beginning at red oak corner of James Brinkley, Henry King and others, running Brinkley's line to white oak, corner tree of Nathan Riddick's on his line to a ditch of William Harrells, to Joseph Riddick and to Henry Walton's, dec. line...
                                                    Pheraba(x)Trotman
Jet.H.Riddick
Ezekiel Trotman

189 15 Apr 1837--Humphrey Parker to Henry Riddick...$400...2 Negro boys, Merida and Bob...
                                                    Humphrey Parker
Mary C. Parker
William(x)Mitchell

189 1 Jul 1837--Julia Ann Briggs to John Rawls...$125...30 acres joining Thomas Twine, Risop Rawls and others, beginning at a pine in Twine's line E to ditch through old field to Robert Riddick's line S to said Rawls and W to Twine's...
                                                    Julia A. Briggs
Miles Briggs
Edward Briggs

190 10 Jun 1837--John Granbury to John Rawls...$442.12...98¼ acres beginning at small pine on Granbury's ditch SW to Thomas Twine's ditch, NE to white oak and NW to a beach corner of said Granburys SW along line of marked trees...
                                                    John G. Granbury
R. Rawls
B.F. Riddick

191 2 Oct 1837--Dempsey Griffith of Hertford to James Gatling...$300...his ¼ part of a 633 acre-undivided tract, which was conveyed by deed of gift in 1836 by Burwell Griffith to Dempsey Griffith, Pleasant Gatling (wife of James Gatling), Nancy Saunders (wife of Jason Saunders) and Martha Griffith. Land adjoins land of Richard Odom (formerly Jacob Odom), Etheldred Cross, William Goodman, Abraham Parker (formerly David Cross) and Willis Cross...
                                                    Dempsey Griffith
John A. Anderson
W.J. Moore

191 12 Aug 1837--Emily Hunter to Edward R. Hunter and Robert Hill Jr...$1000...243 acres beginning at a pine called The Hawks Nest, a corner on William Mathews NW to a sweet gum, SW to a corner of John Matthews, SE to Middle Swamp Road, along road NW; said tract Emily heired from her father, except part sold to John Mathews...
                                                    Emily Hunter
Bn.B. Ballard
Rich'd Parker

192 7 Oct 1837--Isaac R. Hunter to John Gatling and George Costen...$3000...700 acres he received from division of lands of his father, Isaac Hunter, lying on E side of Hunters Mill Pond, adjoining land of Thomas Riddick and separated therefrom by public road, and lands of William Reed and others...
                                                    Isaac R. Hunter
Thomas Riddick
Thos. Twine

193 1 Jul 1837--John B. Baker to Lassiter Riddick...$201...67 3/4 acres beginning at water oak, Simon Roundtree's corner, running down branch to holly corner of John Bakers and Roundtrees SW to road and down road toward Gatesville to a pine, Prior Savage's corner NE to L. Riddicks to a small oak bush nearly opposite Anthony Green's house...
John B. Baker
Wm. B. Wynns
Wm. J. Baker

194 30 Dec 1836--Julia Lawrence to Jethro Howell...$12...8 acres adjoining Lassiter Riddick, Adam Rabey, said Howell and others...
Pryer Savage   Julia(x)Lawrence
Isaa Piland

194 3 Nov 1837--Riddick Smith to Joseph R. Hays...$125...30 acres, part of a tract called Howell Tract, beginning at a pine on Piney woods path, a corner tree on John Walton's line running W by a line of marked trees to William Jones line S to said Smith's line E to James Hare's and on his line to sweet gum and N by line of marked trees...
                                                Riddick(x)Smith
Docton Hays
John W. Hays

195 1 Sep 1828--Thomas Spivey and wife, Mary, to John Roberts... $10...50 acres beginning in Roberts line and along his line to high land and along edge of high land through pocosin to creek...
Daniel S. Ward   Henry Spivey
Jas. T. Hurdle   Mary(x)Spivey

195 25 Mar 1837--Thomas Ellinor, Hertford, to Kedar Hinton...$45 15 acres on Bennetts Creek that his grandfather, William Hays, gave him by deed 15 May 1823, beginning at forked cypress in a botton, a corner tree of John Walton's, up creek bottom by line of marked trees to Kedar Hinton's line E to a pine, a corner of said Hinton's (formerly James Gordons) to creek...
                                                Thomas(x)Ellinor
Timothy Hays
Thomas W. Hays

196 1 Mar 1835--Sally Smith, widow of the late Richard Smith, dec., Dorotha Smith, Thomas Smith and James Rogers and wife, Milly, to Kedar Powell and wife, Mary; all heirs at law of said Richard, who devised his estate to almost exclude his daughter, Mary Powell from any part thereof; said will having been executed some time before her marriage and it appears since her marriage it was his desire that said Mary should share equally with other daughters, therefore they agree she is entitled to an equal share...
                                                Sally Smith
                                                Dortha Smith
                                                James Rogers
Thos. Smith   Milly (x)Rogers

196 26 Mar 1837--William E. Pugh, CME, to Exum Jenkins...$306... 180 acres called Old Mill Tract and belonging to H.L. Blount and wife, Sarah E., and Sophia Odom. Sold by court petition made by said Blount and wife and said Sophia's guardian. Land descended to them from their father, Ira Odom...   Wm E. Pugh
Wm. W. Cowper

196 20 Mar 1837--William E. Pugh, CME, to Dempsey Parker...$113
30 acres, belonging to Elizabeth Beeman, of full age, and Israel
and William Beeman, infants, by their guardian, John C. Gordon.
Land adjoins A. Beeman, William Savage and Reuben Piland and
was sold by court petition...
                Wm. E. Pugh
Wm. L. Boothe

198 20 May 1835--James R. Riddick, sheriff, to William Hudgins...
$600...plantation whereon Seth Morgan lived and died, sold by
court writ against Seth P. Morgan and Samuel R. Morgan, brought
by said Hudgins, administrator of Abraham Morgan, dec...
                J.R. Riddick
Jno. R. Gilliam
A.W. Parker

198 25 Aug 1837--Jason Saunders to William Beasley...$75...50
acres beginning at road in Miles Parker's line at a pine and running
road to Henry Carter's line to Gilbert Saunders line to a red
oak, a corner of said Parkers and up his line...
Miles Howell   Jason Saunders

199 21 Oct 1837--Thomas Twine to Alfred Small of Chowan...$1500...
250 acres formerly belonging to Joseph Gordon and Abraham Spivey,
adjoining lands of George Costen at red oak on causeway and Timothy
Spivey, Timothy Walton, Joseph Brooks, Edward Jones and others.
Joseph Sutton   Thomas Twine
Andrew Johnson

200 2 Oct 1837--Henry Gilliam to Nathan Riddick...$100...37½ acres
adjoining Joseph Hurdle, Wesley Phelps and others; it being tract
purchased at a sheriff's sale and belonging to Abel Rogerson...
James Morgan   H. Gilliam

200 2 Apr 1836--Nathan Riddick to William Simpson...$137...30
acres beginning at main road running Simpson's line S to run of
Catherine Creek Swamp, down swamp to Milton Eason's line and along
his line to main road...
                Nathan Riddick
J.R. Kee
Bushrod Riddick

201 7 Jan 1837--Thomas Smith to Penninah Lee...$55...30 acres on
S side of Cypress Swamp at a corner tree running with David Umphlett's
line to Mire Branch and down run of swamp...
                Thomas Smith
Mills Eure
Benjamin Eure

201 20 Nov 1837--Willis Bunch Sr. to son, Willis Jr...deed of
gift of 88 acres beginning at a pine stump, a corner of Crissey
Twine's, John Felton and others and along said Crissey's line to
a sweet gum in Bull Branch and running along branch to Reuben Nixon's
line to Levi Sumners to a pine, corner of Jesse Hobbs and
others to Jordon Hobbs line...
                Willis(x)Bunch
D. Parker
Robert Simons

202 20 Nov 1837--Jesse P. Wiggens to John Wiggens...$1000...75
acres adjoining land of Wilie Riddick, William Parker's heirs and

others; it being tract which his grandfather, Jesse Wiggens, dec. bequeathed to him...
                  Jesse P. Wiggens
James Morgan
Henry Pearce

202 2 Nov 1837--Susanna Lassiter Sr. to Noah Roundtree...$40...
15 acres on N side of Bennetts Creek beginning at a pine, corner of Roundtrees to run of small branch along Dempsey Bond's land...
                 Susanna(x)Lassiter
Jas. T. Freeman
John (x) Morris

203 6 Jan 1837--James T. Freeman to Noah Roundtree $100...35 acres beginning at a small pine, Jacob N. Parker's line, to a pine near pocosin NE to John Saunder's line, a corner of Dempsey Bonds, then SE along Roundtree's line...
                Jas. T. Freeman
Reuben Lassiter
Seth W. Roundtree

30 Sep 1835--George M. Mullen and wife, Mary, of Murfreesboro in Hertford County, to John Lee...$56...40 or 50 acres adjoining land of Riddick Gatling and others and called Rogers Pocosin...
                George M. Mullen
R. Gatling
                Mary G. Mullen
Bray Parker
Sam'l Mullen

204 3 Dec 1834--John Savage of Nansemond to Louisa Savage...$1.00 deed of gift of six Negroes Ned, Lear, Jinney, Jacob, Miles and Rose...
                John Savage
Caleb Savage

204 20 Nov 1837--Alexander Marshall to Abram Pearce...$16...8¼ acres beginning at dead oak corner on Jethro Blanchard's running SE to Watery Swamp and down run SW...
                Alexander(x)Marshall
Jacob T. Johnson
Allen Smith

205 21 Nov 1837--Robert Marshall to Abram Pearce...$6...8 acres beginning at a pine corner on Jethro Blanchards SW to his own corner, N to a small hickory of Henry Hofler's...
Ezekiel T. Jones   Robert (x)Marshall
Archibald R. Jones

206 4 May 1838--Wiley P. Jones to John C. Gordon...$1.00...deed in trust and to make safe to Joseph Gordon as his security for note to David Benton for $100...123 acre tract of land he bought of Jacob Powell, formerly belonging to Soloman Briggs and joining land of Robert Riddick and others; 74 acres he bought of Abrm. Harrell and 5 acres, whereon he lives. Also, all his cattle, horses, hogs, sheep, household and kitchen furniture, farming tools, corn and fodder...
                Wiley P.(x)Jones
Joseph G. Granbury
Jos. Gordon

207 20 Feb 1838--James Mathias to David Parker...$5.00...deed of trust to secure notes to David Parker for $50, James H. Parker for $95 and Augustus Moore for $105...Negroes Isaac, Penina and Bob

and land called the Brickhouse Tract and one called the Parker Place...
James Mathias
James H. Parker
Thos. R. Costen
D. Parker

208 19 Jan 1838--Hardy C. Jones of the first part, William Jones of the second part and Exum Jenkins of the third part, all of Nansemond, whereas: said Hardy is indebted to Mills Roberts for $370 for which said Jenkins is security...said Hardy to said William for $1.00 and a deed of trust agrees to sell his undivided 1/3 part of tract of land whereon the late Henry Jones lived and known as Vollentine Land and which was devised to his son, Henry Jones, lately deceased; adjoining land of James Sumner, Elijah Hare, Drew Saunders and others and bounded on N and NW by Sumerton Creek; also Negro man, Tom...to secure loan to said Roberts...
H.H.C. Jones
Susan(x)Waters
Wm. M. Jones
John R. Lee
Exum Jenkins

209 19 Jun 1837--Isaac Hyatt to James T. Freeman...$1.00 and to secure to John Hinton and Hance Hofler debt of $96.37½...two tracts of land in Indian Neck 50 a.bought of John Powell and 22 acres whereon he lives...
Isaac(x)Hyatt
John W. Hinton
John Hinton
Asa G. Hofler
Hance Hofler
Jas. T. Freeman

210 1 Dec 1837--Whereas: Robert Hill and Mary Ann Richardson are about to enter into a marriage connection said Robert agrees to settle the following property on said Mary Ann in case she should survive him: plantation whereon he lives beginning at public road at Hollow Bridge in Mary Hunter's line, along ditch on her line to Benjamin Hunter's line to cross ditch SE near Mill Swamp to road. Also, Negroes Soloman and Penny, 1 horse and cart, 2 milch cows, 2 sows and pigs, 1 feather bed and furniture, 1 doz. of his best chairs, 1 beaureau, 1 small walnut table, 1 barrell of brandy, still and 1 years provisions for her and her family. She agrees after her death property will return to said Robert's legal representatives...
Mary Ann Richard
Richard H. Parker
Robert Hill
James D. Parker

211 30 Nov 1837--Lawful heirs of Burwell Griffith and wife, Lovina, agree to the following division of his real estate: No. 4--James Gatling in right of wife, Pleasant...192 acres beginning at large gum in Reedy Branch, up branch to a gum, corner of Richard Odom and James Brady, SE to table pines NE to an oak and gum, corner for James Brady, Jesse Vann and James Williams and SW. No. 1--Nancy Saunders...128 acres, including house, and beginning at an oak and pine, S to corner of Isaac Speights and Etheldred Cross, NE to run of Reedy Branch, up branch NW. No. 2--Dempsey Griffith...128 acres beginning at oak and pine corner running NE to oak and persimmon tree NW to Willis Cross' line then SW to swamp to corner pine of James Brady. No. 3--Martha

Griffith...192 acres beginning at oak and persimmon tree, running NE to James Williams line, SW to Abram Parkers to a small pine and SE. Nancy Saunders to pay Dempsey Griffith $64. Said Dempsey and said Martha Griffith and James and Pleasant Gatling are from Hertford County...

                Dempsey Griffith
                Martha Griffith
Myles Parker   Nancy Saunders
Kinsey Jordon   Pleasant Gatling

212 14 Feb 1838--Charles Jones to Dempsey S. Goodman...$115.64 49 acres beginning at red oak on public road leading from Gates courthouse to Somerton in Nansemond County E to Edwin Cross' corner, then SE to Hillory Willey's NW to blackjack oak on road...
Edwin Cross   Charles Jones

213 10 Nov 1837--Thomas Twine to Henry Costen...$2200...229 acres called Brickhouse Plantation, formerly belonging to James Gregory, dec. adjoining land of Isaac R. Hunter on E, George Costen on S and farm whereon said Twine lives on W and N...
Open Ct Feb 1838   Thomas Twine

214 15 Feb 1838--Richard H. Ballard to Jesse Wiggens...$1.00 deed of trust and to make safe to David Benton debt of $995.90...500 acre tract, called the Marsh Plantation, adjoining land of Tilly W. Carr...
                 R.H. Ballard
Jordon Parker
William Benton

214 20 Feb 1838--Kicheon Norfleet to Abner Harrell of Hertford... for love and good will...deed of gift of Negro woman, Jenny, and her children, Nelson and Charles...
Sipha Smith   Kicheon Norfleet

215 10 Nov 1837--Esther Mitchell to her friend, Jacob Powell and his children, for good will and affection...all her property, reserving life estate...Negro woman Agga and her children Gates, Warwic and Rachael, 1 looking glass, 1 walnut bedstead, 1 walnut table, 6 walnut chairs and cushion bottoms...
Jos Gordon   Easter Mitchell
John Alpin

216 6 Dec 1837--John Hollowell of Pasquotank to Quinton H. Trotman and his son, Calvin, $5.00...deed of gift of 82 acres that was conveyed to him by Phereba Trotman by deed 3 Mar 1837, beginning at a red oak, corner of James Brinkley, Henry King and others, running to Brinkley's line, to Nathan Riddicks to a ditch, William Harrell's line to Joseph Riddicks and to Henry Walton...
C.R. Kinney   John Hollowell
Jet. H. Riddick

216 22 Aug 1837--Joseph Riddick to Job R. Hall...$1600...360 acres beginning at a persimmon stump near Honey Pot Bridge, up side of swamp to run of White Pot Swamp, to a branch, Powell's corner, up branch to new road, Norfleet's line NW to James R. Riddick's line, N to Honey Pot road and down road...
                 Jo. Riddick
R. Rawls
Allen Smith

216 7 Sep 1837--William E. Pugh to R.K. Speed, power of attorney, to transfer 1-acre tract to him, which was left by John Lovett to said Pugh in deed of trust 9 Jun 1835 to secure debt to William G. Daughtry; lot situated in Gates E side of street running N and S and bounded on N by Asa Hill, E by Thomas Saunders and S by John Mathews...
                                                                            W.E. Pugh
H.M. Daughtry

217 5 Feb 1838--Gilbert Harrell to Reuben Lassiter...$40...3 acres beginning at a pine and running S along Henry Walton's Old Path to a post oak, a corner tree, then W to land of Peter B. Minton then to road...
                                                                   Gilbert Harrell
A.G. Hofler
D.S. Hobbs

217 21 Dec 1837--David Parker to Marmaduke Norfleet...$1308.50 Negroes Beck and children, Cassandra, Bob and Lizza, conveyed to him by John H. Felton in deed of trust...
Whit'l Stallings   D. Parker

218 23 Dec 1837--Marmaduke Norfleet to David Parker...$1308.90 Negroes Beck and children, Bob, Cassandra and Liza...
                                                     M. Norfleet
Seth R. Norfleet

218 8 Jun 1838--Quinton Roundtree to John Walton...$1.00 and deed of trust to secure to John Roberts $100 bond...100 acres adjoining said Walton, John Hinton and heirs of William Hinton, dec.; it being same tract whereon said Roundtree lives and devised to him by his father, Thomas Roundtree. Also, 1 mare, 1 horsecart and gear, 3 head cattle, hogs, crop now growing, feather bed, household and kitchen furniture and farm utensils...
                                                 Quinton(x)Roundtr
                                                 John Roberts
W.G. Daughtry   John Walton

219 12 Jan 1838--James Matthews to David Parker...$1.00 and deed of trust to insure payment of $90 note to said Parker, $42.97 to Miles Briggs (assigned to James H. Parker), $30 to James H. Parker...Negroes Isaac, Penina and Bob and two parcels of land: Brickhouse Tract and Parker Place. Also Negroes: Mahala, Charlotte and Martha. Said David to receive a 5 % commission...
                                                 James Mathias
W.G. Daughtry   D. Parker

220 25 Jun 1838--Joseph Jordon to Julia Jordon...50¢ and to cover a $70 debt...deed in trust of crop of corn on land where she lives and the crop growing on estate of John Felton, dec...
                                               Jos.J. Jordon
Thos. A. Jordon   Julia Jordon

221 18 Jul 1838--William Mathias to Soloman Roundtree...$1.00 and to secure debt of $82.23 and another one to W.G. Daughtry for $119.25...4 acre tract of land in Gatesville adjoining Jesse Brown, Henry Gilliam and John P. Savage...
                                               Wm. Mathias
Wm. H. Gwinn   Solo. Roundtree

222 20 Feb 1838--William Mathias and John Lovett, merchants
trading under the name of William Mathias & Co. to Jethro S.
Haslett...$1.00 and to make safe to Henry Gilliam and William
G. Daughtery, who are security for the following debts: John
Roberts for $135 and $150, Henry Herman of Norfolk for $350,
Jethro S. and Fletcher Haslett for $105 and Henry Gilliam for
$29.50...4 acres adjoining Jesse Brown and Henry L. Blount and
now occupied by said Mathias, horse and double gig, cart, house-
hold and kitchen furniture, stock of dry goods, hardware, etc and
all lumber...to hold in trust...
                                        William Mathias
                                        John Lovett
                                        Jethro S. Haslett
Wm.H. Gwinn   H. Gilliam
Rich'd McIntosh   W.G. Daughtry

224 10 Aug 1838--John P. Savage of Halifax County to William G.
Daughtery...legacies bequeated to him in will of Pryer Savage, dec.
and payment of two judgements for $375 and a note for $68.54 to
Henry Gilliam and another suit now in court for $300...
John Walton   John P. Savage
Willis I. Riddick

225 13 Jan 1838--Isaac Hofler to Docton Hayes...$281.75...41¼
acres beginning in road at Hollow Bridge in Deep Branch, corner
on land of Henry Bond running down branch to Indian Swamp to run
of Schoolhouse Branch, George Reeds corner up run to road and SW;
is land where said Hofler now lives and devised to him by his
father, James Hofler, dec....
                                        Isaac Hofler
John Walton
Willis I. Riddick

225 29 Jan 1838--David Parker to Isaac Hofler...41¼ acres described in above deed, which was executed to said Parker in trust
1 Oct 1836; objects of trust having been met...
                                        D. Parker
Hance Hofler

226 30 Nov 1837--Lewis M. Pruden to Elbert H. Riddick...$100...
50-acre plantation whereon Nathaniel Pruden formerly lived and
was allotted to said Lewis in the division of his father's estate, beginning at a pine stump, corner tree of David Riddick
and Prudens, to a pine in James Benton's line and back to Riddicks.
Jno.V.Sumner   Lewis W. Pruden
B. Goodman

226 27 Jan 1838--Hertford: Absylla Morgan to David Riddick...$42
relinquishes her quit claim in Old Pruden Place on 30 acres,
drawn by Lewis W. Pruden and Martha Pruden, wife of Moses Newsom,
in division of their father's estate...
                                        Absylla Morgan
Mich'l E. Newsom

227 15 Oct 1837--Nancy Welch to David F. Felton...$20...6 acres
allotted to her in division of land of Noah Felton, dec. beginn-
ing at a chinquepin oak in Middle Swamp, a corner tree of David
F. and John R. Felton, by house and through plantation W...
                                        Ann Welch
Elbert H. Riddick
Samuel Felton

228 10 Feb 1838--William W. Powell to Soloman Roundtree...$200
70 acres on N side of Kicheon Norfleet's Mill Pond beginning at
a cypress in run of White Pot Swamp at Poly Branch road, along
mill path to land formerly belonging to Mills R. Fields and now
owned by James R. Riddick to Job R. Hall's line back to White Pot
Swamp...
Rich'd H. Parker   Wm.W.Powell
Simmonds Roundtree

228 25 Jan 1838--Mary A. Barnes of Nansemond to Thomas E. Riddick
$500...160 acres, her interest in land which she heired from her
mother, formerly the property of her father, Micajah Riddick, dec.
beginning at a persimmon tree on edge of main road opposite James
M. Riddick's to main run of Bennetts Creek, down run to William S.
Riddick...
Wm. F. Bennett   Mary A. Barnes
James M. Riddick

229 12 Jan 1838--Francis Duke to William Lee...$250...92 acres
beginning at a pine in Lee's line, running his line NE to main
run of Beach Swamp and running up swamp S to beginning pine...
Feb Ct 1828   Francis Duke

229 12 Jan 1838--William Lee to Francis Duke...$200...46¼ acres
beginning at black gum in Pearce's Branch, up branch to red oak
SW to Gall Bush Branch and up branch to a path corner on Joseph
Freeman's SW to sweet gum on corner of Freemans and Mary Ann Eure,
NW to a hickory corner of said Eure and Goodman's heirs and NE...
J. Freeman   William Lee
Wm. H. Lee

230 17 Feb 1838--John P. Benton to Jesse Wiggens...$1.00 and to
make safe to David Benton debt of $1006...170-acre plantation,
whereon he lives, adjoining land of Dempsey Knight, Kedar Taylor,
Miles Parker and others and Negroes Jim, Abram and Caty...
Jos. Wiggens   Jno.P. Benton
Jordan Parker

231 18 Dec 1837--Drew Trotman to Lemuel Morris of Chowan...$800..
170 acres left to him by his father, Noah Trotman, in his will
binding on lands of James Brinkley, Jethro H. Riddick and Nathan
Riddick...   Drew Trotman
Wynns Baker
Edward Felton

232 31 Aug 1837--William Mathias to John B. Baker...$1.00 and
to hold in trust to pay note to William J. Baker...vessel known
by name Lima with all her rigging, sails, cable, anchors, etc...
F. Haslett   Wm. Mathias
Asa Hill   W.J. Baker
John Lovett   Jno.B.Baker

233 10 Aug 1838--Daniel S. Hobbs to Henry Gilliam...$5.00...deed
in trust, to secure the following notes: David Parker for $222
and $120, James Parker for $250, Joseph Riddick for $250, Abel
Rogerson for $900 and Joel B. Hurdle for $850, with Abel Rogerson

and Joel B. Hurdle as security...three tracts of land; 30 acres
devised to him by David Parker, 30 acres adjoining land of Timothy
Walton and heirs of Walton Freeman and 126 acres adjoining Abram
Spivey and Timothy Walton; all household and kitchen furniture
and stock of goods, wares and merchandise...
                    Daniel S. Hobbs
Jet.H. Riddick   Abel Rogerson
Asa Hill   Joel B. Hurdle
                        H. Gilliam

234 Feb Ct 1838--James R. Riddick, sheriff, to Isiah Lassiter...
$1.10 for 50 acres and 50¢ for 2/5 acres in unpaid taxes for 1834
on land listed by Matthew Lassiter and beginning at black gum,
Thomas Lassiter's corner running SE to Cena Lassiter to Timothy
Lassiters and NE...
                        J.R. Riddick
Open Court

234 1 Dec 1837--Bryant Brothers to Warren Brothers...$50...100
acres, his interest in Parker Plantation, where said Bryant now
lives, beginning on N side of Bennetts Creek at channel running
along Garretts line to water oak on E side of main road then SE
down Branch...
                        Bryant Brothers
M. Norfleet
Seth R. Norfleet

235 8 Feb 1838--John Jones to Dempsey Parker (of John)...$75...
his interest in Henry Jones Plantation, which descended to him
as heir of Henry Jones Sr. and Henry Jones Jr., dec.; said land
being at this time dowry of Mrs. Chetta Parker, beginning in run
of Cypress Swamp, adjoining land of James Sumner to a post oak,
to a black gum to a pine in Sumner's line to a maple corner of
Miles Howell, Harrison Hare and Dempsey Parker, to a sweet gum
of said Hare's to a corner of said Harrison and Elijah Hare, to
a dead pine, a corner of D.M. Saunders, E to Hares and Parkers
line, thence to a catawba tree, thence to David Howell's line
binding on said creek, to Cypress Swamp; containing 300 acres,
said Jones owning 1/3 (that is to say after death of said Chetta
Parker)...   John(x)Jones
Elisha Parker
James(x)Sumner

235 1 Sep 1838--Levin Hofler to Henry Gilliam...$1.00 and to
cover debt of $39 due in 3 mos...30 acres adjoining land of
Timothy Walton, Nathan Nixon and others...
S.W. Worrell   Levin(x)Hofler
J.A. Blount   H. Gilliam

236 10 Feb 1838--Enoch Pearce to James Marshall...$8.40...6 1/3
acres beginning in old road and running to Kedar Lassiters line
down line to Abraham Pearce's...
                        Enoch(x)Pearce
Henry E. Blanchard
Jethro Blanchard

238 14 Dec 1837--Margaret Cross to Hardy Cross...$130...30 acres
beginning at side of public road leading from Gates courthouse to
Somerton, along Dempsey S. Goodman's line to William Sears, dec.
line to corner tree in branch, along John Willey's line...
D. Williams   Margaret Cross
J. Willey

239 1 Jan 1838--Henry Willey to William Boothe...$80...100 acres beginning at red oak, corner on Nisum Cuffs and said Boothes, along Boothe's path to line of sliped trees to gum in Frogborough Branch to edge of branch...
James Parker   Henry Willey
Kedar(x)Parker

239 20 Mar 1836--William E. Pugh, CME, to John King...$260...50 acres belonging to Elizabeth Beeman, of full age, and Israel and William Beeman, infants, by their guardian, John C. Gordon, adjoining lands of Levi Eure Jr., John King, Nathaniel Harrell and A.W. Parker...sold by court petition made by owners...
Wm. . Boothe   Wm.E. Pugh

240 10 Nov 1837--Riddick Smith to James Hare...$40...10 acres beginning at a water oak, corner tree between said Hare and Nath'l Jones, along Jones line to a maple, thence to a white oak, Joseph Hays corner...
John Walton   Riddick(x)Smith
Susan Walton

240 25 May 1837--John Mitchell to Thomas W. Stallings...$10... 2 acres beginning at corner of George Outlaw's line running Old Town Road S and back...
John B. Taylor   John Mitchell
Whit'l Stallings

2 Dec 1837--P.B. Minton to Eliza Pearce...$275...40 acres beginning at main road, a corner of John Shepperd's land, running road to Jacob Nixon's line, along his line to Joel B. Hurdle's to Burwell Brothers and back to Shepperds...
B. Brothers   P.B. Minton
Thos. Riddick

241 13 Feb 1838--Peter B. Minton to Joel B. Hurdle...$800...150 acres beginning at a water oak on Virginia Road binding on Walton Freeman's land running along road N to Thomas Harrell's to Henry Walton's line to Timothy Walton's line (the Bagley Land), it being all the land he purchased of James Costen Jr...
Burwell Brothers   P.B. Minton
Abner Eason

242 31 Jan 1838--Abram Riddick Sr. and Abram Riddick Jr. of Nansemond to Joseph Gwin...$105...30 acres beginning at a corner of Joseph Small's heirs, binding on his line W to Powell's ditch and N...
Riddick Jones Jr.   Abram Riddick
Wm. H. McGuire   Abraham Riddick

243 17 Feb 1838--John Arnold to Henry Speight...$50...50 acres whereon Edward Arnold lived and died; John's right in land given to him by his grandfather, John Arnold; adjoining lands of John Pruden, James Benton and Wilie Riddick...
David Riddick   John(x)Arnold
Soloman Roundtree

243 15 Feb 1838--Henry Boothe to William Jones...$9...2¼ acres, part of land formerly owned by John Lewis, beginning at a popular in James Smith's corner binding on Jones former line to main road to a pine in Deep Branch...
                                                          Henry Boothe

244 16 Feb 1838--Joseph Hill to Robert R. Hill...$135...30 acres beginning at a peach tree in said Robert's line S to a pine in Whitmill Hill's line, along his line to a forked water oak in Richard H. Parker's line, to Hill's line...
Bn. B. Ballard   Joseph(x)Hill
David Speight

244 23 Dec 1837--Judith Blanchard to Henry Boothe...$150...right of dower set apart to her by jury to land belonging to Henry Gilliam, adjoining lands of said Boothe, William Jones, Riddick Smith and others...
William Jones   Judith Blanchard
Asa(x)Hays

245 23 Dec 1837--Henry Gilliam to Henry Boothe...$275...100 acres adjoining said Boothe, William Jones, Riddick Smith and others, reserving to Judith Blanchard her right of dower...
Willis J. Riddick   H. Gilliam

246 1 Feb 1833--William W. Cowper to John Clark...farm let of 15 acres of woodland, bounded by B. Wynns, Isaac Pipkin and John Riddick...for 20 years; Said Clark to have all corn fodder for first four years after clearing and fencing and thereafter said Cowper to receive 1/3...
                                                        Wm.W. Cowper
Nicholas Wades

246 6 Mar 1837--James Boyce of Chowan to Guy Hobbs...$275...50 acres beginning at a pine corner in said Hobbs line running E to road that leads through plantation S to Willis Bunch and Kedar Hurdle's heirs land, to Harmon Hurdle and Luke Hollowell's line W to Levi Sumner's line then NW...
                                                        James Boyce
Jordon Hobbs
Amos Hobbs

247 7 Mar 1837--James Boyce of Chowan to Jordon Hobbs...$275... 50 acres beginning at road, adjoining Willis Bunch's line to Jesse Hobbs line, N to line of William Boyce's heirs, and along road; land purchased of Amos Perry and William Boyce 26 Nov 1828.
                                                        James Boyce
Amos Hobbs
Guy Hobbs

248 1 Jan 1838--Elisha Harrell Sr. to William Harrell (of Mills) $59¼...88 acres beginning at white oak, a corner of William Boothes and Mrs. Lucreta Beeman's, thence a line of marked trees to a sweet gum, a corner of Abram and Dempsey Parker and lands belonging to estate of Mills Eure, dec.   Elisha Harrell
Wm. L. Boothe
Bennet Harrell

248 10 Feb 1838--James Marshall to Thomas Lassiter...$11...4½ acres beginning at a pine and running to Watery Swamp in Abraham Pearce's line...   James(x)Marshall
Archibald R. Jones

249 28 May 1836--Thomas Hoggard to William Umphflett...$15...17½ acres beginning at a black gum in Long Branch, a corner of Bray

Eure's to juniper in edge of river pocosin and down run...
Thomas Hoggard
Abraham Pruden

249 19 Feb 1838--Frederick Jones to Blake Baker...$100...57 acres on N side of Mile Branch, beginning at a white oak, a corner tree on Stuard Bond's, NE to a red oak, corner of John Smith's, NE to a bunch of maples in Joshua Allen's line and up branch...
Frederick Jones
Nath'l Doughtie
William Bush

250 22 Nov 1836--James Jones to Simmons Jones...$110...40 acres beginning at a small gum in swamp in Isaac Pipkin's line, along Pipkin's line to Blake Brady's to a white oak near path leading from Sears Mill to Jones Swamp...
James(x)Jones
John Willey
John Brady

251 1 Nov 1836--Henry King to Timothy Walton...$40...his equity in an undivided 200-acre tract near Muddy Cross and bounded by said Walton, Whitmill Stallings, Aaron Spivey and others; plantation whereon Charles Roundtree lived and died and gave to his wife Christian (now Christian Walton) during her life and after her death to her cousin, Charles Roundtree...
Nathaniel Jones
Henry King
John G. Walton

252 7 Mar 1837--Henry King to Quinton H. Trotman...$6...1 acre beginning at post oak on ditch bank of Whitmill Stallings and Jethro H. Riddick's line, thence to a post oak in James Brinkley's line...
Henry King
Calvin R. Brinkley
Rachael Elliott

252 20 Sep 1837--Anthony Matthews to Blake Baker...$18...24 acres near Norfleet's Mill Pond beginning at a red oak, a corner tree in Frederick Jones and John Smith's line E to swamp, to Noah Harrells line, to Richard Smith, dec. line and W...
Anthony Matthews
Nath'l Doughtie
Sam'l Baker

253 27 Feb 1836--Richard Odom to James Smith...$100...132 acres beginning at corner pine in William's line near head of Boyse Swamp, to Asa Odom's, to a corner gum in Mirey Branch, up branch to Isaac Pipkin's line and along his line to edge of Notoway River and running Williams line...
Richard Odom
Nathan Harrell
G.G. Saunders

254 10 Dec 1836--Jason Roundtree to William Umphflet...$16...17½ acres on S side of Cypress Swamp beginning at gum in run of Long Branch, along Henry Harrell's line to run of swamp and down to Bray Eure's line to Umphflet's...
Jason(x)Roundtree
A.W. Parker
John Turner

255 19 Feb 1838--Lassiter Riddick and wife, Jane, to Thomas Hoggard...$700...300 acres, part of a tract that descended to said Jane as an heir at law by death of Taylor Cross, dec. and same land whereon Mrs. Christian Cross, grandmother to said Jane, lived and died; beginning at a persimmon tree in Etheldred Cross's line on E side of outside swamp adjoining land of Abram Pruden, to Wynns Ferry Road and across road and down swamp to Elisha Umphflet's line, N to William G. Daughtry's line, to a pine in Sarah Saunders line, N to a gum in end of Long Pond and along road...
R.K. Speed   Lassiter Riddick
Asa Hill   Margaret J. Riddick

256 19 Feb 1838--Lassiter Riddick and wife, Jane, to Thomas Hoggard...$100...161 acre tract of Sand Banks land, beginning at corner of William G. Daughtry's line to a post oak in side of marsh, E along Umphflet's line to run of outside swamp to A.W. Parker's line of land formerly owned by Samuel Harrell, to a red oak in John Sparkman's heirs and David Lewis heirs...
R.K. Speed   Lassiter Riddick
Asa Hill   Margaret J. Riddick

257 18 Dec 1837--Timothy Spivey to Jethro Blanchard...$150...40 acres beginning at black gum in swamp, a corner tree between said Spivey, William Hofler and Currie Blanchard, thence by strait line of marked trees to a white oak, a corner between Spivey and John Lassiter, to a red oak, a corner in Jethro Blanchards and binding on his line...
Easton Blanchard   Timothy Spivey
Henry Hofler

257 19 Feb 1838--Nannah Umphflet to Abraham Brinkley...$30...40 or 50 acres adjoining land of A.W. Parker, known as the Stallings Tract and she defends such rights as Bray Parker warranted to her...
Abraham Pruden   Nannah(x)Umphflet
Abraham Smith

258 10 Mar 1837--Jethro Willey to Seth R. Morgan...$825...Negroes Alman, Julie and Rose...
John Willey   Jethro Willey

258 24 Aug 1838--Elizabeth Morrice to John W. Hinton...$1.00 and to secure note to James T. Freeman for $104.93...37½ acres in Indian Neck, where Frederick Morrice formerly lived, adjoining land of John Morrice, John Roberts and others...
                                                        Elizabeth(x)Morrice
Starky(x)Trotman   Jas. T. Freeman
L.D. Freeman   John W. Hinton

260 18 May 1838--Thomas A. Small to Jesse Wiggens...$1.00 and to make safe to Humphrey Parker as his security for debet to David Benton of $101.50...101 acres land where said Small lives, adjoining Reuben W. Small and John C. Gordon...
                                                         Thomas A. Small
Jesse L. Hare
Miles(x)Parker

261 11 Apr 1838--Jesse Wiggens to David Benton...$235.90...Four

Negroes Tom, Amey, Sue and Jiles, 1 bay horse, cart and wheels...
John Wiggens   Jesse P. Wiggens

261 11 Apr 1838--James Mathias to Hardy D. Parker....$747.50
Negroes Tiller, Isaac and Martha...
                                                James Mathias
Humphrey Parker

262 26 Mar 1838--Herod Faison and wife, Gulielma Mariah, of Northampton to John Willey...$204...91 acres beginning at Jones path at short strawed pine E to large rosemary pine, binding on heirs of William Sears, to Mills Swamp, down swamp binding on Kindred Parker, to Isaac Pipkin's line and up swamp to Blake Brady's corner NW to a white oak and SW to Pipkins and then N to a sweet gum, a corner in line of land of said Willey, purchased of Tilman Vann and wife, then S on Willey's to Jones path and NE; land that said Gulielma heired from her father...
                                                Herod Faison
J.R. Riddick   Gulielma M. Faiso
M. Norfleet

263 1 Dec 1837--John B. Baker to John Roberts...$500...his man Don Carlos, 25 years old...
                                                Jno. B. Baker
J.R. Riddick

263 22 May 1838--Benjamin Brown to Mary Hudgins...$125...33 acres beginning at Beaver Dam bridge in main road leading from Gatesville to Edenton running up road W to a white oak, a corner tree near Zion Meeting House and along line of meeting house land to a post oak, another corner between said land and on William Pearce line, along Pearce's line to pine on side of Beaver Dam Swamp and down run...
                                                Benjamin Brown
Jet. H. Riddick
John Walton

264 Jan 1838--James Boothe to William Boothe...$100...40 acres commencing at a corner at road on Jesse Arline and cornering at a gum on William J. Smith's, to corner gum in the but swamp, up swamp to road; tract whereon James lives...
                                                Jas. Boothe
Henning Boothe
Crissey A. Dukes

265 10 Mar 1838--James Copeland to Joshua Jones...$81.54...2 gray mares, 12 and 4 years old...
                                                James Copeland
Miles Briggs
Ethel'd Matthews

265 29 Nov 1836--Joseph Gordon and Henry Gilliam to Holloday Walton...$100...29 acres placed in their trust by William W. Stedman, on which he lived and adjoining lands of Richard H. Ballard, John Powell and others; trust not having been met...
                                                Jos. Gordon
Jacob J. Harvey   H. Gilliam
T. Saunders

266 14 Mar 1838--Joseph Gordon to Edward Riddick of Nansemond... $514...257 acres of desert land beginning at a gum in Isaac L.

Harrell's line of land he bought of said Gordon, E with his line
to land where said Gordon now lives, that he bought of John C.
Gordon, executor of Nancy Granbury, dec., on N side of Horsepool Swamp, including 1 acre of high land...to Mary Riddick's
desert patent, E to Mills Riddick's line...
James Briggs   Jos.Gordon
Joseph G. Granbury

267 1 Mar 1837--John D. Hart and wife, Sophia E., of Southamton,
Va. to Thomas Odom of Nansemond...$250...100 acres known at Thomas
P. Smith farm, part of which is in Nansemond and part of which is
in Gates County; it being 2nd deed given for land, bounded by Capt.
Samuel Cross, Col. Hardy Cross and Lee's Mill...
Ro.R. Smith   John D. Hart
John D. Langston   Sophie E. Hart

267 17 Mar 1838--Joshua Levisay to William W. Hayes...$650...224
acres beginning at white oak, corner on Hardy Williams on Mill
Swamp, NE to a pine then SE to a small pine corner of Hillory
Willey and L. Parker, to a post oak and NE to Henry G. Williams,
to a small dogwood on road and down road to land of heirs of Dem-
sey Williams, dec., NW to white oak on margin of Harveys Mill
Swamp...   Joshua Levisay
Dempsey(x)Parker (of Miles)
Jonathan (x) Williams

268 23 Jan 1838--John Lassiter to Jethro Blanchard...$20...10 acres
beginning at a pine and white oak in said Blanchard's line running
NE by line of marked trees, corner on Henry Hofler, William Hofler
and Timothy Spivey lines, S to dead oak stump in Blanchard's line
and down his line...
                                                        John Lassiter
Robert Blanchard   (of Absylla)
John Wesley Blanchard

269 5 Sep 1836--Mildred and Nancy Lee to Rodon Odom...$200...100
acres beginning at corner tree of John Gatling and Levi Eures, a-
long Eure's line to David Umphflets to Elizabeth Briscoe's line
and along her line to heirs of David Lewis, dec. and back to Gatlings...   Mildred(x)Lee
Kichen Taylor   Nancy(x)Lee
Bennet Harrell

270 20 Sep 1838--James Mathias to Willoughby Manning...$375...100
acres bounded by Humphrey Parker's land to run of Joseph Riddick's
mill pond, down run of pond to line of James Morgan's heirs, along
their line and up Thicket Swamp...   James Mathias
Jno.P.Benton
Jesse Wiggens

271 4 Apr 1838--Nathan Nixon and wife, Sally, to Timothy Walton
$300...66 acres commencing at corner oak in Walton's land to Abel
Rogerson's line to branch and then to Catherine Creek to Levin Hof-
ler's line...   Nathan Nixon
                                                        Sally Nixon
Zachariah Nixon
John (x) Polson

271 11 Nov 1837--Lassiter Pearce to Nathan Pearce...$100...50 acres beginning at a pine, a corner tree between said Lassiter Pearce and Jethro Blanchard, running S to another pine, then N to a water oak in Edward Jones line, then running E to Williams line(formerly)...
                                                        Lassiter(x)Pearce
Henry E. Blanchard
Jethro Blanchard

272 14 Feb 1837--Jesse Piland to James Smith...$1.00 for lease for 10 years on 5 acres, beginning at a pine, down ditch to branch, line of Elisha Piland's heirs, to old field and up to corner of Jesse Piland's fence; to clear and tend land four years and there after to give 1/3 production to said Piland...
                                                        Jesse Piland
Washington Harrell
John Turner

272 9 Dec 1837--Nathan Riddick to son, Jason, gift of 137 acres beginning at a red oak, corner tree of Joseph Hurdles and Jethro H. Riddicks, S to Wesley Phelps corner, down branch W to willow oak corner, S to Levi Sumner's corner in Cabbin Swamp, down swamp to Joseph T. Hurdles and James Baker's corner tree, N to Jethro Riddicks...
                                                        Nathan Riddick
Abel Rogerson
Elisha R. Hunter

273 6 Mar 1838--Jason Riddick to Jethro H. Riddick...$875...137 acres described in above deed...
                                                        Jason Riddick
Joseph Hurdle
Levi (x) Sumner

274 29 Oct 1838--William B. Harvey to James R. Riddick...$1.00 and to make safe safe to Ann N. Harvey as his security for bonds to James Coffield for $200, John Roberts for $100, Henry Bond for $200, William B. Wynns for $375, Hardy Cross for $100, Thomas G. Benton for $220, Thomas Harvey for $300 and Ann N. Harvey for $300...1 pannel double gig, 1 faieton, 1 barouche, 1 tray body waggon, 1 chariote, 1 craneneck gig, 1 crane neck sulky, 1 stick sulky, 1 barouche body, 1 sportsman waggon body, 2 old single gigs, 3 old gig bodies, 4 stoves, 1 steamer, 2 sets blacksmith tools, 1 china press, 1 bed and furniture, 1 table, all timber and materials, all tools except wood shop and silver plater tools.
                                                        Wm. B. Harvey
                                                        J.R. Riddick
Eli P. Moore   Ann N. Harvey

275 27 Nov 1837--Nathan Riddick to Elisha R. Hunter...$125...54 acres beginning at a water oak on main road running S to swamp along swamp E to land formerly belonging to Joseph T. Hurdle's N to road...
                                                        Nathan Riddick
J.R. Kee
Wm (x) Simpson

275 30 Jun 1836--Nathan Riddick to his grandson, Harry Hunter, gift of 38 acres of land known as Hurdle Land, adjoining land of Milton Eason, said Riddick and others on S side of road leading from Sandy to Muddy Cross...
                                                        Nathan Riddick
J.R. Kee
Wm. (x) Simpson

276 14 Feb 1838--Lassiter Riddick to John S. Roberts...$500...120 acres adjoining said Roberts, Riddick and Pryor Savage, beginning at red oak on side of new road to Hawtree Branch and up branch W to a pine and SE...
Simmonds Roundtree
Lem'l Riddick
             Lassiter Riddick

278 15 May 1838--James R. Riddick, sheriff, to Rodon Eure...$10 tract of land whereon Samuel Eure lived beginning at a post oak near corner of old field running NE to run of swamp, up run to pappaw gum of Abram W. Parker and William Blades on Parker's line to a maple, corner of Nathaniel and Miles Cullens, to Riddick B. Eure; sold by levy of constable on execution obtained by Levi Beeman, administrator of Riddick B. Eure, dec.
             J.R. Riddick
Elisha Parker
Levi (x) Eure Jr.

279 1 May 1838--James R. Riddick to Benjamin Franklin $34.92... old mill seat and four acres formerly belonging to Abram Riddick, adjoining land of said Franklin, Jason Franklin, Col Joseph Riddick and others...sold by court order to comply with execution obtained by Etheldred Matthews on land of Soloman Riddick...
             J.R. Riddick
A.W. Parker
H.S. Blount

280 28 Feb 1838--Abraham Smith to Rodon Odom...$550...300 acres beginning at a corner gum in run of Mirey Branch, to Humphrey Savage, to corner tree of James Williams, running his line to corner juniper in edge of river pocosin, running along edge of pocosin and across Winton road to a corner gum in river pocosin of John Vann and running his line of marked trees to Mirey Branch and up branch...
Thos. Hoggard   Abraham Smith
Rodon Odom

280 4 Nov 1835--Benbury Walton to Timothy Walton...$500...200 acres beginning at Joseph Sutton's corner along his line to Robert Blanchard's corner, along his line to Henry Bond and Brown's line to Nancy Bonds and along her line...
             B. Walton
George W. Reed
John Walton

281 21 May 1838--Holloday Walton and wife, Linney, to James Small... $50...30 acres, her share of land that she heired from her father, Joseph Small, dec....
Bn. B. Ballard   Holloday Walton
A.R. Harrell   Linney(x)Walton

282 28 Feb 1838--John White to William White...$200...his interest in 75 acres of land, whereon his father lived, adjoining land of John Mitchell, William White, Elmire Ward and others...
Tim. Walton   John White
Seth W. Roundtree

282 24 Nov 1837--Joseph J. Jordon to Miles Briggs...$1.00 and to secure to James A. Small payment of $70...1 bay mare, 8 hogs

and 2 ploughs...
Jos. Jordon
                                              Joseph J. Jordan

283 19 Nov 1838--William L. Boothe to John Riddick and Dempsey Sparkman...$1.00 and to secure the following debts: $575 to John C. Gordon, $50 to A.W. Parker, now going to David Parker, $22.50 to H. Gilliam, $20 to Richard Odom, $10 and $40 to Abraham W. Parker, $9 to John Mathews now paying to Jethro Willey and $10 to Benjamin Wynn now paying to David Parker...plantation whereon he lives and formerly owned by John Beeman, dec., 1 bay horse, 3 head cattle, 30 head of hogs, 1 bed and furniture, 1 walnut table, 12 sitting chairs, 20 barrels corn, 1000 pds. fodder and 1 lot of shucks...
Reuben Piland   W.L. Boothe

284 25 Jan 1838--James Freeman and Martha Moore, both of Madison Co., Tn. appoint John F. Lee of Bertie County as their attorney to prosecute suit against Joseph Freeman for recovery of money, Negroes or property that they maybe entitled to by death of their brothers, John and David Freeman...
                                                Jas. Freeman
Hugh B. Robinson   Martha Moore
F.E. Hill
M.B. Stewart, clerk at office in Jackson
W.T. Benton, justice

285 20 Aug 1838--John Wiggens to Jesse Wiggens...$1.00 and to make safe to David Benton debt of $1015...Negroes Sam, Henry and Dave...
                                                Jno. Wiggens
B. Goodman
W. Hudgins

286 2 Oct 1838--Mary Williams to her beloved children: Penny Parker, John Williams and Mary Parker...3 Negroes, Pat, Mary and Mike; stock of cattle and hogs, farm utensils and household and kitchen furniture...
                                                Mary(x)Williams
Henry Willey
Henry H. Williams

287 10 Aug 1837--John B. Baker to John C. Gordon...$186...tract of land beginning at Wiggens Bridge, running along road to Gates Courthouse, to white oak sapling, Lassiter Riddick's corner, NE to holly in Deep Bottom Swamp to pine stump, Simons Roundtree and Ruth Lawrence's corner NE along line of marked trees to ditch on Isaac Pipkin's line and down branch...
                                                Jno.B.Baker
Benj'n W. Gordon
Jos. Gordon

287 7 Jan 1838--Josiah Briggs to Charlotte Briggs...$50...Negro boy, Justice...
                                                Josiah Briggs
J. Riddick

287 29 Dec 1837--William J. Boothe, administrator for James Boothe, Negro girl, Betty...$601 at six months credit...to Kedar Hinton...
H. Gilliam   Wm.J. Boothe

288 21 Aug 1837--John B. Baker to Mills Piland...$50...50 acres beginning at pawpaw gum on Chowan River between the Island and mouth of Sarum Creek, down river to mouth of said creek and up creek to forked cypress nearly opposite rocking cypress and a strait course...
J.B. Baker
Wm. J. Baker
John(x)Brinkley

288 12 Aug 1838--Joseph Benton to David Benton...$100...20 acres beginning at a beach near main road, Seth R. Morgan's line, along his line to run of Bennett's Creek to said David's corner and along road...
Joseph Benton
Jesse Wiggens
Elizabeth(x)Wiggens

289 12 Aug 1838--David Benton to Joseph Benton...$100...20 acres beginning at a pine stump near main road, said Joseph's line, to said David's line, along new fence...
David(x)Benton
Jesse Wiggens
Elizabeth(x)Wiggens

289 12 Feb 1837--James, Mary and Louisa Boyce to Jesse Hobbs...$200 50 acres, which was allotted to them by death of their father, William Boyce, lying on S side of Catherine Creek near said Hobbs...
James Boyce
Henry W. Hobbs
Mary(x)Boyce
Elijah Smith
Eliza(x)Boyce

289 30 May 1829--Bryant Brothers to Nancy Bond...$44.44....1 horse, 3 feather beds and furniture, 6 windsor chairs, 1 cow and calf, 1 heifer and 1 walnut table...
Bryant Brothers
David Parker

290 20 Jan 1838--James Brown Sr. to Jethro Eure Jr...$17.52...7½ acres beginning at white oak in edge of road (Wynns) under or near Mrs. Susannah Piland's fence, whereon Peter Piland now lives W to a post oak, S to a water oak in Shoulder Hill Branch and down branch...
James(x)Brown
Peter Piland
Wm. L. Boothe

291 3 Jan 1833--Thomas R. Costen to William W. Hayes...$600...89 acres, all the land he purchased of George Costen, beginning at main road leading from Gatesville to Edenton, running down Reuben Hinton's line S to a white oak, a corner tree between Costen, Reuben Hinton and John Roberts, down Robert's line E to corner tree between said Costen and said Roberts and Leah Hinton, up main road.
Thos.R. Costen
I.S. Harrell
Thos. E. Powell

293 15 May 1829--Wills Cowper Jr. and George W. Granbery, both of Portsmouth, Va. and Joseph J. Granbery agree: whereas their mother, Elizabeth Granbery lately died intestate leaving considerable personal property of which they are sole heirs, call in friends Thomas Twine, Rissop Rawls and Jesse Wiggens to make division of said estate, reserving privilege to bid among themselves for any article they think proper...
Wills Cowper
R. Lassiter
Geo.W. Granbery
Jos. Gordon
John J. Granbery

293 20 Aug 1838--William W. Cowper to Ann N. Harvey...$122.50...
relinquishes his right of cutting timber from certain tract of
land...
H. Gilliam   Wm.W.Cowper

293 12 Dec 1838--Gilbert G. Saunders to James Cobb of Hertford
$1.00 and to secure to Abram Riddick of Hertford debt of $987...
232 acres whereon he lives and 10 acres adjoining known as Ballard
Land and 90 acres known as Pipkin Land; also, Negroes Ned and
Lucy, 2 horses, 1 work stear, 4 cows and calves, 2 young stears,
33 fat hogs, 50 out hogs, 4 beds, steads and furniture, 1 buffet
and contents of crockery, glassware etc., 12 chairs, 1 chest, 2
trunks, 4 tables, farm and cooking utensils, 80 barrels of corn,
5000 lbs blade fodder, 30 bushels peas, 50 bushels potatoes, 1
loom and gear, 2 shotguns, 1 riding chair and gear, 2 carts and
gear, 15 turkeys, 1 seine, rope, cork and timber for a new flat...
                                                     G.G. Saunders
B.W. Britt   James Cobb
James W. Britt   A. Riddick

294 7 Apr 1832--Elisha Duke to Joseph Gordon...$22.12½ ...9 acres,
his undivided interest in land belonging to his father, Daniel Duke,
dec., whereon his mother now lives, adjoining lands of James Lassiter, Rissop Rawls and others...
Marmaduke Norfleet   Elisha(x)Duke
George G. Harvey

295 2 Aug 1838--Joseph Gordon to James E. Small...$45...20 acres,
proportional parts of his brothers, William and Daniel, both dec.
of their father, Joseph Small's real estate...
Joseph Mathias   Jos. Gordon
Jas. A. Small

296 7 Jan 1838--Joseph Gordon, trustee of Wiley P. Jones, to Edward Parker...$316 ($4 per acre)...two tracts of land placed in
deed of trust 12 May 1837...first tract of five acres, where he
lives and another adjoining of 74 acres, bought of Abraham Harrell.
Jet. H. Riddick   Jos. Gordon
James Briggs

296 23 May 1838--Richard B. Gatling of Shelby County, Tn. appoints
his friend, Lassiter Riddick, as his attorney to sell 400 acres in
Gates County, which was given to him by his father, Etheldred B.
Gatling...   Rich'd B. Gatling
William Harris, judge of circuit
court of Tennessee and attested to
by Newton Cannon, governor, and Luke
Lee, secretary of state

297 20 Aug 1838--Richard B. Gatling of Shelby County, Tn. to Henry
L. Eure...$502.25...228 acres beginning in path near Beaverdam
Swamp, running NE to head of branch to corner of Short Beaverdam,
said Eure and Gatling's corner, to a small sweet gum on Mary A.
Eure's, SW along her line to water oak stump near some marked
pines SW to an ash to Beaverdam Swamp and up its run. Land was given
to said Riddick by his father, Etheldred B. Gatling...
                                                     Rich'd B. Gatling
Riddick Gatling   by his attorney, Lassiter Riddick
M. Norfleet

298 28 Dec 1836--Ann Gatling and Joseph Gatling to Exum Lewis
$300...99 acres beginning at red oak near edge of road leading
from Mrs. Ann Harveys to Wynns Ferry, a corner of said Gatlings
and Lewis line N to a red oak, corner of Gatling and William W.
Cowper, nearly W to a gum, a corner of Gatlings and Isaac Pipkin
SE to bush near edge of road and down road...
              Ann Gatling
Wm.L. Boothe   Joseph Gatling
Amos Cullens

299 29 May 1838--Riddick Gatling to John Powell...$148...124½
acres beginning at small pine on E side of road leading from
Isaac Pipkin's to Winton, said Gatling's corner, down road to
pine on Samuel Felton's line and along line to a black gum, a
corner in James William's line, to William Sears line and to
William Goodman's line...   R. Gatling
Senea Eure

300 18 Aug 1838--Nancy Harvey to Robert Rogers...$1457...364¼
acres beginning at a water oak on W side of road from Somerton to
Gatesville, near a hollow bridge thence S 73 W 21½ po. to a pine,
thence N 89 W 11 to a white oak, thence S 77 W 15 to an oak, thence
S 80½ W 19 to road, down road 200 po. to run of Hackley Swamp, down
run of swamp to Wiggens Branch and along road to red oak on edge
of old field, thence N 64½ W 68 to large pine, thence N 21 E 148¼
to small persimmon tree thence NE to Pipkin's lane and along road.
Kindred Parker   Ann N. Harvey
William Babb

300 5 Jul 1828--Clement Hill to John B. Baker...$300...land, which
he purchased of Mills Riddick and Charles Townsend, beginning at
Sarum Creek near Capt. William Goodman's, down creek to Chowan River
then up river to Barnes Creek and up creek to a cypress called The
Gentleman and along Goodman's line...
              Clement Hill
Jno. Gatling
T. Saunders

301 23 May 1838--Andrew R. Harrell to Isaac S. Harrell...$1200
230 acres whereon he lives beginning at a red oak on S side of
public road in John Alpin's line S to land belonging to James
Harrell, to Creecy's line N to road and along road E...
             Andrew R. Harrell
Jas. A. Small
Wm. R. Brothers

302 20 Apr 1838--Joel B. Hurdle to Peter B. Minton...$800...150
acres beginning at a water oak on Virginia road binding on Walton
Freeman's line N to land of Thomas or William Harrell's line to
Henry Walton, dec. line, to Timothy Walton's line, the Bagley
land, to Walton Freeman's; land which Hurdle purchased of Minton,
who purchased from James Costen Jr.... Joel B. Hurdle
Willis Walton
Sarah(x)Hobbs

302 29 Nov 1837--Peter B. Minton to Mary Powell and Nathan Parker
$75...land bounded on N by land of Charles Powell, on W by heirs

of John Outlaw, on S by land of John White and on E by land of
Jacob N. Parker and is land now occupied by said Mary Powell...
  C.R. Kinney   P.B. Minton

303 2 Jan 1837--Seth R. Morgan to Allen Daughtry...$283.75...27½ acres, beginning at a sweet gum, corner of said Daughtry, SW to a post and then SE to Jesse Wiggens line, NE to a white oak and holly and NW...
                                                                                           Seth R. Morgan
Jesse Wiggens
Harrison(x)Ellis

303 27 Jul 1838--Absylla Nixon of Chowan to Kedar Riddick...
$60...24 acres that she heired from her brother, Joseph Pearce, dec. beginning at a corner gum on swamp, along said Riddick's line W to Ezekiel Jones, SW to William Jones corner, then SE to Isaac Pearce's to the swamp...
                                                                       Absylla(x)Nixon
D. Riddick
David Nixon

304 16 Nov 1835--William E. Pugh, CME, to Pryor Savage...$462.62 one hundred and ___ acres: whereas in fall term of 1833 court William Parker by his guardian, Hardy D. Parker; Nancy, Mary, Harriett, Martha and Eliza Parker by their next friend, Henry Gilliam, and Daniel Parker, by his guardian, Reuben Harrell, filed for sale of tract, adjoining land of Jesse Brown, William G. Daughtry and others
  H. Gilliam   Wm. E. Pugh

305 3 Aug 1838--Isaac Pipkin to Belver Sears...$96...32 acres beginning in road, corner on said Sears and Pipkin, running NE to a pine, SE to Sears Mill Pond to run of branch, corner on William Goodman's and up branch SW...
                                                                       Isaac Pipkin
Dempsey S. Goodman
Allen Smith

306 1 Aug 1838--Edward Parker to William Miller...$158...40¼ acres beginning at a black gum corner on said Miller, E to Baylis Swamp and down swamp to red oak, corner of Wiley P. Jones, and SE to Millers line of marked trees...
                                                                       Edward Parker
Wm. L. Boothe
Allen Smith

307 Aug Ct 1838--James R. Riddick, sheriff, to John B. Baker... $133.67...land of Mills Riddick...sold by writs of Ven. Expos. made in Feb Term of 1830 court at instance of Elizabeth Goodman to use of Lassiter Riddick and instance of Susannah Piland to use of John Riddick on lands adjoining lands of John Beeman Pintard's heirs and Spivey's patent line...
                                                                       J.R. Riddick
W.G. Daughtry

308 20 Jan 1837--James R. Riddick, sheriff, to Amos Hobbs...$1.17 in taxes for 1834 on 24 acres belonging to Elizabeth Hobbs beginning at a post oak, corner of Dempsey Hobbs, NE to William Hobbs line to run of swamp SE to black gum and NW...
                                                                       J.R. Riddick
W.G. Daughtry
Jet. H. Riddick

308 20 Jan 1838--James R. Riddick to Edward Parker...$30...17 acres beginning at main road in William Miller's line, with his line to edge of Mill Swamp and down swamp to Charles Briggs' fence, with his fence to road; it being land said Briggs sold to James Powell...
Willis F. Riddick   J.R. Riddick
J. Kee

309 6 Aug 1838--Timothy Rogers and wife, Polly, to Elizabeth Lee $18...9 8/10 acres beginning at a pine, a corner of said Elizabeth's in Rogers line, SW to branch in James Saunders line and down branch N to Beaverdam Swamp and up swamp to Lee's line...
A.H. Jones   Timothy(x)Rogers
James P. Gwinn
George H. Gardner

310 27 Jun 1838--William Steward to Elisha Parker...$1.00 and to insure to James Sumner debt of $35...1 sorrell filley...
                                       Elisha Parker
Aaron(x) Johnson   Wm.(x)Steward
Lucinda Parker   Willis(x)Duck

311 24 Mar 1837--Lemuel Smith to Thomas Cornelius...$14...14 acres beginning at a pine on Saunders line to Smith's line thence running a line of blazed trees to Hare's line and along Hare's line to Saunders line...
D.M. Saunders   Lemuel(x)Smith
James Saunders

311 15 Aug 1838--Simon Stallings to Thomas W. Stallings...$5.00 25 acres adjoining lands of Hofler and Welch's Mill Pond, land of heirs of Timothy Walton, dec. and land whereon Nathan Cullen's formerly lived, being swamp land...
                                     Simon Stallings
Whit'l Stallings
James Howard

312 16 Jul 1837--Drew Trotman to his nephew, Richard M. Baker, son of Wynns Baker and wife, Armesia, deed of gift of 10 acres known by name Chimney Fial beginning at willow oak in Jethro Riddick's line running road W to James Brinkley's line...
James(x)Boyce   Drew Trotman
William Baker

313 6 Jun 1838--Jesse P. Wiggens to David Benton...$30...4 feather beds and furniture, 1 buffet, 2 tables, 10 chairs, 7 head of hogs, 1 stear, 1 sorrel horse, cooking utensils and crop of corn in field...
Wm. H. Hudgins   Jesse P. Wiggens

313 24 Dec 1836--Jesse Wiggens to Allen Daughtry...$70...14 acres beginning at a pine, corner of Seth Morgan's, NE to a maple and S.
Seth R. Morgan   Jesse Wiggens
Harrison(x)Ellis

314 5 Dec 1837--Michael Williams to Thomas Umphflet...$40...25 acres beginning at a black gum, a corner of Nannah Umphflet's in swamp, along her line and A.W. Parker's line and down his line to run of swamp and up swamp...
                                     Michael(x)Williams
Wm. L. Boothe

315 1 Mar 1838--Division of estate of Reuben Parker, dec. as follows: Survey No. 1--Syntha...32 acres beginning at a white oak at the fence, corner on Lot No. 2, NW at a strait line of marked trees to a small gum in branch on Dempsey Parker, up branch to large pine corner on Mills Eure's NE to a pine corner and SW. No. 2--Martha...37 acres beginning at a white oak corner of No. 1, SW to a stump, corner of said Eure's NW to water oak in branch, up branch to Dempsey Parkers and SE...No. 3--Ann...22 acres beginning at a large oak at road SE to a small gum corner NE to large oak, SE to pine corner on Mrs. Beeman's, NE to a popular then NW to a post and back NE to road and down road. No. 4--Elisha Harrell...23 acres beginning at a large oak at road SE to small gum corner on Lot 3, thence SW to a sweet gum, corner on Dempsey Parker's NW to road and along road...
Allen Smith, co. s.
Peter Piland, alternate commissioner
                              Wm. L. Boothe
                              Dempsey Sparkman
                              Mills Sparkman

316 1 Sep 1838--William G. Daughtry to Edward Decormis...$128.48½ 1 secretary, 2 walnut tables, 1½ doz. windsor chairs, 1 map, 1 glass, 1 table, 1 sideboard, 1 brass clock, 1 pair andirons, 2 beds and furniture, washstand bason, 1 table, 1 passage lamp, 1 popular table, 1 bedstead, 1 cart and wheels, 1 pair patent balances, 1 sow and pigs...in possession of John Lovett and purchased by said Daughtry at Lovett's sale Aug 1837...
John Walton, P.R.
                              W.G. Daughtry

316 1 Sep 1838--Abel Rogerson to Edward Decormis...$96.19...1 bay horse, 9 hogs, 2 sows and pigs; now in possession of John Lovett...
Wm. H. Gwin
                              Abel Rogerson

316 17 Nov 1838--Richard Blanchard and wife, Margaret, to Edward Hobbs...$10...10 acres bounded on W by Walton Hobbs, N by Easter Mitchell, E by William Perry and S by Edward Hobbs; it being all that tract of land conveyed to Margaret Stallings by said Edward Hobbs...
                              Richard(x)Blanchard
P.B. Minton   Margaret(x)Blanchard
Riddick Gatling and John Willey testified said Margaret signed freely.

317 16 Jun 1838--Washington Blanchard to Riddick Blanchard...$32 all rights in 100 acres of land formerly belonging to Absylla Blanchard, late of county, and adjoining lands of Miles Brown, Benjamin Brown and others...
                              Washington(x)Blancha
Henry E. Blanchard
Mary(x)Blanchard

318 16 Nov 1838--William R. Boothe to James Parker...$125...___ acres beginning at white oak on N side of new road adjoining Nisum Cuff, along his line NE to new road S to main road and along it to William A. Mathews line on land formerly owned by Daniel Field S to a sourwood corner, adjoining land of Allen Smith, thence along Smith's line W to Andrew Easons to a black gum, a corner tree on land belonging to heirs of Harrison Vann, along Vann's line N to red oak on main road...
                              Wm. R. Boothe
John Figg
Andrew Eason

319 13 Jul 1837--James Baker to Abel Rogerson...$10...40 acres of marsh land between Bennetts Creek and Chowan River, beginning at John Roberts upper windless running W to Mud Creek and back to Bennetts Creek...
                 James Baker
Elisha Walton
William H. Goodman

319 6 Feb 1838--Ephraim Bunch to Thomas Forehand, both of Chowan, $150...75 acres beginning at a cypress in Warwick Swamp, a corner betwixt John Felton and said Bunch, running a line of marked trees E along Felton's line then N to Moses Hurdles and along his line to a pine stump and 4 small oaks, Willis Bunch Jr. corner...
                 Ephraim(x)Bunch
Guy Hobbs
Willis Bunch

320 6 Oct 1838--Prisylla Cross to Sarah Cross...$1.00...deed of gift of 1 bed and furniture, 1 chest, 1 bowl and pitcher, coffee pot, 1 pair warping bars and all money I may have at my death and any that may be due me from Henry Gilliam in consequence of sale of my interest in estate of late Daniel Parker, dec...
                 Prisylla(x)Cross
H. Gilliam
Isaac Williams

320 19 Nov 1838--Andrew Doughtie and wife, Barsheba, Washington Blanchard and Rosa Blanchard to Riddick Blanchard...$32...their undivided interest in 100 acres belonging to their sister, Nancy Blanchard, adjoining lands of Miles Brown, William Blanchard, William Pearce, Benjamin Brown and others...

Frederick Blanchard
                 Andrew(x)Dougtie
                 Barsheba(x)Doughtie
Lemuel Riddick and A.W. Parker testified Washington(x)Blanchard
Barsheba signed deed of her own free will. Rosa(x)Blanchard

321 1 Nov 1838--Jesse Eason to Sally, Leah, Barsheba and Seany Perry...$20...tract of land beginning at corner of Elisha Eason in Luke Hollowell line to John Kelly's line and along his line, including 10 acres of parallel land...
Wm. Bunch   Jesse Eason
Jet. H. Riddick

321 20 Nov 1837--Milton Eason to Abel Rogerson...$90...80 acres, his life rights in land his father gave him, beginning at main road at Quinton Trotman's line S along line of marked trees along William Simpson's line to the swamp, to Jesse Hobbs line and down swamp to Amos Hobbs, to Nathan Riddicks and along his line to said Trotmans and main road...
                 Milton Eason
Jas. Blanchard
Wm. H. Goodman

322 30 Oct 1838--James T. Freeman to Elisha Bond...$20...20 acres on S side of Spring Branch, beginning at a gum in run, S to Bond's other land to a pine corner of old field and down field W to pocosin to aforesaid branch and up branch; it being land Jesse Reed purchased of Dempsey Bond, dec....
                 James T. Freeman

Clement Hill

323 18 Sep 1838--Ann Harvey to John C. Gordon...$1300...400 acres on N side of Goff Swamp and on E side of road from Virginia to Gatesville, beginning at foot of Pipkin's avenue near a small oak along avenue to run of swamp to a pine stump, corner on said Gordon and Dempsey Parker, a strait line to corner of Parkers and Harveys SW to road...
                                                             Ann N. Harvey
J.R. Riddick
Nancy Parker

324 25 Jul 1838--William W. Hayes to John Roberts...$650...84 acres on main road leading from Edenton to Gatesville, beginning at a ditch, a corner on Leah Hinton's land, running S down ditch to John Robert's line, W along his line to a corner of Reuben Hinton, dec. N to James Boothe, dec. line to road and down road...
                                                             Wm.W. Hays
Mills Roberts

324 20 Aug 1838--Edward Hare to John Walton...$76...11 acres, whereon his father, John Hare Sr., lived at time of his death and given to him in his will, adjoining lands of said Walton, William Hays and others...
                                                             Edward Hare
T.A. Jordon
James Hare

325 4 Nov 1837--Isaac R. Hunter to Whitmill and Joseph Hill...$900 300 acres adjoining land of William Reed, Willis Harrell and others.
                                                             Isaac R. Hunter
James D. Parker Jr.
Costen Jordan

325 22 Aug 1838--Elijah Harrell to Riddick Cross...$636...172-acre plantation on Bennetts Creek, beginning at Zachariah Hays line, along his line to a pine near Honey Pot Road, along road toward Gatesville, to swamp and to said creek...
                                                             Elijah Harrell
Simmonds Roundtree
Zachariah Hays

326 2 Oct 1838--James Jones to Simmonds Roundtree...$1.00 and to make safe to Soloman Roundtree debt of $270...land which said Jones bought of Soloman Roundtree, joining land of James R. Riddick, Job R. Hall and others...
                                                             James(x)Jones
Henry M. Daughtry
Jet H. Riddick

327 25 Oct 1838--Easter Mitchell to Thomas Hurdle...$25...50 acres beginning at Fox Branch at a black gum, running N to Jesse Hobbs land, along his line E to T.G. Trotman's and along his line to Old Hobbs Track, now the Mitchell land, and along Mitchell's line to black gum at Fox Branch; it being all that land called Richard Walton Tract...
                                                             Easther Mitchell
P.B. Minton
Washington(x)Spivey

328 25 Oct 1838--Easther Mitchell to Charity Spivey...1 cent... farm let on tract of land which William Spivey, dec. had a lease from John Mitchell for 15 years and bounded on N by new road, on W by path and containing 20,000 corn hills. Said Charity to have for 10 years and after first two years, starting 1 Jan, to pay 1/3 of all crops except peas to said Easther...
                                                             Easter Mitchell
    Thomas (x) Hurdle
    P.B. Minton   Charity(x)Spivey

328 17 Nov 1838--Easter Mitchell, being old and infirm in body, but of perfect mind and recollection, appoints Peter B. Minton as her attorney...
Drew Welch   Easther(x)Mitchell

329 12 Aug 1838--Willoughby Manning and wife, Mary, to David Benton...$15...1/6 of a 75-acre tract, it being land which James Wiggens died seized and possessed of, adjoining land of Wilie Riddick, said Benton and others...
                                             Willoughby Manning
Jesse Wiggens   Mary Ann Manning

329 24 Nov 1837--Rodon Odom to Bray Parker...$31.37½...22 acres adjoining lands of said Parker and beginning at a corner of Parker and John Gatling, running SE to road to a sweet gum on said Odoms NW to a marked stake corner on Odoms and Gatlings and NE along Gatlings line...
                                             Rodon Odom
Wm. L. Boothe

330 15 Mar 1838--David Parker to Mills Roberts...$75...50 acres conveyed to him in a deed of trust 11 Aug 1837 by Nathaniel Jones and is land whereon said Jones lived, adjoining land of Henry Trevathan, James Hare, Riddick Smith, Robert Jordon and Reuben Hinton, dec....
                                             D. Parker,
John Walton   trustee
James H. Parker

331 15 Mar 1838--Elizabeth Jones, widow of Nathaniel Jones, relinquishes her rights to above mentioned land, which was conveyed to David Parker by her husband and now conveyed to Mills Roberts by said Parker...
D. Parker   Elizabeth(x)Jones
James H. Parker

332 20 Nov 1838--Mills Roberts to Henry Trevathan...$75...50 acres of land conveyed to him by David Parker and formerly belonging to Nathaniel Jones, dec.
                                             Mills Roberts
D. Parker

332 20 Mar 1837--William E. Pugh, CME, to William G. Daughtry...$529...150 acres belonging to Elizabeth Beeman, of full age, Israel and William Beeman, infants by their guardian, John C. Gordon by their court petition. Land adjoins Wm. G. Daughtry, Reuben Harrell and John B. Baker

332 23 Jan 1838--Elisha N. Riddick, executor of Daniel Stallings, dec. to Joseph Riddick...$500...Negro girl, Ester...
                                             Elisha N. Riddick
J.R. Kee

333 4 Oct 1838--Robert Riddick Sr. to son, Henry...gift of 30 acres of land whereon said Henry lives and bounded on N by ditch, nearly before Richard Briggs door and is dividing line between land reserved by said Robert and his wife, Elizabeth, and a tract given in his will to his son, James A. Riddick, and bounded on E by main road, S by line of fence commencing at road near an old cherry tree, running W across plantation along by still house, down to

branch then N. Also, for $2000...balance of his land, 356 acres bounded on E by main road, S by land of Henry Riddick and W by Edward R. Hunter and Rissop Rawls, another tract on E side of main road beginning at stump in Richard Briggs line E to dead stump on Benjamin Jones line, S to a branch to the line of Wiley P. Jones and SE to Luke Green's to Bee Tree Pond to line between Luke Green, Andrew Harrell and said Robert Riddick, to James Woodwards, to Thomas Rice, to Mrs. Mary Goodman's line NW to Robert Hills and N to said Henry Riddick. Also a 6 acre tract on side of main road before gate to yard and bounded on NE and S by land of Richard and Edward Briggs and W by road; another 25 acre tract on E side of road out of tract given to James A. Riddick...
Edward Briggs   Robert Riddick
J.R. Hunter

334 1 Oct 1838--James R. Riddick, sheriff, to Kedar Powell...85¢ for 1835 taxes on land belonging to Jacob Powell...27 acres beginning at a stump in said Kedar's line, along road SW to lane NW to pine in swamp, corner on Henry Bond's, up swamp NE, corner on Hoflers and SE...
Wm. M. Dorcy   J.R. Riddick
Orren B. Savage

335 1 Sep 1838--Simmonds Roundtree to Soloman Roundtree...$300... 4 acres in Gatesville adjoining land of John P. Savage, Henry Gilliam and Jesse Brown...
                                                            Simmonds Roundtr
John Figg
Job R. Hall

336 1 Sep 1838--Soloman Roundtree to Simmonds Roundtree...$300... 4 acres conveyed to him by deed of trust, lot in Gatesville, bounded by road leading to Somerton, land of John P. Savage, Henry Gilliam and Jesse Brown...
                                                            Soloman Roundtre
Job R. Hall
John Figg

336 5 Dec 1836--Willis I. Riddick to Elizabeth Morress...$25...37½ acres, which was conveyed to him by deed of trust Sep 1834 by Frederick Morris, to insure debt to James T. Freeman...
Jo. Riddick   Willis I. Riddic
Reuben Hinton

337 1 Jan 1838--William E. Pugh to William G. Daughtry...$1000... 2-acre lot in village of Gatesville, conveyed to him by John Lovett, and occupied as store and dwelling by said Lovett, bounded by road leading from Somerton, by lands of Asa Hill, heirs of Thomas Saunders and lands of Allen Daughtry...
Ja. R. Riddick   Wm. E. Pugh by
Thos. A. Jordon   Rufus K. Speed, his attorney

238 19 Nov 1838--John P. Savage to Margaret Savage...$100...4 acres in Gatesville bounded on N by Soloman Roundtree, W by Henry Gilliam, S by Henry S. Blount and E by main street...
H.M. Daughtry   John P. Savage
Wm. F. Cowper

238 24 Aug 1838--Fanny Smith to John W. Odom...$20...15 acres in
fork of Mills Swamp bounded by lands of Samuel Cross, said Smith
and said Odom...
James Arline   Fanny(x)Smith
Purvis Dilday

339 15 Oct 1838--Riddick Smith to William Jones...$40...10 acres
beginning at a white oak in Henry Boothe's line, formerly John
Lewis line, S to Boothe's corner, along branch E to a white oak,
Joseph Hays corner, formerly called the Howell Tract, then N along
Hays line to said Jones and is piece of land that said Smith bought
of John Jones, formerly belonging to Dempsey Jones...
                                            Riddick(x)Smith

340 19 Nov 1838--John P. Savage to Margaret Savage...$200...65
acres bounded by land of Eff Lewis, dec, lands of Isaac Pipkin
and William W. Cowper...
H. Willey   John P. Savage
H.M. Daughtry

340 23 Oct 1837--Thomas Twine to Isaac R. Hunter...$3300...592 acres
adjoining lands of Rissop Rawls, John Granbery, John Rawls and others.
                                            Thomas Twine
George Costen
Andrew Johnson

341 19 Jan 1839--Boon Eure to Willis Cross...$1.00...79 acres to
make safe to Abraham W. Parker, who is his security for three notes
of $50 each to Dempsey Sparkman, beginning at a large corner pine
on said Parker and Jethro Eure's running Eure's line to a red oak
corner on said Eure and Shadrack Felton, thence SW to a pine, then
to a maple NW to a corner of said Sparkman and Wiley Carter to a
line of marked trees...   Boon(x)Eure
Washington Harrell   A.W. Parker
D. Sparkman   Willis Cross

342 11 Sep 1838--Elvey Lewis of Barbour Co., Ala., executor of
will of Molly Lewis, dec., formerly of Gates and Robert Dill and
wife, Mary, late widow of William W. McDaniel, dec. and daughter
of said Elvey, who are both legatees of said Molly...appoint their
friend, Lewis Smith of Barbour Co. as their attorney to recover
for them any property, especially slaves, Peg and Stephen, mentioned in will of said Molly 6 Oct 1821, and lent to Eff Lewis in
North Carolina, now dead...   Elvey Lewis
Anderson Crenshaw, judge of   Robert Dill
6th Jud. Circuit of Ala.   Mary Dill
Neal McDonald, clerk

343 18 Sep 1838--William G. Daughtry to Edward Decormis of borough of Norfolk...$1000...1 acre in village of Gatesville, bounded
by road leading to Somerton, lands of Asa Hill, heirs of Thomas
Saunders and heirs of Allen Daughtry, and now occupied as a store
and dwelling...   W.G. Daughtry
Wm. M. Dorcy
Henry M. Daughtry

344 5 Oct 1838--Mary Haslett to Jethro S. Haslett $1.00...gift of 1 acre in village of Gatesville, bounded on E by road leading to Somerton, S and W by lands of Henry Gilliam and on N by land of Henry S. Blount...
Jennings A. Blount   Mary (x) Haslett
Anna Bond

344 25 Feb 1837--Thomas Rice to John G. Liles...$120...50 acres, part of a tract he bought of James Woodward, adjoining said Woodward, Mary Goodman, Robert Reddick and Andrew Harrell on road...
James Woodward   Thomas Rice
A.R. Harrell

345 30 Oct 1838--Norman King to Joseph Hurdle...$200...50 acres adjoining lands of William King, Christian Twine and others...
Burwell Brothers   Norman(x)King
Isaac Eason

346 7 Mar 1839--Nathaniel Curl to Nathaniel Eure and William W. Cowper...$1.00 and to secure bond to Henry Gilliam for $100.73 46 acres bounded by land of Henry Carter, James Carter and Pleasant Piland; it being land whereon he resides and by a tract he owns in right of his wife, Mildred; it being dower from her former husband. Also, 3 feather beds and furniture, 1 table, 1 desk, household and kitchen furniture, cart and wheels, gear, implements of husbandry, 9 head cattle and 6 head hogs...
                                                 Richard(x)Curl
Blake Brady   Nath'l Eure
Belver Sears   Wm.W. Cowper

347 12 Mar 1839--Richard Curl to William W. Cowper...$37.60...1 bay mare, 4 years old...
Blake Brady   Richard(x)Curl
Belver Sears

347 30 Dec 1837--Holloday Walton to Nathan A. Stedman...$215... 29 acres whereon William W. Stedman lately resided, adjoining lands of Richard H. Ballard, John Powell and others; for sole and separate use of Rebecca Stedman, widow of late Wm. W. Stedman.
Jos. Gordon   Holloday Walton
Whit'l Stallings

348 3 Sep 1838--Dolphin Drew of Perry County, Ala. appoints John P. Savage as his attorney to receive from John Walton, esq., administrator of Pryor Savage, dec. any money to be received in right of his wife, Margaret Jane, daughter of said Pryor...
Lem. Parker   Dolphin Drew

349 29 Jan 1839--John Allen to Jethro Willey...$1.00 and to make safe to John Willey debt of $440...deed in trust of 2 Negro boys, Luke and Charles...
                                                 John Allen
                                                 Jethro Willey
Exum Lewis   John Willey

350 19 Feb 1839--Thomas Edward Riddick to Richard H. Parker, Willis F. Riddick, James R. Riddick and James M. Riddick, trustees of Jane R. Bennett...50¢ and $2000 for 202 acres of land: Whereas, James M. Riddick and William F. Bennett and his wife, said Jane R. have executed unto said Thomas Edward Riddick all

that tract of land bounded on N by land of James M. Riddick,
W by William A. Matthews, S by Willis F. Riddick and E by main
road leading from Gatesville to Middle Swamp. The said James M.
Riddick was entitled to life estate of William F. Bennett, who became tenant by curtesy by his intermarriage with said Jane and
birth of a child, which said estate of said William F. Bennett
was devised by aforesaid James M., having become the purchaser
thereof and said Jane being owner of the fee simple estate in
said land. She consents to conveyance of her interest to be held
in trust and said Thomas Edward Riddick for 50¢ sells 200 acre
tract of land bounded on W by Richard H. Parker, N by Rissop Rawls
and Robert Riddick and on E by land of Isaac R. Hunters heirs and
on S by James Costens land, running down to George's Marsh. All
rents, etc. to be paid to said Jane and if she should die before
her husband land should be conveyed to her child or children...
                                        Thos. E. Riddick   Willis F. Riddick
                                        Rich'd H. Parker   J.R. Riddick
Jacob E. Hunter   James M. Riddick

353 21 Aug 1838--Abraham Pearce to Archibald R. Jones...$1.00...
deed in trust of 100 acres for a note for $59 made 19 Feb 1838 to
Thomas Twine for which Alfred Jones is security and witnessed by
Reuben Lassiter; tract of land adjoins Enoch Pearce, said Archibald Jones and Kedar Lassiter...
                                                           Abraham(x)Pearce
Ezekiel T. Jones

354 1 Feb 1839--John Wiggens to Jesse Wiggens...$1.00 and to make
safe to David Benton $1000 note...300 acres of several tracts, including 40 acres at crossroads, adjoining land of Seth Benton, John
V. Sumner, to Bennetts Creek, down creek to Hog Swamp, up swamp to
road adjoining lands of David Benton...   Jno. Wiggens
Jordon Parker
Henry Pearce

355 2 Jan 1839--James Barnes of Nansemond to William Lee...$150...
95½ acres beginning at said Lee's on tract of land purchased of
Robert Rogers, thence running N to run of Beach Swamp and up run
of swamp to Mrs. Fanny Smith's line and along her line S to a
corner on Mills Rogers' heirs land thence along their line W to
Lee's land...   James Barnes
Francis Duke
Wm. H. Lee

356 3 Jan 1839--James Barnes of Nansemond to Francis Duke...$150...
84 acres beginning at a gum in or near run of Long Branch, corner
on Fanny Smiths and Mills Rogers, dec. heirs, then down branch on
Smith's line to John W. Odom's line and along his line up branch
to Edward Howell's line and along Howell's line to Smiths and along Smith's line...   James Barnes
Wm. Lee
Wm. H. Lee
John Willey

356 23 Apr 1839--Martha Beeman to Mills Sparkman...$300...her interest in 300-acre plantation given to her in will of Abram Beeman
esq., dec., adjoining lands of Dempsey Sparkman, William L. Boothe,

Charney Umphflet, Dempsey Parker and others...
Wm. L. Boothe   Martha Beeman
D. Sparkman

357 23 Apr 1839--Nathaniel Harrell to Dempsey Sparkman...$1.00
and to secure several debts to him...plantation whereon said
Harrell lives commencing at a water oak near Meeting House, corner tree in John King's line, thence a line of marked trees along King's line to a white oak, a corner in Jethro Eure's line
and along Eure's line to Coles Creek, up creek and across road to
Abraham W. Parker's line and along his line...with all crops of
wheat, corn and potatoes and 1 white horse, 1 cart and wheels, 1
gig and harness, 4 head cattle, 11 hogs, 2 beds and furniture, 1
loom, 12 sitting chairs, 1 wood clock, 1 cast pot, 1 dutch oven,
1 kettle and spider, 5 barrels of corn, 200 pds. bacon, 800 pds.
fodder, 4 tables and 3 pine chests...
                                                    Nathaniel Harrell
John Riddick

358 8 Sep 1838--William C. Brooks, executor of his father, William
Brooks Sr., in obedience with wishes in his will dated 18 June 1836,
which was proved in May term of court 1837, offered at public sale
257 acres of land on which Elisha Harrell (agent of Elijah Harrell)
bid $2.60 per acre on land, bounded on W by Coles Creek, commencing
at a maple on S side of creek, running along line of marked trees
to mouth of Trumpet Marsh Branch, and along main run of branch to
main road running from Baker's Mill to Gatesville, along road to
John Worrells corner (formerly Bakers) SW to a stump corner on Worrells thence to run of said creek...
                                                    Will.C. Brooks
H. Gilliam
Thos. A. Jordan
Feb Ct 1839

359 2 Feb 1839--Miles Briggs to Wiley P. Jones...$160...50 acres
beginning at a pine, a corner tree in Richard A. Ballards, Elisha
Small's and Edward Parker's line, thence along Small's line to
said Jones and to said Parkers...
                                                    Miles Briggs
Ben. B. Ballard
John Benton

359 17 Aug 1838--Prissilla Cross to Hardy D. Parker...$525...two
Negroes, Peter and Nelvy...
                                                    Prissilla(x)Cross
James Rogers

359 17 Aug 1838--Prissilla Cross to Henry Gilliam...$150 and for
like sum of $150 annually on 22 Sep each year during her lifetime,
her interest in estate of Daniel Parker, dec...
                                                    Prissilla(x)Cross
Jonathan Williams

360 18 Feb 1839--James Carter and wife, Emma, to Miles Parker...
$1205...her share in division of land of Lewis Eure, dec. being
5, 406 acres, beginning at a sweet gum in Beaverdam Swamp along
Mills Eure Sr.'s line to a pine, a corner tree of Elijah Hare's
line to a white oak, a corner tree on Miles Howell's and John

Everett's, thence up run of said branch to an elm, a corner tree in Beaverdam Swamp and along run of swamp...

Wm. L. Boothe
D.M. Saunders

James Carter
Emma Carter

361 28 Jul 1838--Richard F. Goodwin and wife, Martha E., of Nansemond to Thomas E. Riddick...$500...part of an undivided tract of 160 acres bounded by land of Willis F. Riddick and James M. Riddick; it being part of land of Micajah Riddick, dec. and assigned to said Martha E. (then Martha E. Barnes) and Mary A. Barnes, two of the heirs of said Micajah, dec. being the children of Elizabeth Barnes, who was daughter of said Micajah...

Thos. J. Kilby
Thos. G. Benton

Richard F. Goodwin
Martha E. Goodwin

362 15 Jan 1839--Nansemond: Richard H. Baker, one of judges of General Court and judge in First Circuit in first district of the Circuit Superior Courts of Law and Chancery in state of Virginia, certified to recording of deed and that said Martha signed freely. David Campbell, governor at office in city of Richmond, and William H. Richardson, sec. and keeper of seal, witnessed...

363 21 Aug 1815--James Granbery to Frederick B. Sawyer of Pasquotank...$400...1500 acres, part of a 3000-acre tract in Dismal Swamp, patented by John Fountain and conveyed to William Durant and by him conveyed to John Cowper, beginning at corner of Fontain's 1500-acre purchase of Isaac Hunter, running E and then SW to Fontain's corner.

Jos. Gordon
Wm. S. Barnes
Feb Ct 1839

Ja. Granbery

364 10 Nov 1836--John C. Gordon, executor, of Nancy Granbery, dec. to Joseph Gordon...$680...100 acres of high land on which she lately lived, beginning at public road at said Joseph's corner, E along his line to Horsepool Swamp, N to a pine at end of point of high land at foot of Mills Riddick's shingle road, to George G. Harvey's line W along his line to road and S...

J. Riddick

John C. Gordon

365 27 May 1836--H. Gilliam to Richard Hinton...$227.76...Negro girl Millery sold by him as administrator of Benjamin Hayes, dec. 21 Nov 1833, and purchased by his wife, Martha Hays, who was at that time not married...

H. Gilliam

365 29 Dec 1838--Edward R. Hunter to Thomas E. Riddick...$2000 200 acres beginning at a beach on George's Marsh in Richard H. Parker's line, along his line crossing road near Parker's house, then by a line of marked trees to Rissop Rawls line to Robert and Henry Riddick's line and along said Henry's line to a sweet gum on road S to fork of road and W to branch binding on land of heirs of Isaac R. Hunter, dec. to James Costen's line and along his line...

E.R. Hunter

Ben. B. Ballard
Richard H. Parker

366 12 Dec 1837--Thomas and Amos Hobbs to Dempsey Hobbs...$100 50 acres beginning at post oak, a corner tree in John Mitchell's line and said Dempsey's line N to William Hobbs line to Amos Hobbs line E to a black gum, corner of Guy Hobbs, along his line S to Mordeca Perry's line to John Mitchell's...
Jordon Hobbs Thomas(x)Hobbs
Guy Hobbs Amos Hobbs

366 15 Jan 1839--Zachariah Hays to Marmaduke Norfleet...$350... 58 acres beginning at an ash tree in Hawtree Swamp and down run to Bennetts Creek to Riddick Cross' line...
Zachariah Hays
John Harrell
John M. Beeman

367 24 Sep 1838--Elisha R. Hunter to Calvin R. Brinkley...$210... 55 acres beginning at a water oak on road running S along Daniel S. Ward's line to run of Catherine Swamp and along run to Harry Hunter's line of marked trees to a red oak and W along road...
Elisha R. Hunter
J. Kee
Henry King

368 16 Feb 1839--Edward Howell and wife, Sally, of Nansemond to Jonathan Williams...$150...60 acres beginning at a sweet gum on Lawrence Branch, James Barnes corner tree, along his and Fanny Smith's line to James Rogers and Jonathan Williams corner tree and along William's line to William K. Moore's to Lawrence Branch to Mary Odom's corner tree and down branch...
Feb Ct 1839 Edw'd Howell
Henry Gilliam and Jos. Riddick, justices Sally Howell
testified said Sally signed freely.

369 16 Apr 1838--Edward Hobbs to Whitmill Stallings...$1400...Negro, Prissilla and child, Ellick; Sarah and child, Penelope; Jane and Mary...
Frederick Rooks Edward(x)Hobbs

369 24 Jan 1839--Thomas Hoggard to John Brinkley...$130...60 acres, part of land he bought of Lassiter Riddick, on E side of road from Wynns Ferry to Suffolk, beginning at a pine to Sand Banks, to Elisha Umphflets line to William G. Daughtry's and along his line to Sarah B. Saunders line and along her line to Wynns Ferry Road...
Thomas Hoggard
Arther Smith
John O. Hoggard

70 31 Aug 1838--Whitmill Jones to William Jones...$60...26 acres beginning at a water oak on corner of Nancy Jones running SW to a pine thence NW to a red oak on said William Jones to a water oak in swamp; being land he drew in division of his fathers estate...
J. Willey Whitmill(x)Jones
Jesse Parker

70 4 Feb 1839--William Jones to Joseph Hays...$44...11 acres beginning at a holly, corner on said Hays and Mills Roberts, SW to a white oak corner on John Hays and said Jones SE to Jones and Hays line and NW to said Roberts...
Wm. R. Boothe Wm.P. Jones
James Smith

371 10 Feb 1839--Archibald R. Jones to Nathan Pearce...$500...167 acres binding on lands of David Parker, Kedar Lassiter and others.
Moses Trotman   Archibald R. Jones

372 14 Jan 1839--James Mathias to Riddick Jones...$10...Negro woman, Wina...
                                                 James Mathias
Wm. H. McGuire

372 22 Sep 1838--Willoughby Manning to Jesse Wiggens...$1.00 and to make safe to David Benton debt of $375...100 acres adjoining Humphrey Parker, Riddicks Mill Pond and James Morgan...
Henry Pearce   Willoughby Manning
Jesse P. Wiggens

372 3 May 1838--Jane Miller to William Miller...$50...32 acres, her part in her father's land, adjoining lands of William Miller, Elizabeth Miller and others...
                                                 Jane Miller
William R. Brothers
Elizabeth Duke

The following deed was inadvertently left out of Book 14, my previous volume.

14-412 7 Jan 1832--Sarah Parker to John Matthews...$18...4 acres, her part of land inherited by death of uncle, Robert Parker, and bounded by land of John Matthews, Briant Brothers, John Gatling and others.
Anthony Matthews   Sarah (x) Parker
R. Matthews

Also, witnesses for the deed of Elisha Walton to Reuben Hinton, which precedes the Sarah Parker deed were H. Gilliam and Arodi Draper and not Anthony Matthews and R. Matthews, as I show. Book 14 p. 80

INDEX

Allen, John 38,92,124
  Joshua 9,54,80,86,106
  Nathaniel 85
  Thomas W.G. 87
Alpin, Docton 4
  John 6,24,45,70,75,92,99,115
  Leah 45
Anderson, John A. 18,68,94
Arline, James 40,41,51,123
  Jesse 31,51,81,108
Arnold, Edward 104
  John 37,63,66,104
  Richard 3
  Riddick 44
  William 32,58,63,64,71,86
Austin, Richard 51,81

Babb, William 24,115
Bagley, Martha S. 56
  Thomas 11,56
Baker, Andrew 8,34,58,66,79
  Armesia 117
  Blake 2,47,49,69,106
  Hardy 8
  James 1,8,22,34,35,58,60,
  84,110,119
  James Jr. 1,22,79 Sr. 1
  John B. 2,6,11,15,17,25,38,
  39,49,65,71,72,73,74,76,84,
  95,102,108,112,113,115,116,
  121
  ~~Lemuel 2~~
  ~~Margaret 2~~
  Marmaduke 16
  Richard B. 40
  Richard H. 88,117,127
  Samuel 106
  William 60,117
  Wm. J. 71,72,73,95,102,113
  Wynns 35,84,102,117
Ballard, Alfred 18,20,37
  Benjamin B. 6,9,34,72,75,
  94,105,111,126,127
  James A. 10,25,41,66,71,74
  Jethro A. 10,23
  Kedar 18
  Margaret 18,54
  Mary Jane 18
  Richard A. 126
  Richard H. 19,27,38,41,69,
  76,91,99,108,124
  Robert H. 76,77
  William 21
Barnes, Benjamin 39
  Elizabeth 127

Barnes, James 4,69,125,128
  Jethro 27,28
  John 8,37,76
  Joseph J. 6,11,34
  Louisa R. 34
  Martha E. 127
  Mary A. 102,127
  Mildred 85
  William S. 4,5,22,39,88,127
Barr, Britton 8,51
  John R. 8,46
  Wright 51
  William 51
Beasley, William 96
Beeman, Abraham 13,56,59,96,125
  Elizabeth 96,104,121
  Israel 96,104,121
  John 1,10,41,55,112,128
  Levi 35,59,60,111
  Lucretia 59,105
  Martha 125,126
  William 96,104,121
Bennett, Jane R. 124,125
  William F. 50,66,73,102,124,125
Benton, Abraham 27,46,51,67,77,78
  Benjamin 27
  David 3,5,8,18,27,32,37,44,57,67,
  76,77,84,97,99,102,107,112,113,
  117,121,125
  Elisha 27,77
  Elizabeth 27
  Henry 42
  James 4,5,40,43,62,63,68,85,104
  Jesse 2,42,51
  Jethro 51
  John 2,42,51,61,73,126
  John P. 20,37,92,102,109
  Joseph 27,32,67,77,78,113
  Lemuel 25,42,51
  Margaret 51
  Mary 69
  Miles 16,35
  Noah B. 31
  Seth 4,27,37,73,82,87,89,90,125
  Sidney 27
  Susanna 27
  Thomas G. 15,110,127
  William 38,99
  W.T. 112
Best, Bryant B. 22
  Mary 22
Billups, Joseph R. 61
  Mary 61
Blades, Abraham 38
  William 111

Blanchard, A. 60
  Absolom 7,21,24,58
  Absylla 59,118
  Benjamin Sr. 7
  Currie 71,107
  Easton 9,45,56,57,60,82,107
  Elisha 75
  Frederick 61,119
  Henry E. 9,57,60,61,68,71,
    86,103,110,118
  James 119
  Jethro 19,26,27,47,58,60,61,
    71,86,92,93,103,107,109,110
  Job 68
  John Wesley 5,109
  Josiah 40
  Margaret 118
  Mary 118
  Penelope 62
  Reuben 10
  Richard 118
  Robert 45,71,109,111
  Rosa 119
  Sarah 9,11
  Washington 118,119
  William 7,11,60,119
Blount, Henry S. 35,77,79,87,
    89,91,95,101,111,122,123
  Jennings A. 87,103,123
  Sarah 89,95
Bogue, William 16
Bond, Anna 9,22,124
  Dempsey 19,23,60,97,119
  Dorothy 83
  Elisha 35,119
  Elisha H. 21,35,53,65,67,85
  Elizabeth B. 9
  Henry 3,5,13,24,27,37,43,45,
    49,58,65,67,68,78,80,101,110,
    122
  James 17
  John 11,13,18,49
  John W. 37,45,65,67,70,79,81
  Mary 47
  Mildred 35
  Nancy 12,14,19,24,37,62,111,
    113
  Priscilla 40
  Richard 39
  Samuel S. 39,62
  Stuart S. 83,85,106
  Thomas 47
  Willis 60
  William 39

Booker, A.B. 79
Boon, Zachariah 33,52
Boss, Odah 78
Boothe, Francis 90
  Henning 108
  Henry 58,90,104,105,123
  James 1,11,40,44,47,48,51,52,
    90,91,108,112,120
  John 90
  Martha 90
  Robert 15
  William 80,85,90,104,108
  William L. 2,7,9,10,13,22,31,35,
    38,42,44,45,52,55,56,59,68,72,74,
    81,82,83,96,104,105,112,113,116,
    117,118,121,125,126,127
  William R. 128
Bowden, Robert W. 17,35
Boyce, Deborah 9,10
  Elizabeth (Louisa) 113
  James 2,9,10,14,16,36,41,48,63,
    105,113,117
  John 24
  Mary 113
  William 2,105,113
Boyt, David 8
  Etheldred 62
  Richard 25
Brady, Blake 44,93,106,108,124
  Elizabeth 68
  James 41,68,98
  John 106
Bramble, William 87
Briggs, Allen 32,89
  Benjamin 93
  Charles 39,61,117
  Charlotte 112
  Edward 93,94,122
  Henry S. 9
  James 32,52,62,91,109,114
  Jethro 86
  Josiah 32,39,63,112
  Julia Ann 93,94
  Kedar 19,20,86
  Miles 19,20,36,69,74,86,91,93,
    94,100,109,111,126
  Richard 93,121,122
  Solloman 19,79,86,97
  Thamer 13,50
  Wesley 19
Brinkley, Abraham 107
  Ammon 55
  Benjamin 10,68
  Calvin 23,35,38,106,128

Brinkley, Cynthia 38
  Daniel 87
  David 41,63,68
  Elisha 10,23,41
  Henry 66
  Isaac 55
  James 1,9,10,17,33,41,51,
    54,94,99,102,106,117
  Jerry 55
  Jethro 55
  John 23,113,128
  Louisa 55
  Mary 78,86
  Miles 68,78
  Owen 78
  Penny 10
  Polly 10
  Riddick 86
  Simon 20
  Timothy 55
  William 43,77
Brisco, Elizabeth 109
  Mary 5
Britt, B.W. 114
  Enoch 52
  James 114
Brooks, Catherine 82
  George 8,26,56,61,74
  Joseph 56,60,82,96
  Margaret C. 26,57,61,71
  William 72,82,126
  William C. 82,126
Brothers, Bryant 9,12,40,45,
    59,70,103,113
  Burwell 11,13,57,58,66,79,
    104,124
  Jacob 19
  John 32,69
  Mary 49
  Warren 103
  William 16,36,49,59,72
Brown, Benjamin 7,19,42,58,59,
    60,68,108,118
  Elizabeth 56
  James 12,44,54,55,74,85,90,
    91,116
  James Sr. 113
  Jesse 3,40,56,66,75,81,82,84,
    100,101,122
  John 9,40,53,59,60
  Miles 7,42,58,59,118
  Samuel 7,19,42,56,58,65,79
  William 18,40,53,60

Brown, Willis 12,18
Bullock, Elizabeth 12
Bunch, Ephriam 83,119
  William 119
  Willis 96,105,119
Bunton, James M. 85
Burgess, Elizabeth 36
Bush, John 1
  William 1,16,29,106
Byrum, W.L. 29

Campbell, David 88,127
Cannon, Newton 114
Carr, Samuel W. 85
  Tilley W. 18,23,30,37,44,54,
    69,87,99
Carter, Annis 12
  Charles 34,38,61
  Emma 126,127
  Henry 10,12,79,82,124
  Ira 61
  Isaac 7
  James 12,82,124,126,127
  Lewis 38
  Ludey 61
  Penelope 55,57,82
  Wiley 22,52,64,123
  William 70
Casey, Willis 30
Cobb, James 87,114
Coffield, Elizabeth 16
  James 5,110
  John 16
  Joseph 30
  Josiah 5,39,69
Collins, Nancy 15
  Thomas 15
Copeland, Edwin 20
  James 69,108
  John 14,62
Coriell, Augustus 4,5
Cornelius, Thomas 117
Costen, George 12,13,26,31,44
    59,72,88,94,96,99,113,123
  Henry 4,65,69,99
  James 4,25,33,38,40,89,125,127
  James Sr. 39
  James Jr. 8,69,84,104
  Mary Ann 40
  Thomas 29
  Thomas R. 10,18,36,37,44,57,
    59,60,67,74,83,98,113
Cotter, Frances Ann 48,49
Cowper, John 6,17,36,87,127

Cowper, William 6,17,36,87
　William F. 122
　William W. 21,31,32,35,36,38,
　42,44,45,53,66,68,70,73,74,
　77,87,89,105,114,115,123,124
　Wills 3,6,17,20,22,23,24,42,
　87　Wills Jr. 4,23,113
　Thomas P. 4
Cox, Jesse I. 70,78
Crawford, Abraham 1,41,67
　John J. 74
　Odah 78
　William 15,78
Creecy, Charles 80
　James R. 32,50,91
　Levi 7,13,38,40,42
　William 50,91,92
Crenshaw, Anderson 123
Cross, Abraham 1,15,34,41,63,67
　Charity 39
　Christian 107
　Cyprian 15,42
　Cyprian R. 43
　David 11,14,15,94
　Edwin 19,23,72,73,79,99
　Elisha 23
　Hardy 8,66,69,73,93,103,
　109,110
　Harriett 67
　John 23,79
　Margaret 103
　Monica 19
　Prisylla 119,126
　Richard 33,36
　Riddick 46,120,128
　Samuel 19,51,109,123
　Sarah 119
　Taylor 9, 107
　William 69,72,73
　Willis 6,14,62,66,68,94,
　98,123
Crosslin, Jonas 54
Cuff, Daniel 7,15,84
　John 7,74,75,85
　Kesiah 84
　Levin 7,15
　Mallica 1,52
　Nisum 1,52,90,104,118
Cullens, Amos 115
　Christian 29,53
　Jacob 29,36,69
　Mary 7,44,74

Cullens, Miles 65,68,111
　Nathan 29,42,53,55,117
　Nathaniel 65,58,111
Curl, Abram 1
　Mildred 124
　Nathaniel 124
　Richard 12,124
Daniels, Elizabeth 93
　William 65,79
　Willis 93
Darden, Margaret 39
　Mary 34
　John 34
　John W. 6
　Thomas 30
　Titus 29
Daughtrie, Andrew 59,119
　Allen 39,44,47,51,78,83,116,
　117,122
　Barsheba 59,119
　Henry M. 80,83,91,100,120,121
　122,123
　Lawrence S. 3,11,13,18,21,29,59
　Nathaniel 7,16,66,106
　William G. 3,18,21,29,36,37,38,
　40,42,47,53,58,70,71,82,83,89,
　100,101,107,116,118,123,128
Davidson, William 8
Davis, Abram 1
　Elizabeth 77
　James 91
　Miles M. 7
　Thomas 57
Day, John Davis 17
Deans, John 21
Decormis, Edward 118,123
Dick, John M. 50
Dilday, Purvis 123
Dill, Mary 123
　Robert 123
Draper, Arodi 70
Drew, Dolphin 124
　Margaret Jane 124
Dorcy, William M. 122, 123
Duke, Crissey A. 108
　Daniel 22,114
　David O. 32
　Elisha 114
　Elizabeth 66,129
　Francis 62,89,102,125
　James 19
　John 3,44
　Sophia 19
Duck, Willis 117

Dunsford, David Jr. 30,67
  John 67
Durant, William 127
Dye, Matthew M. 127

Eads, Nancy 7
Eason, Abner 19,42,48,52,
  63,104
  Abraham 34,78
  Agatha 16
  Andrew 16,19,52,118
  Charles 34,40,51,92
  Elisha 89
  Frederick 40,92
  Hardy 32,34,42,67,89
  Isaac 89,124
  Jacob 37,61
  James 29
  Jesse 34,48,51,62,89,119
  Joseph R. 61
  Milton 9,33,67,75,96,
  110,119
  Soloman 34,52,89
  Thomas 34,68,85,86
  Whitty 89
Eley, Sarah 31
  William 31
Ellen, John 1,2
Ellinor, Thomas 57,95
Elliott, Rachael 106
  William H. 49
Ellis, Harrison 32,37,116,117
  Josiah 32
  Kedar 2,10,20,25,41,52,66
  Marmaduke 61
  Soloman 54
  Theresa 34
Eure, Benjamin 96
  Boon 52,55,64,123
  Bray 22,25,27,28,52,64,
  72,83,106
  Burwell 61
  Cyprian 20
  Daniel 64
  Dempsey 54,55,78,79,82
  Euriah(Uriah) 52,83
  Henry 78
  Henry L. 114
  Hillory H. 48,49
  James 10,13,32
  Jethro 71,113,123,126
  Jethro Jr. 71
  John 20,22,41,46,61
  J. Riddick 64
  Levi 64,104,109
  Levi Jr. 111
  Lewis 39,41,52,126

Eure, Mary Ann 10,20,102,114
  Mildred 71
  Mills 2,10,22,25,26,28,46,54,55
  56,64,73,74,78,82,96,105,118,126
  Nancy 12,56
  Nathaniel 10,53,65,91,124
  Peter 10,12,55,92
  Riddick B. 56,65,111
  Rodon 111
  Samuel 55,65,111
  Samuel Jr. 82
  Sarah 27
  Senea 115
  Tinson Y. 65,71
Evans, James 64
  John 12
  Mary 78
  Nancy 78
  Samuel 78
  Willis 78
Everitt, Armety 30
  John 30,92,126

Fairless, Jos. A. 30
Fareboult, J.H. 5
Felton, David 5,25
  David F. 51,70,101
  Edward 102
  Fisher 17,47,90
  John 84,96,100,119
  John H. 78
  John R. 1,17,37,73,101
  Samuel 25,60,70,101,115
  Shadrack 37,123
  Kedar 53,74,80
  Noah 101
Ferebee, George 4,5
Fields, Daniel 24,35,52,74,118
  Mills R. 15,41,47,49,102
  Lemuel K. 47,69
  Richard H. 47,49,69,74
Faison, Gulielma Mariah 108
  Herod 108
Faulk(Fowlkes) Elizabeth 45
  Jeptha 3,11,14,24,29,37,60
  William 45
Figg, James 40,63
  John 7,40,62,63,80,118,122
Flood, Dempsey 16
  Mary 16
Fontaine, John 5,127
Forbes, John 3
Forehand, Thomas 119
Fowler, Charles 3,5,39
Franklin, Benjamin 23,52,66,86,111
  Jason 58,71,111
  Mary 74

Freeman, Alexander 9
  David 112
  Felisha 56
  George 11,67
  Isaac P. 2
  James 34,35,112
  James T. 5,9,17,18,10,24,32,
    36,44,60,64,70,76,97,107
  John 35
  Joseph 35,66,102,112
  L.D. 107
  Walton 8,12,13,58,66,69,
    103,115
Fryer, Isaac 3

Gardner, George H. 117
Garrett, James 66
Gatling, Ann 115
  Arthur 74
  D. 93
  Etheldred B. 85,114
  James 68,94,98,99
  John 2,9,18,25,42,47,65,79,
    83,94,109,115,121
  Joseph 35,115
  Harriett B. 39
  Mary Jane 39
  John B. 35,39
  Miles 74
  Nancy 73
  Pleasant 68,94,98,99
  Riddick 2,7,10,21,28,30,35,44,
    60,72,85,91,97,114,115,118
  R. 92
  Richard B. 39,85,114
  William 30,42,44,79,83,92
Gilliam, Henry 3,6,7,11,12,13,15,
  17,18,19,20,21,23,24,26,31,32,
  34,36,37,38,39,42,48,49,50,53,
  57,59,60,65,67,70,75,76,77,80,
  81,82,83,84,85,87,89,90,96,
  100,101,102,103,105,108,112,
  114,116,119,122,123,124,126,
  127,128
  John R. 50,61,96
Glover, Nancy 18
Gomer, Dempsey 31
  Elizabeth 31
  Nancy 31
  Thomas 31
  William 31
Goodman, Abigail 45
  B. 7,60,85,90,101,112
  Barnes 16,34,38,92

Goodman, Dempsey S. 36,38,85,93
  99,103,116
  Elizabeth 116
  Henry 6
  James 3,72,73
  Jethro D. 3,65
  John C. 22
  Mary 45,78,122,124
  Soloman K. 45
  William 2,6,21,39,46,58,65,66,
    85,94,115,116
  William H. 35,47,71,85,86,93,119
Goodwin, James 42,70
  Martha E. 127
  Richard F. 127
Goomer, John 71
Gordon, Benjamin 50
  Benjamin W. 112
  James 17,36,87,95
  John C. 16,19,21,23,27,30,31,32,
    36,38,40,43,61,67,69,70,72,76,79,
    84,91,92,96,97,104,107,109,112,
    120,121,127
  Joseph 1,6,9,16,22,30,32,36,38,
    39,40,43,45,51,52,53,61,62,65,
    67,69,70,73,74,75,76,78,79,80,
    91,96,97,99,108,109,112,113,
    114,124,127
  Mary E. 43
  Patience B. 43
  William 12
Granbury, Elizabeth 23,113
  George 47
  George W. 23,50,51,113
  James 127
  John 23,31,32,36,47,51,62,78,
    94,123
  John J. 4,5,22,31,47,50,61,109,113
  Joseph G. 78,97,109
Gregory, James 99
  Jane A. 4,5,39
  Richard B. 5,22,39,72
  Richard I. 71
Green, Abram 25,27
  Anthony 95
  Charlotte 67
  Henry 67
  Isaac 25
  Judith 27,37
  Kedar 14,27,37
  Lewis 2,46,86
  Luke 91,122
  Margaret 22,46

Green, Reddick 27,28
  Samuel 34,46,87,89
Griffin, Benbury 10
  James 34
  James B. 50
  John B. 13,50
  James M. 55
  William 10
Griffith, Burwell 36,41,53,
  63,66,68,94,98
  Dempsey 68,94,98,99
  John L. 24,25,68
  Lovina 98
  Martha 68,94,98,99
  Moses 17
  Nathaniel 16
Gwinn, James 20,61
  James P. 117
  Joseph 104
  John 39
  William H. 100,101,118

Hall, Job R. 9,15,17,31,32,39,
54,67,85,90,92,99,102,120
  Emma 35,39
  William W. 36
Hare, Anna 45,46
  Bryan 20,27,63,92
  Burwell 77
  Christian 41
  Edward 120
  Elijah 45,52,71,98,103,126
  Elisha 8
  Eliza 92
  Elizabeth 77
  Esther 77
  Henry 20,25,43,44,45,92
  James 76,77,79,104,120,121
  Jesse 45,46
  Jesse S. 1,107
  Jane 45,46
  John 20,43,45,63,64,66,73,92
  John Sr. 120
  Harrison 33,45,46,52,103
  Joseph 34,46
  Marsha 45,46,92
  Moses D. 7,42,77
  Mary 45,46
  Nancy 92
  Robert 40
  William 40
Harrell, Abner 99
  Abraham 6,79,97,114
  Andrew R. 6,24,36,45,50,54,
  70,91,92,111,115,122,124

Harrell, Bennett 105,109
  Daley 63
  Elijah 21,35,57,77,90,118,120,126
  Elisha 55,56,81,105,126
  George 25,28,64
  Henry 6,106
  Gilbert 8,100
  Isaac 4,8
  Isaac S. 17,18,29,51,70,75,
  83,91,115
  I.L. 70,109
  I.W. 60,78
  James 3,15,70,92,115
  James A. 39,69,75
  John 3,128
  John B. 49
  Jesse 15,92
  Jethro 2
  Joshua M. 6,35,87,88
  Joseph 75
  Mary 22,25,27
  Mills 105
  Moses R. 63,64
  Nancy 22
  Nathan 28,106
  Nathaniel 104,126
  Noah 3,16,23,24,30,47,49,67,106
  Peter 27,72
  Reuben 26,83,116,121
  Samuel R. 3,4,5,30,57,66,107
  Samuel 43,64,72,79
  Thomas 8,53,69,104,115
  Washington 83,110,123
  William 6,10,13,69,81,94,99,
  105,115
  William H. 70,89,92
  William B. 75
  Willis 92,120
  Willis W. 6,16,50,75
Harris, Eliza 45,46
  William 45,46,114
Hart, John D. 107
  Sophie E. 109
Haslett, Fletcher 60,101,102
  Jethro H. 123
  Jethro S. 101,123
  John H. 16,19,24,60
  John M. 38
  Mary 124
Harvey, Ann Mrs. 29,33,39,50,76,
  110,114,115,120
  George E. 76
  George G. 16,22,114,127
  Jacob J. 24,32,39,40,45,62,70,108
  Richard M. 73

Harvey, Thomas 110
  William B. 73,110
Haughton, Jonathan 15
Hays, Ann 19
  Asa 40
  Benjamin 41,64,90,127
  Caroline 90,91
  Docton 40,58,80,82,90,101
  Elisha 44
  Hance 19
  Henry 32,50
  John W. 79,95,128
  Joseph 104,123
  Joseph R. 46,95
  Lovina 16,90
  Martha 127
  Penelope 40
  Richard 46
  Robert P. 16,19,21,41,50,57,
    90,91
  Timothy 9,19,21,41,46,57,
    90,91,95
  William 45,95
  William W. 109,120
  Willis R. 16,21,41,57,90
  Wright 3,35,40
  Zachariah 16,21,41,57,90,
    91,120,128
Herman, Henry 101
Hill, Asa 3,31,36,42,60,70,
    79,80,81,84,100,102,103,
    107,122,123
  Clement 5,10,11,18,36,48,
    115,119
  F.E. 112
  John 51,79
  Joseph 29,65,105,120
  Moses 64
  Richard 65
  Robert 21,98,105,122
  Robert Jr. 94
  Whitmill 17,61,65,105,120
Hinton, Benbury 24
  Diana 48
  Elizabeth 53
  Frederick 12
  James 24
  John 36,60,83,84,98,100
  John Sr. 20,42
  John W. 36,98,107
  Jonas 48,60,73,83
  Kedar 33,47,57,95,112
  Leah 45,113
  Louisa 48
  Noah 39,45,47,50

Hinton, Noah Jr. 24
  Noah B. 4,22,24,36
  Reuben 11,19,22,24,67,76,82,
    90,113,120,121,122,
  Reuben Jr. 24
  Richard 33,48,127
  Sarah 48
  Thomas 45
  William 5,18,39,42,48,84,100
Hobbs, Christian 14
  Daniel 8,22,58,63,66
  Daniel S. 57,102,103
  D.S. 100
  David 8,34,58
  Dempsey 128
  Amos 1,16,36,67,105,116,119,128
  Amos Sr. 2
  Edward 13,42,80,88,118,128
  Elizabeth 14,16
  Guy 1,14,29,105,119,128
  Henry W. 113
  Jacob 2,67
  Jesse 1,2,14,17,29,37,65,67,
    96,113,119,120
  Jordon 2,96,105,128
  Sarah 115
  Samuel 17
  Thomas 14,128
  Walton 88,118
  William 14,82,116,128
Hoefler, Asa G. 70,84,98,100
  Elizabeth 12,33
  G. 5
  Hance 12,16,26,36,60,75,83,
    98,101
  Henry 19,57,58,71,92,93,97,
    107,109
  Isaac 43,58,80,101
  James 58,101
  John 16,19,32,36,38,41,72,90
  Levin 103,109
  Richard 43
  Sarah 90
  William 17,107,109
  Willis 25,26
Hoggard, John O. 128
  Thomas 13,16,20,22,25,26,43,
    52,55,64,67,72,73,74,86,87,
    106,107,111,128
Holland, Lemuel C. 88
Holley, Josiah 3
  Thomas 37,69
Hollowell, John 94,99
  Luke 105,119
Hoskins, Peggy 21

Howard, James 83,117
Howell, David 103
  David Sr. 46
  Dempsey 46
  Edward 6,46,69,90,125,128
  Jethro 53,71,84,95
  Kicheon 25,78
  Miles 14,41,52,62,96,103,126
  Sally 89,128
  Timothy 52
Horton, Martha 19,51
Hudgins, Humphrey 59
  Jesse 35
  Josiah 60
  Mary 5,10,68,108
  William 2,40,43,61,68,69,
  85,96,112
  William H. 117
Humphreys, William 84
Hunter, Benjamin 98
  Edward R. 9,34,50,54,94,
  122,127
  Elisha 9,14,17
  Elisha R. 110
  Emily 94
  Elizabeth 31
  Harry 110,128
  Isaac 32,94,127
  Isaac Sr. 13
  Isaac R. 13,49,94,99,120,
  123,127
  Jacob E. 125
  John 17,72,88
  John O. 1,9,30,32,52,55,58,
  77,85,87
  J.R. 122
  Mary 98
  Riddick 16,22
  Thomas 70
  Thomas B. 31
  Theophelus 79
  Timothy 17,72,88
Hurdle, Abraham 17,32,34,40,42,
  48,62,64,74,92
  Harmon 105
  Henry 9
  James T. 95
  Joel B. 4,17,22,48,60,102,
  103,104,115
  John 1
  Joseph 1,2,33,64,80,96,
  110,124
  Joseph T. 17,51
  Kedar 2,105
  Lewis J. 38

Hurdle, Moses 61,119
  Nancy 48
  Thomas 13,120
  William 65,88
Hyatt, Isaac 70,76,98

Jackson, Andrew 96
Jenkins, Exum 32,33,62,65,75,89,
  95,98
  John B. 87
  John C. 24,33
  Wiley 24
Jocelin, Henry 23
Johnson, Andrew 60,72,96,123
  Jacob T. 78
  James 66
  Margaret 28,66
  Leah 78
Johnston, Molly 25
  Aaron 117
Jones, Alfred 125
  Archibald R. 9,47,54,67,69,82,
  86,97,105,125,129
  Absala 46
  Artemesia G. 85,87
  Benjamin 46,122
  Charles 8,45,51,72,99
  Dempsey 77,123
  Edward 26,74,96,110
  Easter 47
  Eli 28
  Elizabeth 28,51,121
  Elizabeth G. 59
  Ezekiel T. 59,62,69, 97,116,125
  Frederick 22,24,37,40,41,69,72,
  86,88,106
  Hardy H.C. 14,33,36,41,52,68,98
  Henry 8,52,71,79,98,103
  Henry Jr. 103
  Henry Sr. 103
  Jacob P. 8,45
  James 27,28,32,44,45,46,51,106,
  120
  James A. 91
  John 11,25,33,52,77,86,90,
  103,123
  Joshua 8,17,37,76,86,108
  Leah 26
  Lewis 2,20,25
  Margaret 76
  Nancy 28,128
  Parker 1
  Paul 67
  Nathaniel 11,28,50,76,77,82,
  106,121

Jones, Riddick 2,10,20,23,25,
   41,51,64,86
  Simmons 28,32,106
  Thomas 36
  Washington 45
  Whitmill 28,128
  William 11,28,65,77,79,95,98,
   104,105,116,123,128
  William M. 47
  William P. 77
  Wiley P.39,79,80,91,97,114,
   116,122,126
Jordon, Costen 120
  Kinsey 99
  Joseph 100,112
  Joseph J. 111,112
  Julia 100
  Matthew 75
  Robert 76,88,121
  Thomas A. 81,100,120,122,126
Kee, Jesse R. 1,33,37,51,96,
   110,117,121,128
Kelly, John 13,80,119
  Perry 80
Kerr, John 49
Kilby, Thomas J. 127
King, Henry 9,14,21,24,31,35,
   94,99,106,128
  John 7,104,126
  Norman 17,29,124
  Purnel 71
  Simon 17,28,29
  William 17,28,61,64,124
Kinney, Charles R. 2,11,22,31,
   99,116
Kittrell, George 47
  Mildred 47
Knight, Belvedera 93
  Dempsey 20,43,90,92,93,102
  Edward 63
  Garrett 89,90
  John 64
Lang, Joshua 2
Langston, Dempsey 62
  John 40
  John B. 89
  John D. 109
Lassiter, Abner 25
  Abram 27
  Amos 25,36
  Ann 26
  Ann E. 56
  Absylla 109

Lassiter, Arey 26
  Cena 103
  Clement 10
  Ezekiel 12
  Frederick 92
  Henry B. 10,11
  Isaac 26
  Henry 16,21,40,79
  Isiah 103
  James 22,27,41,69,86,114
  Jethro 23,60
  John 23,25,26,56,93,107,109
  Kedar 26,37,69,78,86,103,125,
   129
  Mary 26
  Matthew 103
  Moses 25
  Reuben 35,36,57,88,97,100,113,
   125
  Samuel 78
  Susannah 20,23,60
  Susanna Sr. 97
  Thomas 25,26,74,103,105
  Timothy 103
Landing, Rachael 74
  William 78
Laurence, Christian 53
  Henry 70
  Julia 71,84,95
  Margaret 53
  Ruth 112
  Treacy 53
Lee, Elizabeth 2,39,62,117
  John 2,7,97
  John F. 112
  John R. 89,98
  Luke 114
  Mildred 109
  Nancy 109
  Penina 96
  Robert 31
  William 69,89,102,125
  William H. 102,125
Levisay, Joshua 40,109
Lewis, Christian 38
  David 11,13,52,107,109
  Eff 38,53,65,91,123
  Elizabeth 45
  Elvey 123
  Exum 6,35,75,115,124
  John 42,45,59,74,77,104,123
  Louisa 45
  Luten 38

Lewis, Mollie 123
   Rachael 59
Liles, John 6,16,75,124
Lilley, Joseph 1
Loomis, Hiram 24
Lovet, John 3,29,30,36,42,70,
   75,76,82,83,88,100,101,102,
   118,122
Lucas, Silvester 22

Maget, Thomas 68
March, John A. 6,45,62
   Mary 45
Marshall, Alexander 93,97
   Elizabeth 78
   James 93,105
   Robert 93
   William 16,17,92
Manning, Mary 121
   Willoughsby 109,121,129
Matthews(Mathias), Andrew P.
   43,46
   Anthony 106
   Edwin 10,20,23,85,87
   Etheldred 68,108,111
   James 32,47,57,58,63,69,
   82,97,98,100,108,109,129
   James E. 2,70
   Jacob 25
   Jesse 2,10,20,25,41,64,68
   Jesse S. 74,84
   Jesse M. 74
   John 9,12,14,15,36,40,42,43,
   49,59,60,70,75,79,80,89,94,
   100,112
   Joseph 41,64,68,86,114
   Julie 10
   Margaret E. 46
   Mary 86
   Peggy 46
   Polly 2
   Riddick 49,89
   William 64,76,77,82,88,94,100,
   101,102
   William A. 74,118,125
McDaniel, William W. 123
McGuire, William H. 71,76,104,129
Menchew, Bond 27,57
Meltear, Abraham 52,66
McDonald, Neal 123
McIntosh, Richard 101
McPherson, Willie 3,4,5
Miller, Elizabeth 91,129
   Jane 91,129
   Martha 91

Miller, Moses 91
   Reuben 91
   Thomas I. 65,70,80,84,88
   William 39,80,91,116,117,129
Minton, Peter B. 10,55,57,60,69,
   78,83,100,104,115,116,120,121
Mitchell, Esther 99,118,120,121
   John 13,30,36,42,64,65,70,80,
   83,84,104,111,120,128
   William 94
Morgan, Absylla 101
   Abraham 3,4,5,6,15,17,18,22,23,
   24,27,31,32,39,43,61,62,81,82,96
   James 1,3,32,37,44,45,57,58,67,
   71,73,84,86,87,90,96,97,109,129
   John M. 74
   Seth P. 61,96
   Seth R. 3,4,17,18,20,22,31,32,
   62,78,116,117
   Seth 3,47,51,78,96,117
   Seth Sr.61
   Thomas 89
   Thomas P. 3,22,31,32,67
Morris, Elizabeth 107,122
   Frederick 17,20,107,122
   John 17,20,23,107
   Lemuel 102
Moore, Augustus 82,97
   Eli P. 110
   Martha 34,35,112
   William 30,31
   William H. 3
   William K. 9,51,81,128
Moran, John Jr. 42
Mullen, George M. 60,72,97
   Mary 97
   Samuel 97
Murdaugh, James 50,59

Neal, Edward S. 2,49
Newsom, Martha 101
   Michael E. 101
   Moses 101
   Polly 10
   Robert 61
Nixon, Absylla 116
   David 116
   Jacob 4,60,64,104
   John 60
   Nathan 21,24,37,53,69,72,74,
   79,88,103,109
   Reuben 18,29,37,60,69,74,80,96
   Samuel 69
   Sally 109
   Sarah W. 53

Nixon, Zachariah 69,84,109
Norfleet, John R. 1,20,41,44,
  50,67
  Kicheon 6,7,15,63,65,
  66, 74,76,84,99,102
  Harriett W. 1,41
  Marmaduke 50,59,65,66,100,
  103,108,114,128
Nowell, Mary 45
  Seth 45
Nurney, Mary 65

Odom, Asa 43,63,67,106
  Benjamin 51
  Ira 62,89,91,95
  Jacob 41,68,94
  John W. 19,35,51,81,123,125
  Mary 128
  Richard 28,35,41,42,43,53,
  60,63,64,65,67,74,79,89,
  94,98,106,112
  Rodon 7,53,63,67,109,111,
  121
  Sophia 89,91,95
  Susan 1
  Thomas 109
Outlaw, David 22,38
  George 29,104
  John 115,116
Overman, Charles 13
  William 12,13

Paine, Robert T. 80
Parker, Abram 66,85,99
  Abraham W. 6,7,8,12,13,15,
  18,22,25,32,35,38,40,42,54,55,
  56,57,65,66,73,82,83,94,96,104,
  105,106,107,111,112,117,119,123,
  126
  Alfred 18,44
  Amos 66
  Ann(Nancy) 118
  Bray 64,72,97,107,121
  Cherry 15
  Chetta 103
  Daniel 116,119,126
  David 3,10,11,12,16,22,27,
  36,47,51,53,58,73,75,76,
  80,82,86,92,96,97,98,100,
  101,102,103,112,113,121,
  129
  Dempsey 7,8,11,12,12,15,33,46,
  52,55,56,57,59,66,82,86,96,
  103,105,109,118,120,126

Parker, Edward 44,57,84,114-6-7,126
  Elisha 82,111,117
  Elizabeth 12,56
  Eliza 116
  Hardy D. 16,31,49,83,85,108,
  116,126
  Hardy 5
  Henry 15
  Harriett 116
  Humphrey 1,8,20,23,27,37,45,
  50,53,58,63,66,84,86,102,104,
  107,108,109,118
  Jacob N. 48,53,72,97,116
  James 11,17,22,24,44,47,50,53,
  58,77,86,102,104,118
  James D. 98
  James D. Jr. 120
  James H. 76,80,97,98,100,121
  Jesse 27,41,128
  John 63,66,85
  John F. 32,56,75
  John W. 5
  Jordon 18,44,54,57,63,84,99,
  102,125
  Kedar 104
  Kindred 28,49,55,56,93,108,115
  L. 109
  Lem. 124
  Levi W. 54
  Louisa 12,55
  Lucinda 117
  Margaret 14
  Martha 1,116,118
  Mary 15,33,112,116
  Mary C. 94
  Miles 2,7,8,10,13,18,19,25,30,
  33,34,41,45,62,66,71,84,89,90,
  92,96,99,102,107,109,126
  Nancy 15,70,116,120
  Nathan 115
  Penina 12,56
  Penny 7,112
  Reuben 55,56,57,118
  Rex 78
  Richard H. 4,44,49,54,61,65,73
  98,102,105
  Richard 85,94
  R.B. 15
  Robert 12,15,59
  Robert B. 29,30,41,49
  Sarah 12,15
  Sophia 12
  Sydney 12

Parker, Theopulis 12
  Thursey 12
  Thomas 54,63,77
  William 7,8,32,42,51,63,
    66,74,116
  William W. 38
  Willis 18,32,43,59
Peal, Dempsey 63,73,87
  Thomas 2
Pearce, Aaron 47,69
  Abner 25,26,78
  Abram 26,37,92,93,103,105
  Daniel 32
  Eliza 104
  Enoch 27,37,78,103,125
  Frederick 11,67
  Henry 58,87,96,125,129
  Isaac 116
  Jacob 129
  Joseph 116
  Lassiter 25,26,27,110
  Nathan 25,27,33,47,86,110
  William 7,108
Pearson, Richard M. 80
Perry, Amos 105
  Caleb 55
  Barsheba 119
  James 8
  James D. 2,46
  Josiah 55
  Lucinda 88
  Leah 119
  Mordecia 2,128
  Pleasant 46
  Sarah 17 (Sally) 119
  Seany 119
  Timothy 88
  William 13,118
Petty, Sarah 15
  William 14,15,37
Phelps, Wesley 96,110
Piland, Asa 26
  Elisha 26,110
  Isaac 26,95
  James 26
  George 70
  Jesse 12,26,83,88,110
  Mills 26,70,113
  Peter 6,10,35,42,113,118
  Pleasant 12,124
  Reuben 26,28,52,96,112
  Seth 26,70
  Stephen 15
  Susan 42
  Susannah 113,116

Piland, William 70
Pipkin, Isaac 6,21,28,32,36,38,39,
  42,49,60,76,85,91,105,106,108,
  112,115,116,123
  Isaac Sr. 79
  John D. 12,18,39
  Penelope 91,92
Pintard, John Beeman 116
Polson, George 41
  John 109
Pool, Thomas 5
Porter, Jesse 66
  Sabra 66
Popleston, John 5,15
Powell, Charles 69,115
  Daniel 20
  Jacob 39,48,60,62,79,83,97,99,
    122
  James 20,61,72,83,91,117
  John 20,36,61,62,108,115,124
  Kedar 48,83,95,122
  Mary 61,95,115,116
  Millicent 72
  Thomas E. 9,33,113
  William W. 37,38,102
Proctor, Albert G. 5
  Ann E. 5
  Frederick 5
  Lovely L. 5
  Mary V. 4
  Samuel 5
Pruden, Abraham 16,22,25,28,41,64
  67,72,73,87,106,107
  Celia 31,82
  James 35,39,85
  John 42,51,104
  Lewis W. 101
  Martha 22,28,39,73,101
  Nathaniel 101
Pulle, James E. 45
  Ruth 45
Pugh, Henry R. 29,39,41
  William E. 3,14,15,31,36,38,39,
    40,41,45,48,49,53,59,61,70,75,
    77,80,81,85,87,89,95,96,100,104,
    116,121,122

Rabey, Adam 84,95
Randolph, Jeremiah F. 29
Rawls, John E. 44,62,94,123
  Risop 3,4,22,31,38,39,47,62,65,
    86,94,99,113,114,122,123,125,
    127
  Wiley 87
Reed, George W. 43,58,64,67,80,
  101,111

Reed, Jesse 119
  Jethro 42
  Micajah 84
  Sarah E. 44
  William 32,44,50,94,120
Rice, David 50,91
  Thomas 36,45,54,122,124
Richardson, Mary Ann 98
  William H. 127
Riddick, Abram 87,111,114
  Abraham 2,15,25,39,43,58,62,
  68 Jr. 104 Sr. 104
  Anna Maria 88
  Bushrod 1,33,37,78,92,96
  B.F. 94
  Christopher 9
  D. 116
  David 3,31,40,49,70,82,85,
  101,104
  Edward 81,108
  Edward F. 87
  Elbert H. 19,25,31,51,70,
  82,85,101
  Elizabeth 49,121
  Elisha N. 121
  Esther 35,51
  Henry 9,14,36,82,94,121,
  122,127
  I. 22,42
  Isaiah 19,48,52
  J. 4,16,17,23,25,29,34,51,
  52,89,112,127
  James 65,70,81
  James A. 121,122
  James B. 53
  James C. 3,54,65,84
  James M. 49,61,73,85,102,124,
  125,126
  James R. 9,12,18,19,21,22,23,
  31,32,37,38,40,47,49,57,60,
  61,62,64,67,68,70,73,75,76,77,
  80,82,83,84,85,90,91,96,99,102,
  103,111,116,117,120,122,124,125
  Jason 1,33,51,83,110
  Jethro H. 1,4,12,13,17,19,20,
  21,22,31,32,33,34,37,42,48,53,
  54,56,67,74,76,85,87,94,102,
  103,106,108,110,114,116,117,
  119,120
  John 7,19,31,34,38,44,73,74,
  81,105,112,116,126
  Joseph 12,17,29,40,42,47,48,
  50,62,63,64,65,75,77,79,80,
  81,83,85,92,94,95,99,102,
  108,109,111,121,122,128

Riddick, Josiah 4,5,10,19,32,41,
  52,55,68,71,86
  Kedar 60
  Lassiter 9,14,25,27,38,39,41,
  53,54,55,59,64,71,84,91,107,
  111,112,114,116,128
  Leah 38
  Lemuel 7,71,73,111,119
  Margaret Jane 107
  Mary Ann 31,81,109
  Micajah 39,102,127
  Mills 4,5,10,11,13,15,20,60,68,
  76,77,109,115,116,127
  Nancy 6,44
  Nathan 4,9,17,20,29,30,33,35,37,
  55,78,81,89,92,94,99,102,110,119
  Robert 14,18,24,25,31,36,39,42,45,
  79,91,94,97,121,122,124,125,127
  Solloman 111
  Thomas 25,67,72,88,89,92,94
  Thomas E. 6,102,124,125,127
  W. 50,66
  William S. 5,88
  William 19,41,68
  Willis 74
  Willis F. 3,16,40,44,49,40,54,
  59,66,85,87,88,117,124,124,127
  Willis I. 7,11,17,18,24,27,84,
  101,122
  Willis J. 70,105
  Wilie 3,4,6,31,42,62,75,104,
  121
  Wilty 36
Roberts, John 3,5,9,11,13,15,17,
  18,20,22,29,31,39,48,49,60,65,
  70,73,75,77,81,84,90,95,100,
  101,107,108,119,120
  John A. 32,62,63
  John S. 54,60
  Mary B. 49
  Mills 14,18,65,70,84,85,87,98,
  120,121,128
  Thomas V. 15
Robins, William W. 70,76
Robinson, Hugh B. 112
Rochell, Clement 43
  John 35
Righton, Agnes 91
Rogers, James 23,61,72,73,83,95
  126,128
  Levi 9,13,41,47
  Millicent(Milly) 61,95
  Mills 125
  Robert 7,19,28,36,40,42,44,50,
  69,93,115,125

Rogers, Timothy 39,40,117
Rogerson, Abel 1,21,24,28,30,
  43,46,50,54,58,65,74,75,76,
  80,96,102,109,110,118,119,
  127
  Jeremiah 18,74,80
  Jesse 80
Rooks, David 38,49
  Frederick 3,30,128
  Sarah 49
Roundtree, Charles 106
  Christian 106
  Elizabeth 22
  James 82
  Jason 2,3,22,25,46,73,106
  John 2
  Noah 64,70,76,97
  Quinton 84,100
  Seth 14,37
  Seth W. 97,111
  Simmonds 6,9,37,71,84,95,102,
    111,112,120,122
  Solloman 15,75,82,100,102,104,
    120,122
  Thomas 84,100
  William 60
Rudolph, Titan K. 52,66
Russell, James 62,66

Saunders, Briant 14
  Benjamin 14,19,40,62,77,85
  Drew M. 25,33,42,45,49,62,79,
    87,98,103,117,126
  Gilbert G. 10,13,18,33,45,
    79,87,96,106,114
  James 14,45,62,117
  Jason 10,13,14,25,33,49,68,
    79,94,96
  Jesse 6,45
  Jesse Sr. 14
  John 23,28,36,39,45,49,83
  Elizabeth 23
  Nancy 68,94,98,99
  Robert 14,45
  Sarah 107
  Sarah B. 6,128
  Thomas 6,9,12,13,14,19,30,36,
    42,45,46,59,63,65,81,82,83,
    91,100,108,115,122,123
Santos, M.A. 3
Savage, Benjamin 85
  Caleb 15,16,31,97
  Humphrey D. 89,111
  James 15,16,24,31,75,79,83

Savage, Jesse 15
  Jesse M. 15,31
  John 3,5,16,31,39,85,97
  John P. 88,100,101,122,123,124
  Louisa 97
  Margaret 122,123
  Orrin B. 88,122
  Pryor 3,6,26,40,53,54,60,70,71,
    72,73,75,82,91,95,101,111,116,
    124
  Sarah 31
  William 96
  William H. 18,20,22,25,41,46,73
Sawyer, Frederick B. 127
Sears, Barsheba 32
  Belver 38,93,116,124
  James 34,93
  William 33,34,37,38,49,85,93,
    103,108,115
  William H. 93
Seguin, James S. 5
Simons, Robert 36,73,76,96
Simpson, James 34,38,52
  William 96,110,119
Shaw, Edward 10
Sheppard, John 57,66,78,104
  Thomas 14
Sherard, Randolph 54
Skinner, Henry A. 50,91
  Mary 50,91,92
Slocum, E. 3
Small, Alfred 96
  Christian 21,22
  Elisha 91,126
  James A. 111,114,115
  James E. 114
  James P. 16,21,22,43
  John 17,19,36,39,72,87
  Joseph 104,114
  Moses H. 19,43
  Reuben W. 107
  Thomas A. 84,107
  Soloman 39
  Daniel 114
  William 114
Sowerly, Lucy 15
Speed, Rufus K. 18,38,44,67,81,88,
  100,107,122
Smith, Abraham 22,35,43,79,107,111
  Allen 2,24,48,52,53,67,74,75,80,
    85,89,90,91,92,93,99,116,118
  Arthur 55,128
  Britton 13,20,22,46,55,79
  Charles 50,77

Smith, Edwin 8
　Emily 61
　Dorthea 61,83,95
　George W. 8,30,31
　Fanny 123,125,128
　H.T. 36
　James 12,33,76,77,79,104,
　　106,110,128
　James C. 11,19,51,81
　John 86,106
　Joseph 46
　Lemuel 71,117
　Lewis 123
　Marmaduke 77
　Millicent 83
　Nancy 11
　Nathan 22
　Pleasant 77
　Richard 9,61,83,95,106,123
　Riddick 11,65,76,77,95,104,
　　105,121
　Rachael 55
　Sally 95
　Sarah 54,61
　Silpha 99
　Robert R. 19,55,109
　Thomas 61,75,86,95,96
　Thomas P. 109
　Willis B. 77,79
　William J. 81,108
Sparkman, Dempsey 28,35,55,56,59,
　　82,83,112,118,123,125,126
　John 2,7,13,20,35,46,54,55,67,
　　86,107
　Margaret 56
　Mills 56,59,118,125
　Cherry 70
Speight, Ann 33,66
　David 105
　Emmy 87
　Francis 6
　Isaac 98
　Henry 9,72,92,104
　Jacob 43
　John 91
　Jonas 29
　Joseph 61,62,87,93
　Mary 93
　Sophia 92
　Wesley W. 19,58
Spivey, Aaron 106
　Abraham 8,63,79,96,103
　Christian 120
　Henry S. 4,38,48,55,60

Spivey, Jonas 29
　Mary 95
　Moses 70
　Seth 8,29,84
　Thomas 9,95
　Timothy 8,19,26,58,96,107,109
　Washington 120
　Wesley 8
　William 13,29,84,120
Southall, Daniel 54
Stafford, William 117
Stallings, Daniel 18,121
　Henry 13,42
　Joseph 26
　Margaret 118
　Mills 72
　Nancy 72
　Peggy 13
　Shadrack 1,13,72
　Simon 14,30,64,117
　Thomas W. 3,29,30,49,84,104,117
　Whitmill 3,17,29,30,31,32,33,35,
　　36,44,53,63,76,78,82,100,104,106,
　　117,124,128
Stedman, Nathan A. 124
　Rebecca 124
　William W. 1,3,6,30,35,36,38,38,
　　39,43,62,64,72,108,124
Stewart, M.B. 112
　William 117
Strode, Eliza 39
　William 39
Summers, James 8,33,52,98,103,117
　Jethro 15,34,45,62,63
　John V. 73,89,90,92,101,125
　Josiah 79
　Martha R. 6
　Nancy (Ann) 62
　Levy 35,37,96,105,110
Sutton, Benjamin 3
　Joseph 70,96,111
　Martha H. 37
　William J. 78
Swann, Thomas 19

Taber, Charles C. 15
Taylor, Fruzy 30
　Hillory 55,70
　John 43 John B. 104
　Joseph 29,64,72
　Kedar 18,44,86,102
　Kicheon 46,109
　Martha 10,52,55
　Mary 3,8

Taylor, Nathaniel 8,16,29,84
   Pleasant 25,27,28
   Robert 30,70,83,84
   William 64
Teabout, Jethro 2,3
Thornton, Jimimy 62,63
Tines, Nicholas 15
Townsend, Charles 115
Trevathan, Henry 50,76,121
   John 50
Trotman, Calvin 99
   Drew 1,33,102,117
   Elisha 1
   Ezekiel 9,14,16,33,50,72,75,81,94
   Jasper 1,9,20
   Moses 129
   Noah 102
   Pherba 10,13,50,94,99
   Riddick 10,14,16,64,72,75
   Quinton H. 4,37,99,106,119
   Starky 107
   Timothy G. 36,70,83,84,120
Turner, John 106,110
Twine, Abraham 16
   Christian 61,96,124
   Thomas 4,8,47,65,74,78,93,94,96,99,113,123
   William Israel Noah 78

Umphlett, Charney 56,59,79,126
   David 96,109
   Elisha 1,20,41,57,67,86,107,128
   Nannah 72,107,117
   Thomas 117
   William 105,106

Vann, Albert G. 15
   Cintha 68
   Dempsey 10,20,41,64,86
   Harrison 15,24,52,118
   Jesse 67,68,98
   John 15,50,111
   Tilman 108
Vincent, William P. 14

Waddle, John 29
Walters, Charles 74
   Simon 24,38,47,74
   Susan 98
Walton, Ann 72
   Asa 84,87
   Benbury 11,12,18,19,24,27,29,37,43,44,47,53,58,64,81,111

Walton, Christian 106
   Daniel 84
   Elisha 31,35,84,87,119
   Holloday 27,36,39,50,62,92,108,111,124
   J. 91
   Jacob 13
   John 5,7,11,12,18,27,31,43,45,46,48,50,58,64,70,76,79,80,81,84,87,89,95,100,101,104,108,111,118,121,124
   John B. 12
   John G. 106
   Henry 8,84,87,99,100,104,115
   Linney 111
   Lucy 21,24
   Thomas 21,24,106
   Timothy 5,8,11,12,21,22,24,31,34,48,53,54,58,59,66,69,96,103,104,106,109,111,115,117
   Treasy 1
   Richard 120
   W. 11,21,24
   William 21,24,72
   Willis 31,35,84,87,115
   Susan 104
Waddae, James 87
Ward, Daniel 95
   Daniel S. 8,25,65,128
   Eliza 82
   Elmira 10,111
   Leah 82
   Nathan 14,19,38,48,52,60
   Thomas 9
Warren, Peggy 68
Watson, Sarah 23
Welch, Baker F. 49
   Drew 84,121
   Miles 84
   Nancy (Ann) 101
Weston, Carey 5
Wheeler, John 14
White, Jeremiah 87
   Jesse 72
   John 9,48,80,111
   Mary 10,48
   Miles 26
   Robertson 89
   Thomas 15
   William 10,111
Wiggens, Ann 4,31
   Benjamin 34
   Elizabeth 113
   James 76,121

Wiggens, Jesse 3,4,5,6,22,23,
  31,32,39,44,45,47,50,51,63,
  74,78,97,99,102,107,109,
  112,113,116,121,125,129
  Jesse P. 96,97,108,117,129
  John 17,32,37,63,73,76,87,
  89,96,108,112,125
  Joseph 102
  Nancy 5,39
Wilkins, Moses 38
Willey, H. 40,47,72,103
  Henry 1,7,9,13,15,23,24,38,
  49,52,69,74,75,104,112
  Hillory 7,13,19,23,42,73,
  99,109
  J. 49,55,76,84,90,128
  Jethro 3,4,7,11,18,22,38,39,
  40,41,53,69,72,73,79,207,112,
  124
  John 3,20,28,38,60,75,86,90,
  103,106,107,108,118,124,125
  Mary 72
Williford, Richard 34
Williams, Allen 21,54
  Anson 86
  Benjamin 21,54
  Christian 38
  D. 103
  Daniel 19,47,49,69,74
  Dempsey 13,40,109
  Elisha 41
  Hardy 7,40,42,50,109
  Henry H. 112
  H. 38
  Henry G. 7,13,31,33,40,53,
  66,109
  Isaac 1,28,40,47,85,91,119
  James 21,34,42,52,60,61,63,
  67,68,85,91,98,99,111,115
  James Sr. 68
  Jethro 31
  Jonathan 7,9,13,19,23,33,42,
  47,66,79,109,126,128
  Jonathan Jr. 52
  John 52,82,90,112
  Jordon 21,38,54
  Lavinia 21,54
  Mary 112
  Michael 43,117
  Mills 21,54
  Mourning 13
  Nancy 54
  Sarah 54
  Sophia 21,54

Wilson, Jesse 18
  John G. 76
  Robert 51
Winslow, John 53
Woodley, Willis 79
Woodward, James 24,45,79,91,122,124
Worrell, Eli 59
  John 26,71,73,126
  Nancy 93
  S.W. 83,103
Writen, Ann 92
  Jane 92

Yates, Rachael 23,24,47,50
  Christian 55

PLACES

Acamons Corner 33
Alstons Road 41
Arkansas Territory 55
Arnolds Tract 4

Bagleys Swamp 58,67
Bakers Mill 126
Baltimore 88
Bank of Virginia 6,87
Barbour Co., Ala. 123
Barnes Creek 2,115
Barnes Land 4,6
Bay Branch 15,85
Bear Creek 59
Bear Branch 38,49
Beef Creek 81
Blue Hill, Maine 77

Ballard Land 114
Baptist Meeting House 88
Bassy Swamp 91
Beach Swamp 69,81,102,125
Beaverdam Swamp 7,21,30,67,108,
  114,117,126
Bentons Creek 2 Great Ditch 27
Bertie 3,78,112
Baylis Swamp 36,61,116
Bennetts Creek 1,9,13,23,25,27,39,
  41,42,44,51,61,66,67,77,79,81,
  88,90,95,97,102,103,113,119,120,
  125,128
Bee Pond Swamp 26
Big Mare Branch 16
Big Cypress Swamp 20
Black Fishing Hole 74
Boyse Swamp 106

Brick Hole 27,66
Brick House Plantation 58,98,99,
    100
Brinkley Land 33
Bull Branch 37,70,75,96

Cambridge, Md. 15
Camden County 4,5
Catherine Creek Swamp 1,9,14,16,
    29,33,57,72, 75,87,96,109,113,
    128
Chowan 1,5,9,14,24,32,36,37,
    43,44,48,50,61,62,64,81,86,
    96,102,105,113,115,116,119
Charleston 76
Chinquapin 51
Cabin Branch 29,43,45,61,110
Canal Bridge 4
Coldman's Creek 26,27
Collins Tract 93
Coles Creek 26,65,70,126
Copeland's Fishery 25
Cow Creek 81
Cross Swamp 1
Cypress Swamp 2,10,12,22,23,27,
    28,47,50,51,52,75,77,85,92,96,
    103,106

Darlington, SC 51
Davis Tract 36,57
Deep Branch 25,29,30,42,53,101
Deep Bottom Swamp 65,104,112
Deep Gut 25,27,78,
Dismal Swamp 127
Duke's Land 23,36,39

Edenton 15,32,34,35,43,49,50,
    64,76,77,79,80,90,108,113,120
Elm Swamp 63
Ellen Tract 90
Edgecomb 54

Flat Cypress Swamp 62,Branch 40
Folly Branch 63
Fort Branch 20
Fort Island 56
Fox Branch 120
Frogborrow Branch 53,104
Foster Tract 90

Gallbush 102
Gallbery Pocosin 74
Gatesville 2,12,13,18,31,33,36,
    42,43,48,49,53,57,59,60,63,64,
    66,72,75,81,82,83,84,86,95,100,
    108,113,115,122,123,124,125,126

Goff Swamp 120
George Marsh 125,127
Great Dismal Swamp 36,87
Great Mare Branch 16
Great Marsh 19,40
Great Pocosin 35
Great Thicket 70
Granbery Tract 4
Gregory Tract 6,39,52
Griffen Place 12,50
Guilford 50
Gum Pond 43 Swamp 63,74
Gut Landing 25

Hackley Swamp 35,115
Harrell & Costen 57
Halifax 56,61,101
Harris Plantation 59
Halfway Run Swamp 73
Harveys Mill Swamp 109
Hawtree Branch 16,55,57,111,128
Holly Island 6 Holly Tree Branch 33
Hollow Bridge 33,42,46,61,75,98,101
Hog Swamp 125
Hertford 15,21,25,42,53,60,63,67,
    68,74,76,78,87,94,95,97,99,101,
    114
Honey Pot Street,Swamp, Road 9,18,
    24,34,35,40,53,59,66,70,75,78,80,
    99,120
Hill Tract 63,93
Hunter Tract 62
Hunters Mill Swamp 75,94
Hudgins Tract 80
Hughes Road 52
Horsepool Swamp 75,109,127
Howell Tract 95,123

Indian Neck 9,10,17,20,107
Indian Road 9
Indian Swamp 43,64,101
Island 113

Jones Path 108
Jones Swamp 106
Jones Tract 93

Knotty Pine Swamp 33
Knights Tract 90

Lawrence Branch 128
Lickingroot Branch 55
Large Cypress Branch 22
Little Cypress 22,46,55
Little Causeway 2,3,46
Little Field 22

Little Hawtree Branch 41
Long Branch 9,19,22,23,27,28,
64,70,73,105,106,125
Long Pond 107
Lumberton 17,25

Madison County, Tn. 34,112
Manneys Ferry 18,71
Maple Pocosin 22
Marsh Plantation 99
Marsh Road 41
Methodist Meeting House 7,68
Menchew Tract 36
Methodist Episcopal Church 35
Mesway, Montgomery County 36
Middle Swamp 1,85,88,94,105,
125 Pocosin 15
Mills Swamp 6,9,32,44,58,70,
83,98,108,109,117
Mills Dam 24, Pond 83,93,106
Mill Race 43
Mintonville 83,89
Mirey Swamp 63,89,96,106
Mirey Branch 43,52,111
Mile Branch 106
Monroe Co., Ga. 9
Montgomery Co., Mo. 41
Murfhreesborough 76,97
Muddy Cross 34,58,63,79,89,
106,110,119

Nansemond 2,3,6,19,30,31,32,
35,43,51,55,61,63,66,68,70,
71,72,74,76,77,81,83,85,87,
88,89,98,99,102,104,108,109,
125,127,128
Newbern Merchants Bank 80
New York 88
Norfleets Mill 24 Swamp 106
Norfolk 4,5,6,14,17,24,35,82,
86,88,101,123
Northampton Co. 15,45,108
Notaway River 42,106

Old Canal Road 1
Old Ferry Road 1
Old Flax Hole 9,34
Old Field 43,65
Old Indian Field 43
Old Hobbs Tract 120
Old Mill Branch 77
Old Mill Neck 84
Old Mill Tract 95
Old Nichols Line 77
Old Path 31

Old Plantation 6
Old Town 83
Old Town Road 29,104
Old Town Tract 55
Old Woman 34
Orapeak Swamp 1,58

Parkers Path 8,34
Parkers Place 58,98,100,103
Parkers Landing 11,48
Patience Branch 43,64
Pasquotank 5,62,82,99,127
Perquimans Co. 18,25,61,74,80,94
Perry Tract 89
Perry Co., Ala. 124
Pearces Branch 102
Pickens Co., Ala. 54
Pintards Upper Corner 81
Peters Swamp 86,93
Pipkin Land 114
Poley Bridge Branch 9,16,75,86,102
Polson Tract 77
Popular Stump Branch 25
Portsmouth, Va. 48,113
Pruden Place 101
Pugh Road 1

Quarter Plantation 65,76

Reedy Branch 41,98
Richmond 127
Riddicks Mill Pond 129
Rogers Branch 2 Pocosin 97

Sand Banks 14,44,45,66,87,107,128
Sandy Cross 4,34,60,62,78,79,110
Sarum Creek (Road) 10,15,26,42,45,
55,65,71,83,113,115
Sears Mill Race (Pond) 38,49,106,
116
Schoolhouse Branch 43,101
Shelby Co., Tn. 114
Shoulder Hill Branch 113
Speights Mill Pond 44,62
Spring Branch 119
Somerton Creek (Road) 11,18,24,45,
46,53,98,99, 115,122,123,124
Southampton 45,109
South Quay 86
Stallings Tract 72,89,107
Suffolk Road 21,31,49,60,62,70,
71,73,128
Sunbury 12,31,46,57

Talladega Co., Ala. 43
The Barnes Tract 81

The Granbery Tract 5
The Gregory Tract 81
The Grove 66
The Gentleman 115
The Harbour 3
The Hawks Nest 94
The Landing 81
The Ridge Land 41
The Ridges 20
The Wharf 81
Thicket Road 2,54
Thicket Swamp 109
Two Sisters 76,88
Trumpet Marsh Branch 126

Virginia Road 69,81,104,115,120
Vollentine Land 98
Voss Creek 26

Wainsak Ferry 46
Warrick Swamp 5,13,119
White House Tract 93
White Pot Pocosin 99,122
White Oak Branch 45,74
White Oak Spring Marsh 68
Wharf 13
Watery Swamp 8,26,56,57,60,
61,71,74,92,93
Wiggens Branch 112,115
Wiggens Crossroads 63
Washington 55
Winton 38,60,73,111,115
Winton Causeway 15
Watering Hole Branch 47
Wild Cat Creek 59
Wynns Ferry 45,64,74,107
Wynns Ferry Road 113,115,128

Yalobusha Co., Miss. 85
Yazoo Co., Miss. 85,87

Zion Meeting House 108

www.ingramcontent.com/pod-product-compliance
Lightning Source LLC
LaVergne TN
LVHW091552060526
838200LV00036B/804